AN ANVIL ORIGINAL
Under the general editorship of Louis L. Snyder

A SHORT HISTORY
OF THE INDIANS
OF THE UNITED STATES

EDWARD H. SPICER
Professor of Anthropology, University of Arizona

ROBERT E. KRIEGER PUBLISHING COMPANY
MALABAR, FLORIDA
1983

Original Edition   1969
Reprint Edition   1983

Printed and Published by
ROBERT E. KRIEGER PUBLISHING COMPANY, INC.
KRIEGER DRIVE
MALABAR, FLORIDA 32950

Printed in the United States of America

Library of Congress Cataloging in Publication Data

Spicer, Edward Holland, 1906-
    A short history of the Indians of the United
States.

    "An anvil orginal."
    Reprint. Originally published: New York : D. Van
Nostrand, 1969.
    Includes index.
    1. Indians of North America—History.   I. Title.
E77.S749   1983   973'.0497   83-11320
ISBN 0-89874-656-6

Preface

Members of dominant societies habitually see the social universe as oriented around the states which they control. Minority groups may be viewed sympathetically, but always the frame of reference is the necessity for adjustment to the dominant society's aims and institutions. Thus Indian history in the United States has rather consistently been presented as the record of Indian-White relations. This is certainly a legitimate field of history, but it is not an adequate frame of reference for the subject in hand. However influential White policies have been, the development of Indian life involves a great deal more than response to those policies.

This account proceeds from the standpoint that Indian-Indian relations, both within Indian communities and among different Indian nations, have been and are of great importance in Indian lives. The fact that White policies have rarely, if ever, had the results that Whites hoped for suggests that there are other historical factors of decisive importance which must be taken into account. If we are to face squarely the problem of writing Indian history it is necessary, first, to recognize the continuity of Indian societies and, second, to discover the various frames of reference in terms of which Indians view themselves and the people with whom they are in contact.

This book is an effort along the first line. The simple fact of continuing existence of Indian groups, strangely enough, needs emphasis in the United States. This is true because of a prevailing illusion that Indian societies are vanishing, that one after another each Indian group is taking the road to disappearance. Under the influence of this illusion, historians readily overlook the fact that Indian societies have existed for longer periods than the currently dominant society of the United States.

The illusion has moreover fostered a static conception of Indian life. It has come to be believed that what is truly Indian consisted of the Indian life-ways which had taken form before the arrival of Europeans. This view of Indians differs greatly from Europeans' views of Themselves. No European thinks that the Irish ceased to exist when they came into contact with the Danes or the Normans, or even the English. It is customary to speak of Catalonian, or Basque, history as extending through more than two millennia. The history of these and other people is not seen as ending with involvement in the Spanish, or British, or other states. The succession of transformations which the Cherokees, the Papagos, the Navajos, the Iroquois, and the many other Indian groups have undergone does not require a different approach. Like Europeans, the Indians have suffered and survived conquests; and they have continued to adapt in their own styles to successive changes in their social environments. The fact is that in the United States there has obtained a combination of circumstances which has stimulated an unusual ethnic continuity among Indians—and these circumstances are currently stronger than ever.

EDWARD H. SPICER

Grateful acknowledgment is made to the following for permission to reprint excerpts from copyrighted material:

University of California Press for Lesley Byrd Simpson, *The Encomienda in New Spain,* 1966, pp. 127–128.

Indiana Historical Society for *Walam Olum or Red Score. The Migration Legend of the Lenni Lenape or Delaware Indians, A New Translation,* edited by Carl Voegelin and Others, 1954, pp. 209–215.

Harper & Row, Publishers, for Harold E. Fey and D'Arcy McNickle, *Indians and Other Americans,* 1959, pp. 131–133.

Prentice-Hall, Inc. for *The Indian in America's Past,* edited by Jack D. Forbes, 1964, p. 70.

Mrs. Arnold M. Rose for Arnold M. Rose, *Prejudice and Discrimination, Readings in Intergroup Relations,* published by Alfred A. Knopf, 1951, pp. 43–49.

University of Wisconsin Press for Francis La Flesche, *The Middle Five,* 1963, pp. xvi–xix, and xx.

Table of Contents

WHITE POLICY

WHITE VIEWPOINTS

INDIAN PROPHETS AND SPOKESMEN

Part I

THE INDIANS OF THE
UNITED STATES

CHAPTER 1

Many Nations, 1540-1794

For 250 years following the first European invasions of the region that became the United States no one people was politically dominant. From 1540, when Spaniards initiated the first extensive inland marches under Coronado in the west and De Soto in the east, the struggle for dominance continued for nearly three centuries.

For the Indians, both in the east and in the west, there was certainly no clear indication until perhaps the late 1700s that any one of the five newcomer European nations would emerge triumphant. Until that time the view of most of the Indians seems to have been that some kind of balance of power might be struck among the warlike Europeans and themselves and that a new equilibrium of many nations would thus be established.

By the 1790s only a few of the smaller tribes of Indians had been completely eliminated as contenders for independence or dominance. On the east coast in areas of most intensive European settlement, small groups such as the Wampanoag in Massachusetts or the Chickahominy in Virginia were reduced to dependency, although not to extinction as peoples. However, elsewhere throughout the territory between the Atlantic Ocean and the Mississippi River, Indians remained as political bodies —either as persisting confederations such as the Creeks in the southeast and the Iroquois of the northeast, or as autonomous groups like the Kickapoos of the northwest. These political bodies made successive alliances with one another and with various of the Europeans.

On the other hand, some of the Europeans had been eliminated. Even before 1700 the few Swedes and Dutch had been ousted or absorbed. But during the following century Frenchmen, Spaniards, and Englishmen were still in the contest. It was only by the end of the century that the settler offspring of the British had emerged as the major contenders in the east. By hindsight it appears clear enough that the "Americans" as

11

early as the 1790s were on the road to dominance. Indeed the year 1794 might be taken to mark the end of an era. In that year in what became the state of Ohio the triumph of the "Americans" in the Battle of Fallen Timbers was the clearest indication thus far that they were destined for military dominance. Until about the same time the Spaniards had had serious difficulty merely in maintaining a foothold against the Apaches, Comanches, and other tribes of the southwest. Not until the 1790s did the Spaniards, in close alliance with the Pueblo Indians, establish something like a secure position against the still unconquered southwestern tribes.

It is wholly misleading to call this phase of Indian history, as many historians have, a "colonial period." That label may be applied only if the viewpoint is that of one or another of the European peoples. The very great majority of Indians were not living, even by the end of the period, as politically subordinated and culturally dominated people. Except for the few disintegrating eastern tribes of the Atlantic seaboard, the Indians were operating in an active political arena where there was the possibility, through fighting or negotiation, of maintaining an accustomed independence, of escaping domination, or of winning new power over others. It was a period for the Indians during which introduced trade goods led to new objectives, resulting in new kinds of conflict and changing political alignments. It was a period during which persistent, aggressive invasion of their lands led to awareness of new kinds of people and to efforts to adapt their traditional forms of diplomacy and organization to getting along with the threateningly different newcomers. It was a period of competition for trade, of forced migrations, of shifting alliances, of political instability, and of drastic cultural change. It was only as the eighteenth century drew to a close that Indians east of the Mississippi began to be aware that the struggle to escape domination had become desperate and that not only their lands, but also their ways of life, were threatened.

→ This arena in which Indians and Europeans vied for land, trade advantages, political power, and peace presented a complex human scene. The peoples in contact were many, the ways of life (both European and Indian) were varied, and the working relations which they developed followed no single pattern. It is doubtful that any of the invaders attained an overall view of this complexity until the last quarter of the eighteenth century, and then only an approximate one. Certainly no Indian until sometime later gained such a general view, although in the early 1700s there were Iroquois leaders who, as a result of the widespread forays of the Five Nations, knew something of what was taking place from New England to Illinois.

If we use the concept "nation," which English-speaking invaders employed throughout the period and which many Indians have continued to use to the present, we may come close to understanding the situation as it was then viewed. For Europeans the term "nation" was applied to people with common language and customs and usually a name for themselves who shaded imperceptibly into one another. In Europe nations were not coterminous with political organizations. A kingdom might embrace several nations. A principality or an overlordship might include a single nation or a part of a nation. The British were inclined to look for "kings" among the Indians, to apply the term nation to each language group of which they became conscious, and often to assume that a "king" ruled such a group. Their information usually came from the Indians who thought in similar terms about the cultural divisions among themselves, although political authority within the groupings was never so centralized or absolute as the Europeans, projecting their feudal background, imagined it to be.

The Indian nations of the seventeenth and eighteenth centuries were many. (a) East of the Mississippi River and south of the Ohio the greater part of the population spoke languages of the Muskogean family, of which there were four major groups which came to be called Creeks, Choctaws, Chickasaws, and Seminoles. The Seminoles, however, did not come into existence as an entity until the late 1700s when they were formed under White pressure from several smaller groups including some Creeks, Apalachicolas, Alabamas, and others. (Such fusions of smaller groups into larger ones, which then became separately identified by the Europeans, were very common throughout the period.) (b) Widespread in the north from the Mississippi to the coast were many Algonkian speaking peoples—for instance, those of the central coast who came to be called the Delawares; those of New England, such as the Narragansetts, Pequots, Mahicans, Abnakis, and others; the Powatans, Chickahominies, and others in tidewater Virginia; the Ottawas, Chippewas, Potawatomis, Kickapoos, Fox, and numerous others of the Great Lakes region. (c) The Iroquoian Five Nations of the New York area and the Cherokees of Tennessee spoke related languages as did some others who belonged neither to the great Muskogean or Algonkian families.

No sure enumeration of how many "nations" existed east of the Mississippi River has ever been made, and any even approximate count would have to be in terms of different twenty or thirty year periods, for the consolidation of smaller groups into larger and the disappearance of some small groups were constantly going on. In order to suggest the complexity of the scene it may be stated conservatively that at about 1700 the Europeans had become aware of some fifty or sixty "nations" whom they and the Indians thought of as more or less distinct entities. These may have comprised as many as 300,000 individuals.

At about the same time the Europeans numbered no more than 200,000 and, as the Indians saw them, constituted not three, but rather at least some dozen different nations. In the northeast were the French who behaved rather differently from the French who were beginning to come in from the south, the Puritans and two or three other kinds of British in New England, the descendants of the Dutch in New York and Connecticut, the Quakers, the upper and lower class Virginians, the Carolinians, the ever aggressive Georgians, the Spaniards, and the growing nation of Cumberland settlers or "Long Knives" who were clearly a different breed from the others farther east.

In the west there was equal diversity among the Indians, although the Europeans there were more homogeneous. The Pueblo Indians speaking ten or eleven different languages lived along or to the west of the Rio Grande River. Surrounding them were a variety of roving Athabascan-speaking peoples, whom the Spaniards had begun to call Apaches and Navajos, as well as Comanches on the east and Piman- and Yuman-speaking peoples to the west. Here again there were some 50 different Indian nations in the midst of whom had settled Spaniards and some Aztec-speaking Indians brought up from central Mexico.

Into this variety, east and west, the Europeans brought still more diversity, not only in ways of dress and speech and useful tools, but also in ways of carrying on trade, in religious rites, in warfare, in political organization and diplomacy. The two and one-half centuries from the first European invasions until the emergence of the United States as the major military power was a phase in Indian history characterized by a wide variety of adaptive measures. For some Indians, particularly in the far west where Spaniards had colonized as early as 1598, the technological introductions were of relatively minor importance because the material adaptation was already at a high level. This was the case for the Pueblo Indians and also for the majority of the eastern Indians, who were agricultural. The new tools effected primarily hunting and warfare. The new warfare among the Indians of the northeast became a means for expanding trade advantages. The basic way of life, however, was not transformed and the material innovations were integrated in terms of dominant Indian values into Indian cultures. It was chiefly among the Indians in the west, whose ways of life had been based on simple techniques of hunting and gathering, that domestic animals and the new weapons wrought the most profound changes—the Athabascans of the Southwest and such people as the Comanches of the southern plains. The new technology very promptly led them to radically changed ways of life.

For the great majority of Indians in contact with Whites at this period the major realm of adaptation was political, and the major instrument employed was the political confederation. The alliance as an instrument of both offense and defense, sometimes purely Indian in composition but more often including Indians and one or another of the European nations, became of major importance. Some confederations were successful as the means for survival and some were not. Some were developments of forms of organization which had existed before the coming of the Europeans; a few were wholly new. Whatever the variety of forms and whatever their degree of success, most of the Indians tried to meet the new conditions which the European invasions created by means of new political organization.

The Creek Confederacy. The coming of Europeans to the present southeastern United States stimulated the growth of what came to be called a "confederacy." The Indians composing it were for the most part speakers of the Muskogean languages. This confederacy was dominated by several nations whom the English-speaking invaders called Creek, a corruption of an Indian name for the Ocmulgee River in present Georgia. Between 1700 and 1790 the Creek Confederacy increased in numbers and in influence so that by 1770 it was spoken of by a British official as "the most powerful" Indian confederation known to them. Numbering perhaps 20,000 by 1770 the Creeks had become a major focus of the complex diplomatic maneuvers of the British, the Spanish, the French, and the other Indian nations of the southeast. Historians have frequently spoken of them as holding the balance of power in the region. In the 1780s a Creek leader, Alexander McGillivray, was recognized as the brilliant equal in diplomacy of representatives of any of the competing nations and was even held by later historians to be the most distinguished man born on Alabama soil.

The Creek Confederacy was by no means wholly a product of the European invasion. It already existed as early as 1540 when De Soto made his pillaging expedition through present Florida, Georgia, Alabama, Tennessee, and Mississippi. However, the power struggle that developed during the seventeenth and eighteenth centuries stimulated its development and increased its influence. It appears, nevertheless, that the Europeans remained ignorant of its existence as a political entity until about 1716. In 1715 a Muskogean-speaking nation on the Georgia coast rebelled against mistreatment by the British settlers and a conflict known as the Yamassee War broke out. The war was bloody and there is indication that Creeks who lived inland gave support to the Yamassee or urged them on. However, with the complete defeat of the Yamassee by the Carolinians the Creeks withdrew not only from further fighting but also geographically to the Chattahoochee River where for the next hundred years one important group of their towns was centered. From this time on, British as well as French and Spanish were aware of the Creeks and considered them as an entity in their respective efforts to dominate the trade and politics of the southeast.

The withdrawal to the Chattahoochee at about 1716 marked the beginning of a second phase in Creek history as we know it. Even before the Yamassee War the Creeks had become involved in the rivalry of the Europeans. Their settlements extended from the Georgia coast inland to Alabama when the Spaniards in 1563 began their colony at St. Augustine. A century later in 1663 when the British established Charleston, the Creeks took sides with the British against the Spanish. They raided into Florida and helped spread destruction among the Indians there, a foray which brought them into conflict with the Apalachicolas, a Muskogee group like themselves. However, they had meanwhile begun their withdrawal from the coast. The defeat of the Yamassee led not only to further withdrawal but to the development of a new policy by the newly consolidating Creeks.

The Policy of "Neutrality." Under the leadership of the headman of the Creek town of Coweta, whom the English referred to as Old Brims, or Briminus, a policy of minimum involvement in the Europeans' mutual raids and competition was instituted. The Creek confederacy was so loose in structure that it would be a mistake to regard this as a foreign policy comparable to that which a European nation of the time might have adopted. Nevertheless non-involvement was a leading principle which the majority of Creeks tended whenever possible to follow during the next eighty or more years. No extended wars took place between the Creeks and any of the European nations during this time, despite frequent efforts to involve them.

The French who established themselves at Mobile Bay in 1702 were resisted at first by the Muskogee-speaking Alabamas; one group of Creek towns allowed the French to build a fort (Toulouse) in Creek territory in 1714. The Creeks maintained their trade agreement with the British and did not give support either to the French military or to the French Jesuits who were frustrated in their efforts to establish missions among the Creeks.

In fact, when the French attacked the Natchez nation on the Mississippi, none of the confederacy became involved. The British tried to provoke them to war with the French, but they refused. The Creeks ridiculed the Choctaws who split and fought among themselves over alliance with the French in the latter's aggressive aims. Instead of participating in the aggression, the Creeks accepted the larger part of the remnant of the Natchez into their own territory and thereafter the Natchez refugees became a part of the Creek confederacy.

This process of absorption was standard procedure for the Creeks and constituted an important feature of the foundations of their "confederacy." They had apparently, before the coming of the White invaders, customarily taken as allies and residents in their towns many groups whom they had fought and conquered. There was thus a constant increment to the Creek confederation. The process was augmented by the increase in warfare and disorder which the Europeans caused. Following their own raids into Florida under British instigation against the Apalachicolas, about 1704, they had absorbed some 1,400 prisoners. These Muskogean-speaking people became a permanent part of the confederation. The remnant of the Yamassee after 1715 was similarly absorbed, as were the Alabamas who resisted the early settlement of the French at Mobile Bay. Throughout the century the absorption went on, so that at least fifteen different Indian nations were taken into the territory and the councils of the Creek confederacy. Most of these were Muskogee-speaking people, but they included also others such as the Yuchi from the area of Tennessee and some few Shawnees from north of the Ohio River who spoke Algonkian. The absorption process contributed in an important way to the increase in numbers and influence of the Creeks during the late seventeenth and the whole of the eighteenth centuries.

The maintenance of the policy of neutrality depended also on the existence of buffer groups around the territory occupied by the Creeks. On the south and west the Choctaws, almost as large in the early 1700s as the Creeks themselves, were such a buffer group against the French and the Spanish in the European settlements on the Gulf Coast. The Choctaws, allowing themselves to be involved in the French aggression, became divided and constituted no serious threat to Creek territory or independence. On the northwest the Chickasaw became something of a buffer against the advancing English and French north of the Ohio. On the northeast the Cherokees constituted an even more important buffer for a time against the settlers of the Cumberland, the Virginians, and other Long Knives of the British-American frontier. The pressure of the Europeans on the Choctaws and Cherokees to be sure resulted in border disputes and intermittent raiding between those Indians and some Creeks, but in the main these tribes took the brunt of the pressures, and the main body of Creeks was able to remain more or less at peace and to avoid devastating wars.

It was on the east that the Creek frontier was most threatened by the Europeans. In the Carolinas, Georgia, and Florida the Creeks steadily absorbed defeated and disrupted Indian groups, leaving no buffer nations between themselves and the English-speaking invaders. Inevitably this made for a special relationship with the British. More or less consistently the Creeks gave preference in trade to the British, so that most Creek towns by the middle of the eighteenth century had a resident British trader. There were also, however, Spanish sponsored traders and trading companies, so that it was clear that the Creeks were not in alliance with either British or Spaniards and could on occasion play one against the other.

The buffer basis of neutrality was ultimately penetrated by the Georgians who after 1733 became the major foreign problem of the Creeks. Aggressive and unscrupulous from the first, they recognized no land rights of the Creeks and refused to accept general British policy. As their aggression accelerated, it was conflict with the Georgians, working through the most vulnerable spot on the Creek borders, that led to the first serious threat to the Creek program of neutrality.

Creek neutrality in the welter of nations in the southeast was joined with another aspect of policy, which crystallized clearly only after 1739. In contrast with their successes in the north, the French Jesuits were not effective with the Muskogean people. The aggressive French policy, as in the destruction of the Natchez, defeated efforts to spread Christianity or French customs. The Spaniards made almost no missionary efforts. It was the British who seriously attempted to "civilize," and it was they who developed the most effective working relations with the Creeks. The Carolinians offered to establish schools among the Creeks several times during the 1700s. The Creeks were indifferent at first. Later their leaders maintained that school-trained Creeks created only discord and bad leadership. In 1735 the Moravian missionaries sought to extend their program from Savannah into the Creek country. In Savannah they had established a school for Indians which met with some success. Between 1735 and 1739 Moravian missionaries moved out among the Creeks on the Chattahoochee. They built schools and missions, but their behavior displeased both the Creeks and the British and they were expelled in 1739. Frustrated they turned their attention to the broken tribes in eastern Pennsylvania and never came back.

The Creeks remained without direct missionary influence or European type schools throughout the 1700s. We may speak therefore of a policy of cultural, as well as political, independence which characterized the Indians of the confederacy. The Creeks wanted neither close political involvement nor educational or religious influences from the Europeans.

Creek Political Organization. The people who maintained this area of Indian equilibrium for some 70 years in the midst of accelerating change and instability sparked by the Europeans were a "stone age" people before trade with the Europeans began in the 1600s. They lived in settled communities, some containing as many as several thousand inhabitants. They were farmers and placed heavy dependence on the raising of corn, beans, and squash. They also relied on the fairly abundant game and fish of their fertile region. One of the most remarkable things about them was certainly their capacity for organization of large numbers of people. It was this that caused them to stand out among the Indians of the region and it was this which made them an important influence in the power struggle.

The political organization of the Creeks was not unique among the southeastern Indians. It was not indeed the most highly developed form of organization that obtained there. Possibly the Natchez before their destruction by the French had achieved that. The Creek kind of organization was standard for the region, but the various accidents of geography, circumstance, and leadership resulted in the Creeks—among all the Indians of the region—developing the most viable structure. It was not complex, although it may at some times have seemed so to the British and Spanish. The Creeks at the height of their influence in the 1770s held council meetings to which came 400 or 500 officials and 10,000 or 12,000 people. They were reported at this time to be able to raise a fighting force of 6,000. Put in these terms Creek power and organization probably seems more unified than it really was. The fact is that the large general council meetings were held ordinarily only once a year in May and were by no means exclusively for political purposes. They were ceremonial and recreational as well. They did constitute an important source of solidarity and common understanding for the people of the 100 or more "towns" which constituted the Creek nation.

The nature of the political organization, it should be emphasized, was not of a sort with which the Europeans were familiar. It was an organization by consensus or agreement rather than by command or hierarchical organization. The effectiveness depended on much time for consideration of issues and on opportunity for extensive oratory and persuasion. It did not focus up to a "king" with absolute power, although the Europeans often assumed that it did. Each of the major concentrations of settlement was autonomous. The settlement unit of from 100 to as many as two thousand or more persons was called in Creek the *talwa*. It has gone down in history as the "town." It was not compact but consisted of groups of scattered family dwellings with surrounding fields. Each town had a central group of public and ceremonial buildings and enclosures. Clans based on female descent were important in the local community.

Although each talwa was autonomous and ultimately free to negotiate, fight, or make peace with others, the unity of the Creek confederacy lay in the desire for peace and protection from aggressive neighbors which it could insure by its pooling of warrior power. The organization consisted of a number of peace leaders with functions ranging from foreign relations to public works, usually chosen from particular clan groups, within which frequently one man emerged as able in oratory and respected in judgment, as well as a group of elders or "beloved persons." This peace organization was dominant in confederacy affairs, but there was in addition a hierarchy of war leaders with functions for organization of war parties and for policing at the time of council meetings. Thus, there was a division of labor which brought most of the men into the political organization. There was no codified system of regulations or law. There was great solemnity in deliberations. Nevertheless the organization had a certain fluidity and informality, since it did not rest on the principle of command and absolute authority but rather on mechanisms for deliberation and wide consultation which sought unanimity by consensus.

It happened, therefore, that under various pressures from surrounding nations a town or group of towns might act in ways not in concert with other participating towns in the confederacy, as for example when some of the towns permitted the French to build Fort Toulouse and when other towns at different times waged war or retaliated independently against British settlers, Cherokees, or Choctaws. It was this lack of continuous and consistent concert of action which frequently masked the nature of the basic Creek unity.

The Creeks traditionally recognized the primacy of four of the larger towns. Two of these were towns of the Lower Creeks (as the British came to regard them) on the Chattahoochee—Coweta and Kasihta. Two were of the Upper Creek division on the headwaters of the Alabama River—Tukabahchee and Abihka. Coweta and Tukabahchee emerged during the 1700s as the dominant towns and seemed to the British to be the capitals of the Creek Confederacy. Subject to differing pressures from surrounding nations, the towns recognizing Coweta authority and prestige sometimes operated independently from those recognizing Tukabahchee.

The third phase of Creek history as we know it began to be apparent in the 1780s. By this time the French had been eliminated, following the "French and Indian Wars" and the British were engaged in the struggle with their colonists for dominance. The Spanish hovered more or less passively at the southern margins of the southeast. The Creeks had experienced pressure from and conflict with the Georgians who had become the most warlike people in the whole region. The Cherokees, often in conflict with the Long Knives of the Cumberland invasion area, were developing some unity, but without the broad base of absorbed Indian neighbors. The Cherokee-Creek frontier remained unstable. Under these circumstances the Creek policy of non-involvement was becoming more and more difficult to maintain.

Alexander McGillivray. It was at this time that Alexander McGillivray began to dominate Creek affairs. Of mixed blood, he was nevertheless Creek in basic outlook. He had received some formal European schooling in Charleston and had prospered as a trader representing a Spanish-sponsored trading company. He understood the European interests well and how to play one nation against another. He was from a minor Lower Creek town, but his effectiveness in dealing with Europeans gave him increasing prominence among the Creeks as a beloved man or elder.

When the British ceased to be a power in the region in 1782, McGillivray assumed the role not only of spokesman for the Creeks generally in the competition between Spaniards and Americans, but also sought to take a leading role within the Creek confederacy. He accomplished this by reorganizing the traditional structure. In the towns where his influence was strongest he encouraged the war hierarchy of leaders to dominate the peace leaders or miccos. At the same time he gathered about himself a body of retainers, which was possible because of his personal wealth and resources. The overturn of the old organization was by no means complete. It was in fact resisted strongly by Opilth Micco of the Upper Creek town of Tallassee and by others, who regarded McGillivray as a "boy" and a usurper and who tried to deal separately with the viciously troublesome Georgians. McGillivray built much support for himself by threatening to remove traders established in the various Creek towns. Creeks were interested in maintaining these relationships because they had become dependent on what the traders brought into the communities.

McGillivray was therefore a force for disunity in his efforts to reorganize the Creeks, and later disrupting factionalism may be traced in part to his activities during the 1780s and 1790s. Nevertheless it was McGillivray with whom the Spanish and the

Americans began to negotiate for their respective positions. As had been true for many years, the Creeks under this leadership found it impossible to deal satisfactorily with the Georgians who ignored treaties once made and sought constantly to make the semblance of a treaty with any few Creek headmen they could make contact with or force into signing papers.

McGillivray turned his attention increasingly to the new United States government in New York. In 1890 attempting to hold back the Georgians and while still regarded by the Spaniards in New Orleans as in their pay, McGillivray with 26 Creek leaders went to New York. A treaty was negotiated with President Washington. McGillivray was secretly given a salary as a general. The treaty guaranteed Creek lands. He had proposed a separate Creek state without success. The Georgians refused to accept the treaty and, more significant, the main body of Creeks repudiated it.

The terms of the treaty signalized the end of the second phase of Creek history. McGillivray and those who supported him accepted the status of a protectorate of the United States. This was the first time in an important negotiation that Creeks had accepted the idea of any dependent relationship with any other nation. A major power was emerging in the struggle of the many nations to a position of dominance. The Creeks were to be dealt with on terms quite different from those under which they had successfully maintained independence in their dealings with the Spanish and the British. It was indeed a new era in Creek affairs, as well as in the affairs of all the other Indians of the southeast.

The Creek towns by this time were in a very different situation from that which had obtained in the middle of the century. Many of the important major towns, such as Coweta and even Tukabahchee, were becoming depopulated. The prosperity which had characterized them had given way to a state of economic decline. They had lost large tracts of land. The depredations of the Georgians were becoming steadily more serious, and the Choctaw and Cherokee borders were no longer stable.

The disruption of the Creek Confederacy during the McGillivray regime was only a part of the impact on all southeastern Indians of the rising dominance of the Americans. The Choctaws had begun their decline into factional disorganization under the influence of the French 60 years before. They had long since ceased to be a unified nation. The Cherokees, on the other hand, had begun to develop some unity; events were shaping which were to result in their becoming the dominant Indian group of the region. Elsewhere in the southeast, Indians had either been absorbed into the Creek towns and were suffering the Creek fate, had been pushed out of their homelands to the north like-the Shawnees, or had in a very few cases begun to be absorbed into the advancing settler population, a process which was to be long drawn out. The theater of culture contacts was changing sharply as a result of the decline of the stabilizing influence of the Creek Confederacy and the unmistakable gathering of military strength by the people who were assuming the name of Americans.

The League of the Iroquois. In contrast with the neutral-tending Creeks, the confederacy of the Iroquois in the northeast was as bellicose as any of the European nations. It is unlikely that it came into existence quite as early as the Creek Confederacy, and it seems clear that the major impetus to its rise to dominance among northeastern Indians was the fur trade with Europeans. The League of the Iroquois was very much a part of the trade rivalry, the warfare, the mutually destructive raids, and the general disorder which the Europeans brought to the North American continent. It was probably responsible for more massacres of Indians and more devastated Indian settlements between 1640 and 1755 than the French and British together. The Dutch, the French, and the British maintained great respect for the Iroquois confederacy and for more than a hundred years the last two sought in their respective ways to gain its support.

The invading Europeans became aware of the Iroquois confederacy much earlier than they were of the Creek. The French Jesuits seem to have distinguished it as a political entity by 1634 and the Dutch made a trade treaty with the Iroquois in the mid-1640s. This was at a time when the five Iroquoian nations had been organized for concerted action for perhaps 50 or 60 years. When the Dutch made their treaty for a "covenant chain" of trade relations, the Iroquois were already embarked on a highly aggressive program of securing for themselves a favored position in the European trade in which they had been engaged since the early 1600s.

Rise of the League. The Iroquois military action was nearly continuous from 1644 until about 1700. During this period they reached their peak in population and in military and diplomatic power. The Iroquois program had two aspects. On the one hand, they were engaged in destroying or subordinating all the Indian nations from New England to Illinois and from the St. Lawrence to the Ohio. On the other hand, they were concerned with resisting any sort of domination or control by the French. (*See Document No. 8A.*) In the first of these objectives they were highly successful and in the course of achieving it they were thrown into incessant conflict with the French. To achieve the second objective they sought alliance with the British who were also seeking to combat the French and eliminate them from the theater of trade and political influence in what is now the northeastern United States. As the Iroquois became the dominant Indian power in the whole area by 1700, they emerged as a political entity which the British accepted as a foreign power.

This phase of Iroquois development was characterized by increasingly effective military operation and by more and more definite political organization. Just prior to the coming of the Europeans the Iroquois had been engaged in establishing themselves in the area of the present New York state. This had involved the ousting of Algonkian-speaking peoples. During the first 40 years of the seventeenth century, five Iroquoian-speaking nations became established in the territory between the Hudson River and the Genesee in western New York. They comprised between 25,000 and 30,000 people. On the east the Mohawks lived in some eight groups of settlements and numbered possibly 5,000. There were 3,000 or more Oneidas immediately to their west who operated as satellites of the Mohawks. Below the western end of Lake Erie the Senecas constituted the largest and westernmost of the five nations; numbering perhaps 10,000 they occupied a dozen settlements. The Cayugas on their east functioned somewhat as their satellite, adding some 3,000 to their population. In the center of the Iroquois territory were the Onondagas who constituted 4,000 to 5,000. Their influence as the original organizers of the League was very high, despite the relative smallness of their numbers. It was these Five Nations who achieved the domination of the Indians from the Hudson to the Illinois between 1644 and 1680.

Their first major campaign was against a related Iroquoian people, the Hurons, who occupied the upper St. Lawrence valley. Even by this time the fur trade with the French and the Dutch had become so intensive that beaver and other game had been greatly depleted, not only within the territory of the Five Nations but also on its western margin in the territory of the Hurons. The Iroquois were determined to eliminate the Hurons, and others if necessary, from a dominant position in the trade with the French. By 1649 the Iroquois succeeded through ferocious raids in killing hundreds of Hurons and forcing the remaining few into subordination. Then in successive series of fights, they dealt similarly with two other Iroquoian groups on their west, the so-called Neuters (who tried to remain neutral in the Iroquois wars) and the Eries. By 1670 they had control of territory from the Hudson through present Ohio, and their war parties were feared farther west where they had raided into the territory of the Miamis and the Potawatomis and had made themselves felt by the Kickapoos and others in Michigan and Illinois. They were dominant in an area 600 miles east and west and from the Great Lakes south to the Ohio River range of the Cherokees and Shawnees.

Having consolidated their western position deep into the territory being tapped by the French traders, they did not rest content. They continued as they had for some time harassing the remnants of the New England tribes, forcing them into ever greater subordination to the British colonists there. They now moved southeast at the same time that they were raiding into Illinois and instituted a successful campaign to subordinate the Algonkian-speaking peoples in New Jersey and Pennsylvania. By 1680 they had succeeded in dominating the Delawares, the Nanticokes, and smaller groups of Algonkians.

At the same time that the Iroquois were achieving their dominant position among all the Iroquoian- and Algonkian-speaking Indians of the northeast, they had been waging offensive and defensive war against the French. After the British eliminated the Dutch in the favored trading position with the Iroquois in 1664, the French sought to swing the Iroquois to their side (*See Document No. 8B.*) Negotiations and treaties prior to that time had failed to bring about any dependable alliance with the Iroquois. The French then tried for forty years to conquer the Iroquois. In 1666 they began with attacks on the Mohawks in the east, destroying a major settlement and forcing a temporary truce, the Indians having also suffered great population loss through disease. Periodic attacks by the French on Mohawk, Onondaga, and Seneca villages with reprisal attacks by the Iroquois resulted in much destruction. It was not until 1696 after a vigorous attack by the French on the Mohawk villages that something like a lasting peace was agreed to and kept, more or less, until the beginning of the French and Indian War in 1755.

During the first half of the 1700s there were three major powers in the northeast—the French along the St. Lawrence, the Iroquois in the greater part of New York with their subordinated tribes west and south, and the British along the Atlantic seaboard. The British worked closely with the Iroquois. The facts that they met almost as frequently with the Iroquois as in their own councils and that they made and scrupulously observed treaties with the Iroquois indicated that they had accepted the Iroquois as a sovereign nation and as a valued ally against the French in their struggle for control of the northeast. This resulted in a phase of relative stability in Iroquois affairs which lasted until the American Revolution, except for the interlude of the French and Indian War in 1755–63 when the Iroquois assisted the British in their successful efforts to oust the French.

Iroquois Political Organization. The Iroquois confederacy which had succeeded in making such a place for itself in the European-Indian milieu was a different kind of entity from the Creek Confederacy. It was different in that it achieved a higher degree of formality in its organization and that it was able to maintain more unified action with respect to military operations. It adopted a quite different policy from the Creek Confederacy in accepting involvement in the European wars and in aggressive expansion of territorial control. Although the Creek Confederacy seemed less formal and was certainly less belligerent than the Iroquois, it should be recalled that the British in 1770 regarded it nevertheless as "the most powerful" confederation of Indians known to them. This probably is a reflection of the fact that by 1770 there had been a decline in the affairs of the Iroquois while the Creeks were still in the ascendancy.

The territorial units of the Iroquois were less definite, aside from the basic operating unit, than were the Creek towns. The Iroquois basic unit was the kinship unit of the extended maternal family within the clan. While such kinship units were also important among the Creeks, there was also a stronger local territorial unit. It should be noted that the different nations of the Iroquois remained distinct as tribal entities within the whole of the confederacy while the Creeks tended to absorb more completely those Indians who joined them. This gave more the character of a real "confederacy" to the Iroquois.

The Iroquois confederation was not a unique instrument among the northeastern Indians. Other Iroquoians such as the Hurons were leagued together for offensive and defensive purposes. Algonkians east and west of the Iroquois, such as the Kickapoos of Wisconsin and the Wampanoags of Rhode Island and Massachusetts, had the idea of confederation and acted on it. What was unique about the Iroquois was their success in adapting to the new war-ridden milieu. They destroyed, helped destroy, or drove out of the region the other coalitions of nations among the Indians. It is usually held that the nature of the organization of the Iroquois, however, was unique and that the form of organization which they developed was superior to that which any other Indians of the region managed to invent. It is certainly true that there are remarkable features of their League which, by the time of its ascendancy, were not to be found among any other Indian groups in the present United States.

The legendary history of the founding of the League of the Iroquois attributes it to two very wise and able Onondagas— Deganawida and Hiawatha. The first was a wise man of visionary experiences, the second a warrior. There is no such standard legend regarding the origins of the Creek Confederacy, probably because it was not conceptualized so clearly as a special form of organization by the Creeks. It was Deganawida, according to legend, who persuaded the Iroquois to set up a council of leading men (sachems) designed to insure peace within the Five

Nations and to coordinate aggressive action of all the warriors. The organization gave a central place to the Onondagas with the greatest representation, although the Senecas seem to have been the largest of the nations. There was stress on representation by clan, on a hierarchy of titles hereditary in clan lines, on an interlocking system of sub-councils, and on summit deliberation by 50 sachems who took action only when there was unanimity.

There was a surface similarity between Creek and Iroquois in the way in which they handled conquered groups. Like the Creeks, the Iroquois absorbed many other Indian groups, but this they handled in a different way. While there was some direct absorption into the settlements of the Five Nations, the dominated groups generally remained separate geographically and, most important, did not gain representation in the League council. Sometimes as on the northern shore of Lake Ontario, Iroquois set up colonies of their own people to maintain surveillance and prevent war-making except in concert with all members of the League. They placed subject groups like the Delawares in a status which was spoken of as being "women." That is, the Iroquois prohibited such tribes from making war, but kept them in the position of women without voice in the League council, for only the hereditary titles restricted to clans of the Five Nations gave entry to the councils. This was a species of colonialism. Not even the Iroquoian-speaking Tuscaroras, who in 1715 came north after defeats by the Carolinians, were admitted to full participation in the council. No Algonkian-speaking peoples were of any status within the realm of Iroquois power other than as "Women." The League of the Iroquois was thus essentially less democratic than the town-based Creek Confederacy.

Decline of the League. The Iroquois, especially the Mohawks, Onondagas, and Senecas suffered greatly at the hands of the French during the last 30 years of the seventeenth century. These three in an important general council meeting in 1690 had agreed that they would support the British as against the French, but the Oneidas and Cayugas did not concur. Hence there was no general League policy on the matter of European alliance. Nevertheless their relations with the British were generally friendly until the American Revolution. They remained neutral in

1702 when the French and British fought an episode of Queen Anne's War on American soil. In 1713 the members of the Iroquois League were defined in a treaty as British subjects, but how the Iroquois viewed such a concept is by no means clear. They joined in irregular fashion to support the British during the French and Indian War and found themselves on the winning side at the end of that conflict in 1763. (*See Document No. 9.*) This rapprochement, never very precisely defined except from the British side, led to strong efforts by the British to Anglicize the Iroquois.

The French had sent Jesuit missionaries to the Mohawks and other Iroquois and they had had some influence although far less than among the Algonkians. The Mohawks recognized that trade relations with the French or British led to missionaries. After several efforts by the Church of England in the early 1700s to missionize the Iroquois, a vigorous campaign was launched in 1735 under the auspices of the British Society for the Propagation of the Gospel. All the Mohawks were baptized by the 1760s and two thirds of them moved to Canada in Ontario. The Oneidas and Cayugas were also strongly Christianized. Factionalism had developed among the Iroquois, chiefly over the issue of the relationship to be maintained with the British. All Iroquois except some Senecas fought in 1755 to 1760 with the British against the French. But the seeds of disunity were strongly sowed. In contrast with the Creeks who had maintained a degree of cultural isolation, the Iroquois had permitted a myriad of influences to come among them. The Mohawks had built schools for themselves in 1712, maintaining a system of their own. Perhaps the Senecas and the Onondagas were the least influenced by the European schools and missionaries.

The trend toward differences over relations with the Europeans and their cultural offerings came to a head during the American Revolution. Only the Cayuga and the Seneca gave full support to the British cause. After strenuous efforts on the part of the Americans to persuade all the Iroquois to neutrality, the division of opinion became clear. The Oneida and the Tuscarora officially declared neutrality, but in fact gave support to the Americans. The Mohawks and the Onondagas were both split internally, a few of each turning to the American side. But the most influential Mohawk, Joseph Brant, supported the British and cast the lot of most Mohawks with them. The trend toward dissolution of the League of the Iroquois had run its course. It was no longer an organization embracing all the members of all the Six Nations.[1] As the Americans demonstrated their military power, there was no more unanimity among the Iroquois.

In 1779 the Americans asserted their dominance by means of a scorched earth policy. Seneca and other villages were burned, crops and stores were destroyed, and fields were devastated. Joseph Brant in Canada tried to establish the old political entity again, demanding and getting from the British a reservation for the Six Nations. Only 1600 Iroquois responded by migrating to Canada, the greater number being Mohawk, but also including some of each of the other Five Nations. All the other Iroquois remained for the time being in New York where a separate treaty, the Pickering Treaty, was made with them in 1796. (*See Document No. 10.*)

Federations that Failed.   On the Atlantic seaboard confederations of Indians also sprang up in attempts to restore the balance between men and land and among men which White settlement upset. During the 1600s the Indians, most notably of New England and Virginia, formed federations which sought by force of arms to check the Europeans as their expansive intentions and growing strength became fully apparent. These federations were quickly defeated by the settlers and their adherents reduced promptly to subordinate status. At the very time that the Iroquois were achieving their greatest power and the Creeks were gathering influence, the New England and Virginia Indians were eliminated as political entities. Their efforts at concerted resistance to domination had in fact failed by 1680. The story of the last stands of "King Philip" in the north and Opechancanough in the south have often been regarded as typical of what happened to the eastern Indians. Actually this kind of complete conquest of Indian societies was the exception rather than the rule during the first long phase of Indian-White contacts.

In the early 1600s there were not less than 15,000 Indians in the New England area. They constituted some nine major na-

---

[1] The Five Nations became the Six Nations in 1722, when the Tuscaroras were accepted in the League.

tions, all speakers of Algonkian languages. They differed not only in language but also in other fundamental ways from the Iroquoian and the Muskogean people. For example, the female line of descent was not of primary importance in placing people in the society. Leading men were described by the British as exhibiting an over-weening pride, a sort of disdainful, regal behavior which was not the rule among headmen in the Creek and Iroquois councils. What political organization existed was based on loyalty to a particular man of relatively great wealth. Leading men had personal followings, in other words, in contrast with the more widely extended and highly organized political structure of Creeks and Iroquois. The Algonkian ways of organization thus tended to be more understandable to Europeans of the age of kings—and, as it turned out, also more vulnerable.

The fate of the New England Indians occurred largely independently of the neighboring Iroquois. It is true that Mohawks raided into the settlements of the Mohegans and Mahicans directly to their east, helped disrupt these people, and made them easier for the Puritans to defeat. The major interest of the Iroquois was the control of the fur trade and New England was not important in this respect. Ultimately some straggling survivors of the New England tribes joined the Iroquois, but their struggle with the colonists was carried on in isolation from the Iroquois expansion of the seventeenth century.

The Wampanoags. The Mohegans, the Narragansetts, the Massachusetts, the Wampanoags, and the Pequots were the New England Indians of whom history has taken most account. Massasaoit, leading man of the Wampanoags, Miantonomo of the Narragansetts, and Uncas of the Mohegans were all very friendly to the colonists during the first decade of settlement in the 1620s. Within fifteen years, however, serious friction had developed, coming to a focus in 1636 in what was known as the Pequot War. This "war" was indicative of the steadily rising level of hostility between Indians and the Puritan colonists. Beginning with the killing by Indians of a profane sea captain, followed by an impetuous and ruthless reprisal against a Pequot village by a Pilgrim father, it ended in the subjugation of the several thousand Pequots of the Connecticut Valley. The colonists, however, were not content at having defeated the Indians, but decided that the Pequots must be erased as a people. They assigned the 800 or more surviving Pequots to the Mohegans, Narragansetts, and Wampanoags, forbidding them to set up their own independent communities again.

Thirty years later, by 1670, the White population of New England had increased to nearly 75,000 while the Indian population, largely as a result of devastating diseases, had declined to barely 10,000. Indians had sold a great deal of land, so that the colonists possessed more land than did the Indians in eastern Massachusetts, Rhode Island, and Connecticut. The Indian areas of settlement were penetrated everywhere. Several thousand Indians had been converted and lived in what were called "praying towns." (*See Document No. 7.*) No whole tribe, however, had accepted Christianity. Friction was increasing rather than decreasing. The colonists wrestled earnestly with the problems of Indian relations, but always from the standpoint of political subordination of the Indians.

Under these circumstances, the traditions of friendly cooperation began to break down. Pometacom ("King Philip"), the son and successor of Massasoit, became increasingly hostile to the colonists, as he saw the land base of the Wampanoags being invaded and his personal power declining. He made an effort to bring together in a federation the small, similarly situated tribes of eastern Massachusetts, the Niantics, the Pucmucs, and the Massachusetts. In 1675 war broke out, but the federation was not effective. King Philip's allies were weak and uncertain, and the Narragansetts and Mohegans sided with the colonists. King Philip, along with other Wampanoag leaders, was hunted down and killed. The federation was dead and the infiltration of the Indian country continued, as some Indians fled west and the remnants settled down to live under the British regime.

Powhatan and Opechancanough. In another area of intensive early European settlement on the Atlantic Coast—Virginia—an Indian federation rose and failed even before 1650. This was, however, very different from Pometacom's quickly improvised federation of Wampanoags. The Indians were, like those of New England, speakers of Algonkian languages and their traditional organization had the same general emphasis on authoritarian command. Before the British began to settle at

Jamestown, in the last decades of the 1500s a consolidation of small tribes had begun in what became tidewater Virginia. A leading man named Powhatan was engaged in expanding this association of relatively small groups when the first settlement of Europeans took place. Powhatan seemed to the settlers so aristocratic in bearing and so powerful among the Indians in the vicinity of Jamestown that they felt he merited the title of king. They sometimes spoke of his tributary tribes as consisting of an "empire." It is probable that some 30 tribes comprising most, but not all, the 12,000 Indians of coastal Virginia, recognized Powhatan as the dominant leader among them, and his federation (principality or fiefdom might be a better term) was still expanding.

The Jamestown settlers proceeded to deal with Powhatan as they might have with princes in Europe. They sought to make treaties of alliance for trade and defense advantages and to cement these with marriage ties. Powhatan held back, although he was not consistently unfriendly. The British then seized his daughter, Pocahontas, baptized her, and had her married to an Englishman. She became a sort of hostage for the pro-British behavior of Powhatan and his followers. The method worked for as long as Powhatan lived. Other tribes which had not been part of Powhatan's tributaries, like the Chickahominy, signed treaties similar to those made by Powhatan which asserted that the Indians were "true subjects" of the King of England.

When Powhatan died in 1618 the situation began to change. Another able and widely respected leader, of the Pamunkey group, Opechancanough became dominant. He had learned to be wary of the British. Their land hunger was ever more apparent. About 1620 the Virginians began efforts at Christian evangelization and to put Indian children in a school to be trained for missionary work among their people. The influence of Powhatan, plus the increasingly aggressive behavior of the Virginians, had forced some sense of common cause among not only the tribes under Powhatan's direct influence but also the others of the area. Under Opechancanough's leadership a concerted attack on various British settlements was made in 1622. The result was the immediate death of some 350 colonists and a state of intermittent warfare for the next nine years. Treaties in 1629 and 1631 following the adoption of a policy of crop destruction by the British led to shaky peace. Opechancanough remained the dominant patriarch among the Indians. The conditions of land loss and European interference in Indian autonomy did not of course lessen, and in 1644 acting again in concert with most of the other Indians, the Pamunkeys under Opechancanough struck the British settlements again. The results this time were far more decisive. Opechancanough was killed, the Indians suffered more serious loss of crops, and treaties were concluded which defined the Indians as tributaries of the British, holding their land on sufferance of the King's representatives. The tribes which had constituted something of a unified group politically were now separated by British seizure of a land corridor between the northern and the southern groups. The Treaty of 1646 further defined British dominance and Indian subjection. From this time on the Indians who had achieved some degree of unity under Powhatan and Opechancanough were no longer capable of effective military organization.

By 1669 the Indian population of the areas of the federation had been reduced to about 3,500, little more than a quarter of the population in 1607. Most of the tribes continued in existence for another hundred years, as more or less distinct entities. Their population continued to diminish, and each consolidated into fewer and fewer town groupings. They were now under more intensive pressures from the settlers and were pushed from one area, granted to them by the British, to another. They were forced to pay annual tribute and became entirely subject to British convenience in the assignment and re-assignment of land. The British recognized a woman descendant of the Pamunkey Opechancanough, whom they called Queen Anne, as the official representative of the Indians. But she was obviously possessed of no real power, as political organization among the Indians steadily disintegrated. De-tribalization proceeded, despite the fact that as late as 1722 representatives of the Virginia Indians took part in the making of a treaty of peace at Albany with the Iroquois, who had during the first two decades of the eighteenth century frequently raided into Virginia.

During the fifty years preceding the American Revolution the coastal Indians of Virginia became completely atomized.

Families and groups of families sought isolation from the advancing settlers. Many were converted by the Baptists. The remnants of the Powhatan federation were scattered and completely subordinated politically and culturally. They persisted nevertheless through the eighteenth century as tiny remnants speaking their own languages and maintaining a few distinctive customs.

Displaced Persons. Between the two centers of successful Indian confederation north and south were other tribes besides the defeated remnants of Powhatan's and Pometacom's people. Some were Indians who had been moving about east of the Mississippi River before the Europeans came and continued to move during the first centuries of upsetting contact with the Whites. Some were Indians rather recently settled in the areas where the Europeans encountered them. Some were people who broke down almost immediately into associated family groups who developed more unity under the contact conditions than they had before. Some were demoralized and disorganized remnants of groups defeated by the Europeans or by other Indians in the troublous times of the late seventeenth and early eighteenth centuries. Prominent among these displaced people were the Shawnees, the Tuscaroras, and the Delawares. It must be emphasized however that there were a number of others whose fates were linked with these or who underwent similar experiences.

Shawnees. The Shawnees were an Algonkian-speaking people numbering probably about 3,000 who were in process of movement from the north at the time of the arrival of the Europeans. In the late 1600s divisions of the Shawnees were settled in places as far apart as Carolina and central Tennessee. The British in the Carolinas named the Savannah River for them since they seemed to be a principal group settled along that river. The main body of Shawnees lived at this time in Tennessee. Bands of Shawnees shifted about widely between 1700 and 1794, to some extent no doubt merely in continuation of their migrations before the European invasion. However, some of their movements were definitely a consequence of the new conditions of contact and conflict. The Iroquois about 1675 laid claim to a portion of what became Pennsylvania along the upper drainage of the Susquehanna River. The claim was based on conquest by the Iroquois of the Susquehannocks and others. The Iroquois then proceeded for nearly a hundred years to encourage other Indian tribes to settle in this area, by way of maintaining a buffer against the British settlers on the Iroquois southern boundary. The Shawnees were among those who accepted an invitation to settle in the Wyoming Valley of Pennsylvania. The invitation involved accepting also a state of subordination to the Iroquois, that is, the status of "women" without rights in the Iroquois League or the right to make war without Iroquois consent. The Iroquois on their part accepted the obligation to defend such subordinated tribes. The Shawnee readiness to move under such conditions indicated their own lack of power, of established ownership of territory, or of position in the milieu of the many nations. Only a portion of the Shawnees moved to Pennsylvania from their settlements along the Cumberland River in Tennessee, but there was a steady small migration from about 1707 until 1731. During this same period Shawnees after the disturbances of the Yamassee War in 1715 disappeared from their location along the Savannah River, becoming absorbed in part into the Creek Confederacy. Still others, the main body of those in the Tennessee settlements, moved northward in response to the disturbances of the Chickasaw-Choctaw borderlands. In 1730 this larger group obtained permission from the Wyandots to settle along the northern affluents of the Ohio River. In 1742 the Shawnees who had settled in Pennsylvania began to move out from under Iroquois control, as the Iroquois invited still more tribes to settle in their buffer zone in the Wyoming Valley. All the Shawnees of this area had moved west by 1745 and joined the other Shawnees in Ohio. Here they were associated with other Algonkian-speaking people, such as the Miamis and later the Delawares and Kickapoos. Re-forming here as a tribe or nation, they became an important group in the affairs of the Algonkians from the time of Pontiac's revolt through the early years of the nineteenth century.

Tuscaroras. Another group which had been settled inland in the Carolinas at the time of European colonization were also completely displaced. The Tuscaroras were an Iroquoian-speaking tribe who may have numbered as many as 5,000 in the late 1600s. Settled along the Roanoke River and southward into

North Carolina, conflicts between the Tuscaroras and the White settlers became intense in 1711–1713. More or less disrupted and also in conflict with neighboring Indians such as the Catawbas, the Tuscaroras sought alliance with the still vigorous League of the Iroquois to the north. From this time until the end of the century the Tuscaroras moved north and were accepted into the League. As Iroquois-speaking people, they were the only Indians given status as a distinct nation along with the Iroquois Five Nations, so that the League, after 1722, became known as the Six Nations. The Tuscaroras were not, however, given equal status with the others, but remained without hereditary titles in the League council. The association with the Iroquois was nevertheless permanent and the fate of the Tuscaroras was closely bound up from the early 1700s with the Iroquois, especially with the Oneidas who had given them land.

Delawares. The most dramatic displacement of peoples of the early frontier was that of the Delawares. We have record in great detail of the phases through which they went in the process of displacement. Like the Shawnees they were an Algonkian-speaking people. They were a large but not politically unified group numbering 8,000 in the early 1600s. They occupied Manhattan Island, all of New Jersey, eastern Pennsylvania, and northern Delaware at the time of the Dutch and Swedish invasions. In the late 1600s they were between two fires, the advancing settlers of the Middle Atlantic area and the Iroquois. They never were able to form an effective military organization, although the pressures by about 1700 were leading them to greater political unity than they seem to have had before. Their name for themselves was Lenni Lenape, but the term Delaware was used in treaties with the British beginning in 1736. By the first decade of the 1700s they were largely dominated by the Iroquois, and in 1744 the Iroquois ordered them to move westward into the Susquehanna buffer zone. Meanwhile the Delawares had become pretty fully atomized. Groups of families lived in poverty at the edge of British settlements. Other groups moved in no concerted fashion westward. In 1724 there were Delawares already in western Pennsylvania. A slow, piecemeal movement had begun which brought most of them eventually into Ohio. Those disorganized families who accepted Iroquois domination were the atomized Delawares from the Delaware River valley. They had sold or been cheated out of land in one way or another and moved without clear purpose a little westward.

One famous deal resulting in the loss of a large tract of land was known as the Walking Purchase. It became a *cause celèbre* in Delaware affairs. One man among them who was largely responsible for the fame of this deal became known as "King of the Delawares." His name was Teedyuscung. He was a Jersey Delaware who had lived for more than fifty years at the margins of advancing European settlement. He typified the disoriented condition of most of the Indians who had neither accepted European domination nor been successful in dealing with it in the persisting Indian societies. He was a man without a country, merely a member of an unwillingly itinerant family. He greatly admired the British and wanted to become like them; he could be easily influenced in his spokesmanship for the Indians by the British officials, but he was accepted by them only as an Indian. He spent much of his time drunk. Yet, broken personality without a real community association, he nevertheless became a famous figure for a time in the role of eloquent spokesman for the Delawares concerning wrongs done the Indians that most of the British officials recognized as wrongs.

Teedyuscung gained fame first in 1757. There had been border fights and atrocities between the settlers and the displaced bands of Delawares. In the treaty making pursuant to ending the disorders, Teedyuscung pushed by certain Quakers and others made an eloquent speech with regard to the injustice of the Walking Purchase and the desperate plight generally of the Indians. For the next dozen years Teedyuscung became the spokesman for the Delawares remaining in the east and was spoken of as "King" by the settlers. His recorded speeches seem to have, other than the theme of the right to secure title in land, chiefly the repeated theme of the pitiable condition of the Indians. They are the speeches of a confused man uncertain of any standpoint from which to deal with events. Teedyuscung was a typical product of the disrupting conditions of the border conflict between Whites and Indians. He died without influence, murdered by Whites in his cabin, as a Connecticut land company moved settlers into the Wyoming Valley and pushed out the few remaining Delawares and Nanticokes.

As the eastern remnants of the Delawares became a disintegrating people of the border, those who had moved westward and gained permission from the Algonkian tribes to settle in eastern Ohio, were trying to reconstitute themselves. One indication was the appearance of the "Delaware Prophet," a religious leader from whom Pontiac derived support and inspiration. The Delawares settled along the rivers of eastern Ohio in some dozen towns. Here they maintained a record on bark of their legendary history, called the Walam Olum (*see Document No. 1*), and in some measure reorganized. However, they were split over the American Revolution, with one important leader favoring the British, Hopokam (known to the Whites as Captain Pipe), and another, White Eyes, who was pro-American. The Delawares fought in the Battle of Fallen Timbers with the multi-tribal army of Algonkians and suffered defeat with the rest in 1794.

The Pueblo Revolt of 1680. Like oases in a vast desert, the Pueblo Indians of what became New Mexico and Arizona constituted clusters of settled farmers among nomadic or less highly organized village peoples of the Southwest. It was the Pueblos who were the immediate target of the Spanish gold-seekers and missionaries. Coronado, like De Soto in the east, fought with and pillaged the Indian towns he encountered in 1540. Later in 1598 the Spaniards set up a colony in the heart of the largest cluster of Pueblo towns on the Rio Grande. Without competition from other Europeans, the Spaniards proceeded to establish an administrative center of New Spain in this colony at Santa Fe. The Pueblos, lacking interest in aggressive warfare and without inter-village organization, allowed themselves to be brought under the political and ecclesiastical domination of the Spaniards. The greater part of a century passed before the Spanish system of tribute and religious imposition goaded the Pueblos into military resistance.

The Pueblo villages were highly organized compact communities of from several hundred to 1,500 or more people. Along the Rio Grande alone there were some sixty, and in various parts of the arid lands to the west there were another twelve.

Each was an independent political unit. Confederations such as
the eastern Indians developed were absent. Yet intensive agriculture, by irrigation where possible, stone house construction,
elaborately organized religious life, and well-developed crafts
such as the weaving of native cotton and the making of fine
painted pottery were common to all the Pueblos. The development of a high culture focused in politically autonomous communities had been in progress for more than a thousand years.
The dominance of the Spaniards who laid immediate claim to
all the land in the name of the King of Spain (*see Document No.
6*) was nominally accepted, and the Pueblos submitted to the
adjustment of their town organization to the administrative
system of the Spaniards. It was the interference of the missionaries in their religious life which finally proved too much for
the Pueblos to accept. Despite a certain tolerance on the part of
the Spanish civil authorities, the missionaries became increasingly
determined to wipe out Pueblo religion. They developed a special
prejudice against the use of masks in religious ceremony, and
conducted raids on the sacred rooms of the Pueblo towns. The
raids resulted in collections of masks and other ceremonial
equipment which were publicly burned. Some Pueblo leaders who
protested were hanged, and this led in the 1670s to an underground effort to organize all the Pueblo towns in a resistance
movement.

A man named Popé from the town of San Juan near Santa Fe
took the lead with several others. Spanish domination now led
to an entirely new development in Pueblo culture—large scale
political organization for military resistance. Despite a near
betrayal of the secret plans, the revolt which broke out in 1680
was remarkably successful. There was unity against the Spaniards
from one end of the Pueblo country to the other. More than
1,000 Spaniards were killed, and all the others were driven
southward out of the Pueblo country. At El Paso the Spaniards
reformed their disorganized forces along with a few Indians
from the southern Pueblos and began a fifteen-year effort to
regain their foothold in the Pueblo towns. Meanwhile the organization of the Indians proved to be without permanence. It had
formed for a specific purpose—to get rid of the Spaniards. It
was successful, but it was immediately apparent that no lasting

framework of organized cooperation had been developed. The Pueblos reverted to their autonomous town way of life. As the Spaniards mustered more military force and carried out expeditions to the north, the Pueblos exhibited no further unity. By 1696 the towns along the Rio Grande were conquered and again under Spanish control, and some towns to the west were gradually also re-conquered. Only the Hopi towns in northern Arizona continued free of Spanish administrators and missionaries. They were never again brought under Spanish control.

Like almost every tribe east of the Mississippi, even though their cultural patterns militated against it, the Pueblos had tried military resistance against the Europeans. They failed ultimately, but after immediate and sweeping success. They did not try again, but instead during the eighteenth century cooperated more and more completely with the Spaniards in a military alliance against the largely nomadic tribes of the region. The acceptance of political domination and military cooperation with the Spaniards did not, however, mean, as in the case of many small groups of Indians in the east, cultural domination. The Pueblos developed an accommodation to Spanish controls which enabled them to maintain their own distinctive religious life and with that most of the core values of their total way of life. They were unique in this respect among the Indians of the United States, in that their traditional way of life underwent no basic re-orientation. Some Christian concepts and ritual were accepted, but as an adjunct, not a central part, of Pueblo religion. Likewise Spanish administrative roles were accepted, but only as peripheral features of the traditional politico-ceremonial organization of the towns. Many Pueblos learned to speak Spanish, but none through this period ceased to speak Indian languages. Pueblo adaptation involved a kind of compartmentalization of Spanish influences.

New Ways of Life in the Southwest.   In contrast with the Pueblos who learned how to keep European influences at arm's length and still make the necessary adjustments for survival, other peoples of the Southwest experienced profound transformation as a result of the European invasion. Paradoxically those whose ways of life changed most were people who remained beyond the sphere of effective Spanish political control. The Athabascan-speaking Apaches and Navajos and the Shoshonean-speaking Comanches of the southern plains became during the late 16th and the 17th centuries more interested in warfare than they had been before. This constituted a fundamental change in way of life. The instruments of the transformation were the horse which increased the range and intensified the striking power of war parties, new weapons including guns and metal for lance heads, and new settlements of the Spaniards where the domestic animals and the new tools could be acquired by raiding. During the last half of the 1600s the Comanches moved out onto the southern plains under the stimulus of the new possibilities and simultaneously pushed most of the Apaches southwestward to press against the Apaches already settling in the New Mexico area before the arrival of the Spaniards. Thus a changing and volatile situation was in process by the end of the 1600s.

The Spaniards had unwittingly released forces which were to threaten their very existence in New Mexico. Between 1685 when the first definite appearance of raiding Apaches in northeastern Sonora is recorded and about 1795 when the Pueblo-Spanish alliance had established itself as able to withstand the raiding Indians, there were decades when the frontier of Spanish settlement was pushed southward and dozens of recently made settlements had to be abandoned. The Spaniards and Pueblos on the Rio Grande became the target of constant attack. Raids and counter-raids led to a state of intermittent war. Almost throughout the 1700s neither Spaniards nor Indians were in control on this northern frontier. The Athabascans and Comanches were putting an effective northern limit on the Spanish invasion.

CHAPTER 2

New Orientations, 1763-1848

Events of the 1780s and '90s began to make clear to the Indians of the east that a new era was at hand. The devastation of the Seneca and other Iroquois villages by American troops in 1779 demonstrated that the once important League had become as powerless as "King Philip's" tiny confederation had proved to be more than a century earlier. The signing of the New York Treaty in 1790 by the McGillivray Creeks indicated that Creek leadership no longer thought in terms of freedom from dominating involvement with the Whites. The displaced Algonkians massing in the Northwest for renewed resistance suffered decisive defeat in the Battle of Fallen Timbers in 1794, and the memory of Pontiac's failure thirty years before added to a sense of desperation. These events took place in the context of disintegrating and dividing Indian communities. The Iroquois had begun to regard drunkenness and aimless apathy, like that which had characterized the harassed Delawares at the margins of Pennsylvania settlement a half century earlier, as major problems. The depopulated Creek and Choctaw towns were no longer prosperous in the face of the endless depredations of the Georgians and other settlers of the southeast, and their leaders were at odds with one another. The Algonkians were experiencing the same relentless pressures, as the Long Knives, the new border breed, moved steadily into what had been the refuge area of Ohio and Indiana.

What had happened was the emergence of a single nation from among the European invaders as a dominant and determined power. The British had eliminated the French in 1763. The Americans had in turn nearly eliminated the British in 1781, and it was apparent by 1812, if not before, that neither the British nor the Spanish were powers to be reckoned with in the territory east of the Mississippi. The determination of the Americans to push the Indians on in front of their advance became clear and definite in the Northwest within the decade after the Battle of Fallen Timbers. Every parley with the Americans resulted in demands that the Indians give up more land and move west. (*See Document No. 6.*) The United States government had obligated itself in a treaty with the Georgians to help them get Indians out of their territory, and thus the pressure to cede land for other land west of the Mississippi had become constant on the Choctaws, Creeks, and Cherokees. The typical treaty of the times—and there were many—contained an agreement by whatever Indians happened to sign to give up all or most of the land they were then living on in return for a grant of land from the federal government somewhere farther west. The United States agreed in turn to guarantee protection in perpetuity, but typically within a decade or less the settlers brought pressure again for cession of the recently guaranteed lands.

Under these conditions the borderlands of settlement were zones where Indians and Whites were in constant conflict. The effect on an emerging American public consciousness at the national level was the growth of strong support for a policy of isolation of Indians in the unsettled west. The view which was crystallizing was that Indians, for their own well-being (*see Document No. 21*), should be moved into the still dimly conceived lands beyond the Mississippi, perhaps concentrated together somewhere, where they could lead their own lives pretty much as they pleased out of the way of the settlers. The national Congress passed a Removal Act in 1830 which embodied this idea. (*See Document No. 23.*) It empowered the president to remove and make certain provisions for the eastern Indians in territory west of the Mississippi. The act authorized such removal only on condition that the Indians gave consent. In practice the presidents and their representatives continued to act on the basis of getting any Indians whatsoever, by whatever means possible, to sign treaties providing for their removal. Removal was already fixed policy before the passage of the act and this policy had been executed with little or no regard for existing Indian political organization.

The political arena of the many nations had changed profoundly. The aspirations for cultural autonomy and some degree of separate political existence still prevailed among the yet unbroken Indian nations. But the organization for achieving the aims was breaking down, as the exercise of American power pulled Indians one way and another. The efforts toward confederation along traditional lines no longer had meaning, except for the Algonkians of the Northwest where unmodified tribal life was strongest. The times called for new ideas, new forms of organization, new conceptions of the future. Indians everywhere accepted the challenge. The new phase of Indian adaptation involved re-orientation, in some instances, of religious faith, in others, of political organization. The first quarter of the nineteenth century was a period of remarkable recasting of ways of life among the Indians. In some respects what took place among them was parallel with what was taking place also among the Americans.

Two thousand miles away in the southwest a somewhat reverse process went on. The one European nation which had invaded this region was declining in power. Spain had never been able to complete the conquest of the southwestern tribes, had managed only with difficulty to maintain, with the help of the Pueblo Indians, its small foothold in New Mexico in the midst of the rapidly changing and increasingly powerful surrounding tribes. Here from the 1790s until 1848 Spanish power steadily declined. Spanish cultural influence, direct and indirect, had brought great changes, but the trend toward European domination, in contrast with what was happening in the east, was on the wane.

The Handsome Lake Religion. In the 1790s Americans experienced what came to be called a "Second Awakening" of the religious life. There was a ferment of religious feeling which was expressed in new kinds of gatherings under the fluid conditions of frontier settlement. This new intensity of religious life was fanned by travelling ministers of Methodist, Baptist, and Presbyterian persuasion. They set up tents in clearings where thousands of people gathered. The camp meetings were places of frenzied preaching and action. The biggest of all camp meetings was reputed to have taken place at Cain Ridge in Kentucky in 1801. The religious excitement extended through most of the areas of new settlement, as well as within the longer settled areas. New religions of several different kinds arose. Between 1785 and 1848 the settlers of the state of New York received new revelations or revitalized older ones and embarked on new ways of life. The Shakers, the Mormons, the Oneida Community, and the spiritualists had their beginnings, or American foundations, in frontier New York.

One of the new religious teachings of this area was confined to Indians. About 1800 some twenty-five years before Joseph Smith received the revelations which became the basis of the Mormon Church, an elderly Seneca Indian began to be aware of new teachings being revealed to him. His name was Ganeodiyo which was translated as Handsome Lake and his teachings became know to Iroquois-speaking people as Kaiwiyoh, referred to in English as the Code of Handsome Lake. (*See Document No. 34.*)

Handsome Lake was a Seneca with the hereditary title of sachem but of no reputation. Like a good many men of the Six Nations in the period of the decline of the League after the defeats of the American Revolution, he had been a heavy drinker—a man with no particular purpose in life. When he was about 60 he became ill and suffered from illness for a number of years. In 1800 he began to have unusual dreams in which he was in touch with supernatural beings who told him that a new way of life must be opened up for the Senecas. Handsome Lake began to preach to others about what he was hearing in his dreams. Many listened. Within a few years Handsome Lake's teaching was known among all the Iroquois of New York and by 1807 was spreading among those who had gone to Canada.

At the time of Handsome Lake's revelations, the Iroquois had reached a nadir in their history. Their League and its principle of unanimity had been disintegrating for 60 years. Always involved in European rivalries the growth of division of opinion had proceeded steadily, so that by the time of the American Revolution no concerted action was possible among the Six Nations. The Senecas were perhaps the most united in support of the British, while others had been divided or had supported the Americans. It was the Senecas in their villages in Western New York who suffered the most drastic physical destruction of all the Six Nations at the hands of the Americans.

Yet it was also the Senecas by 1794 who possessed more land than any Indians who stayed in New York. They had probably suffered the least disruption as a result of missionary and other European influences. Unlike the Mohawks who had been badly split by both political and religious influences and removal to Canada, the Senecas were in the 1790s less divided into factions. Unlike their neighbors, the Cayugas, they were not yet infiltrated deeply by White settlement. Unlike the Oneidas who were the first of the Iroquois to leave for the west, hoping for peace out of the range of European settlers, the main body of Senecas had remained in what they had regarded as their homeland for a century or more.

They were, of course, not untouched by European influences. On the contrary, they had early involved themselves just as heartily in the wars for the fur trade as any other of the Five Nations, and had continued to align themselves in the conflicts between English and French, being responsible, for example, for the destruction of the British traders in their territory at the time of the French and Indian Wars. They did not welcome but they harbored for a time a few Jesuits, and their sachems, Red Jacket (*see Document No. 35*) and Cornplanter, had become well-known in parleys with the British and Americans. Moreover, they had welcomed missionaries of the Society of Friends or Quakers, for whom they had a great deal of respect. The Senecas were unusual among the Iroquois in the degree to which they had preserved territorial integrity and avoided shattering factionalism. Nevertheless about 1800 they were undergoing the same processes as all the other Iroquois, namely, loss of purpose and social disorganization.

The New Code. It was in this milieu that Handsome Lake began to preach. What he presented was not merely new religious doctrine; rather the emphasis was on a way to bring about moral regeneration. He taught that there was a heaven such as the Christians believed in and also that President George Washington was an important figure like St. Peter at the gates of heaven. He taught that there was a God such as his Quaker friends believed in, but he did not preach that God was to be served in the way the Christians believed. He held that the so-called mourning rites of the traditional Iroquois religion should be observed and did not advocate the rejection of the other aspects of Iroquois religious belief and ceremony. More important than his theology, which did not call for much change from what was already traditionally dominant among the Senecas, was his spirited preaching of a new system of morals with specific rules of behavior. It was this that his listeners among the Indians were most struck with and led to their regarding his preaching as pointing to a new way of life.

The new rules showed some influence from the Quakers in Seneca country. They embodied both traditional Iroquois ways and some White ways in a new synthesis. Handsome Lake had nothing to say about the matrilineal clan system of the Iroquois, but he had a great deal to say about the importance of hard work as farmers and about the need for education. Handsome Lake preached against certain evils, especially drunkenness and witchcraft. He was most interested in advocating certain virtuous behavior, which included the recognition of kinship obligations, especially within the nuclear family. He advocated hospitality and was concerned about orphans and waifs, suggesting that these were serious problems among the Senecas at that time. He emphasized the importance of learning White ways as taught in the schools, proposing that two students from each Nation be appointed to go to White schools, but he opposed the sending of all Iroquois children to American schools; he held that it was important for Iroquois to know how to deal with the American ways, but he thought such knowledge should be a specialty. Iroquois education should be on a different base. He urged that men should farm, build timber houses instead of bark houses, and should keep and carefully manage domestic animals. He also had a good deal to say about political behavior, urging the importance of unanimity in decisions and neutrality in the wars between Whites, as in the War of 1812.

It is clear that this code was a fusion, involving a selective acceptance of White ways. It did not advocate the abandonment of Iroquois ways. On the contrary it was an assertion of the importance of Iroquois religious belief and custom.

Handsome Lake preached the Code for fifteen years, from 1800 until his death in 1815. During these years he was widely accepted by the Iroquois. He immediately found followers among Onondagas, the few remaining Cayugas in New York state, and within a few years his teaching had spread to the Six Nations reserve in Ontario and elsewhere among Iroquois in Canada. What he preached was beginning, in the hands of a few followers, to be memorized or closely paraphrased and then repeated like sacred texts. There were public recitals of the Handsome Lake Code. The Code was regarded as a revolutionary religious system and Handsome Lake as a great innovator for reform and change, especially since some obviously Christian beliefs were a part of his doctrine. He was not, in short, a traditionalist urging a return to the old.

Nevertheless, during the next thirty years the Handsome Lake religion became the bulwark of those Senecas and other Iroquois who were resisting the pressures for change by the Whites. Between 1815 and 1845 several land companies attempted to acquire the Seneca land. Their representatives, often with the assistance of federal government agents, tried by various means to get the Indians to sell their land and move west. Quaker missionaries and others supported those Indians who resisted. As a result of various shady deals and constant pressures large parts of the land remaining after the 1794 treaty were sold, so that the Indians were concentrated into smaller and smaller sections of their old territory. Equally serious for Iroquois welfare was the crystallization of two sharp factions, one opposed to removal and one favoring it. Those Iroquois who favored removal were chiefly those who had been converted to a Christian denomination. Those who opposed had not, which meant in most cases that they were adherents with greater or lesser intensity of the Code of Handsome Lake. The Code in fact held specifically that the Indians should retain their land, that they should remain Iroquois in identity and in distinctive religious belief, while at the same time accepting the need for change in work customs, family life, and interpersonal relations.

The pressures for removal and intrigues regarding the land built to a crisis after 1826. As this happened the factionalism intensified. Most of the traditional sachems appointed by the clan groups had become Christians and were aligned with those who favored giving up the lands and moving west. In response to anti-removal sentiment some of the councils were reorganized so that the sachems became elected rather than hereditary. Paradoxically, what had been a revolutionary new development in religion became the bulwark of those Iroquois who were conservative in the sense that they advocated holding the traditional lands and to an Iroquois oriented religion rather than Christianity. At the same time they tended to support the most European features of a domestic economy and the reorganization of the old council system toward democratic election, instead of family controlled selection. They became known as "pagans" despite the fact that the way of life to which Handsome Lake had led them was so much influenced by Christianity and by European civilization. In the 1820s about three-quarters of the Senecas remained opposed to removal and were devotees of the Handsome Lake Code and religion. Under the leadership of Red Jacket and with the help of some Whites they successfully fought the efforts to push the Iroquois west. The Handsome Lake religion gave them unity and a program.

In 1845 the followers of Handsome Lake began to write down the oral statements of the code which it had become customary to recite. From this time on a sacred written text became available. The one-time revolutionary teaching had become the basis for an established religion. It continued as such among the Iroquois for the next century and a half.

The Algonkian Prophets. The good hunting lands of what became the Northwest Territory were already a gathering place for displaced Indians (chiefly Algonkian-speaking) by the early 1700s. People from various regions had claimed collective hunting rights in Ohio, Indiana, and western Pennsylvania. The Cherokees maintained such a claim until 1764 when in the Treaty of Fort Stanwix they relinquished their rights to all land north of the Ohio.

Not all the Algonkians were displaced from the east. There were Shawnees from the south, Ottawas from the north, Kickapoos from the west. They spoke related languages, although they had been widely separated at the arrival of the Europeans.

By 1763, when Pontiac tried to give leadership to this motley group of re-forming nations, there may have been 15,000 to 20,000 Indians in the area from the headwaters of the Ohio River in western Pennsylvania to the Illinois and between the

Ohio and the Great Lakes. Delawares had been gathering for some years on the Muskingum River in eastern Ohio. The Shawnees had sought relief from the Carolina and Virginia settlers below the Ohio and had established themselves on the Miami River west of the Delawares. The Ottawas had been moving southward out of the Michigan Peninsula and the Potawatomis were moving similarly on the other side of Lake Michigan. The Fox, the Sac, and the Illinois were trying to move out of range of the French and hence southward. One of the most noted of the nations were the Kickapoos who had been associated with the French in the mid-1600s, but had rejected Jesuit missionaries in 1670, and since that time had sought through association with other Algonkians, such as the Mascoutens and Fox, to dominate the Northwest. They were reputed to have developed a confederacy of some strength in the 1680s which challenged the Iroquois. It is certainly true that they raided as far east as Niagara in the late 1680s and that they seem to have sought an alliance against the French with the British-leaning Iroquois. They were ranging widely from their villages in Indiana and were well-known as fighting men.

In this newly forming and fermenting population of embattled Algonkians from many parts, all of whom had had intensive contact with some Europeans, the leadership of any one nation or any one man was not apparent by 1750. Unity of action was far less than among either the Creeks or the Iroquois. The amalgam was too new. There were no very consistent trends or policies among the Indians with regard to alliances with Europeans. A general tendency toward the hostile rejection of European ways and contacts appeared intermittently even though there was a reality of trade interests which pulled groups into the orbit of European contacts.

The Delaware Prophet. Most, like the Delawares, the Shawnees, and the Kickapoos, had experienced bitter fighting and much destruction at the hands of Europeans. Under these circumstances there appeared in the early 1760s a Delaware prophet. (*See Document No. 32.*) His name seems to be lost to history, but his activities beginning in the vicinity of the Delaware settlements on the Muskingum River have been recorded. The Delaware Prophet under the influence of supernatural revelation prepared a "map" about fifteen inches square which he carried with him as he preached among the Algonkian-speaking peoples. The burden of what he taught was in sharp contrast with the Code of Handsome Lake. He preached the rejection of European things and a return to a way of life which Indians practiced before the coming of the Europeans. The path to this restoration of the old ways was the rejection of European trade.

The Delaware Prophet's doctrine was based on his graphic representation of the Path. There was a direct route to a better, or heavenly, land. To follow the Path Indians should get rid of domestic animals introduced by Europeans and should adhere to special rituals which had been revealed to the Prophet. The re-gathering Algonkians were ripe for such teaching. Following the French and Indian War, with the French out of the way, an Ottawa leader named Pontiac, obviously influenced by the teachings of the Delaware Prophet, made an effort to unite the Algonkians for an all-out attack on the British to eliminate them from the Northwest. The attack resulted in the destruction of the British controlled trading posts in western Pennsylvania, Ohio, and Michigan and focused in a siege of Fort Detroit. The British ultimately in 1763 defeated the forces of Wyandots, Ottawas, Kickapoos, Shawnees, and Delawares which Pontiac was able to inspire for a year. Thereafter the Delaware Prophet was not heard from, and Pontiac was killed by the British.

The Open Door and Tecumseh. The defeat of Pontiac, a second major defeat at Fallen Timbers in 1794, and the establishment of American military forces in the northwest to protect the incoming settlers kept the Algonkians in turmoil. They were under constant pressure to cede their lands and move west. The Delawares, the Shawnees, and others were forced to make treaties and move. Border warfare with the American settlers who respected no treaties was constant. In the midst of the turmoil the tradition of the Delaware Prophet remained alive. Two brothers of Shawnee descent began to espouse a cause based in the same kind of vision of the future as characterized the Delaware Prophet. One brother named Laulewasika, who later changed his name to Tenskwatawa, received a revelation in 1805. (*See Document No. 36.*) This had general features similar to the earlier revelation, but clearly constituted something new with respect to specific doctrine and ritual. White men's weapons, animals, and ways in general were to be rejected. A period of darkness or some other natural catastrophe would take place by which the White men would be destroyed, or at least the Americans, for there was a focus on opposition to the Americans rather than all White men. The Indians should follow certain rituals and practice certain acts in common, including the killing of all their dogs. Sacred paraphernalia including sacred strings and a ritual connected with them, called shaking the hand of the Prophet, were employed. Dances, songs, and ceremonies were specified which were based in existing religious practice. This doctrine of the regeneration of Indian life as the result of a millennium was preached by many followers of Tenskwatawa throughout the Algonkian tribes around the Great Lakes and was carried as far as the Creeks in Alabama.

The movement was centered at what was called the Prophet's Town, later Greenville. As developed the doctrine included the idea that all tribes were one and none could make a separate treaty with Whites regarding the land. Pilgrims came from great distances to the Prophet's Town, where ceremonies were attended by thousands of Indians of many tribes, but all Algonkian. It remained a peaceful religious movement until 1810. From 1807 on, the brother of the prophet, Tecumseh, assumed leadership in councils and held conferences with American officials at which he took a determined stand with regard to no further relinquishment of Indian lands. (*See Document No. 37.*) Tecumseh also claimed that previous treaties were invalid because Indians who signed them had acted as individuals.

In 1811 Tecumseh reaffirmed the position that the Indians were determined to stand together. He told the Americans that the Indians wished to be peaceful, but that they would fight if necessary. The Americans refused to accept the position and, like dominant peoples always in the face of prophets of the oppressed, regarded Tenskwatawa as an "impostor." Tecumseh after a council with the Americans made a tour to the south (*see Document No. 38*), going to Tukabahchee of the Creek Nation where he made the effort to persuade the Creeks to join in a last stand with the Algonkians in Indiana and Ohio. He went as far as Florida and persuaded the Seminoles. It was clear that he was an able speaker and that the doctrine which he preached rested ultimately on religious revelation. While Tecumseh was in the south the Americans in Ohio decided to strike. They attacked Prophet's Town, destroyed it and others, and defeated the Indians who opposed them.

On his return Tecumseh was ready for war. As the War of 1812 between the British and the Americans broke out, he joined the British and fought with his supporters against the Americans. He was killed in 1813. His brother, the Prophet, survived until 1827. The movement disintegrated, and the Indians of the Northwest gradually moved west beyond the Mississippi.

Kennekuk, the Kickapoo. Prophecy and new religion were not dead among the Algonkians. By 1827 a new prophet had arisen among the Kickapoos. A man named Kennekuk had revelations which like the earlier ones urged a peaceful approach to relations between Whites and Indians. Also like the others this revelation contained a prescription for getting to heaven. Its ritual centered about prayer sticks with which the people recited prayers. Kennekuk's teaching opposed drinking whiskey. His influence was never very wide, not extending beyond several hundred of the northern branch of Kickapoos in Illinois and perhaps one hundred Potawatomis whom he converted.

Kennekuk refused to leave the northern Kickapoo villages in Illinois, even though the southern branch had by that time agreed to go west. He remained peaceful but yielded to pressure and signed a treaty in 1832 to exchange the Illinois lands for some in Kansas, where his followers settled to the number of about 350. They remained there and took up farming, raising truck produce for Fort Leavenworth. His influence continued strong until his death in 1852. His leadership resulted in an unhealable breach between the northern and southern Kickapoos.

The line of the Algonkian prophets maintained continuity through nearly a hundred years and involved the conscious rejection of Christianity for specific reasons and the rejection of selected White customs, especially drinking whiskey. Each prophet began with peaceful aims, but two of the movements ended in violence under the leadership of men who had not themselves experienced the revelations. Each became an organized religion, and each emphasized Indian identity as distinct from White. The distinctive features of the Algonkian movements as compared with the Iroquois were the millennial teaching and the strong reaction against White customs.

The Cherokee Nation.   The Iroquois and the Algonkian efforts to find ways of adapting to the new conditions of life contrasted sharply. The Iroquois sought some combination of new and old in a working synthesis while the Algonkians rejected the new and sought return of the old. Both, nevertheless, rested on supernatural revelation. In the southeast a very different sort of adaptation took place. Here during the 1820s among the Cherokees a new way of life crystallized which was not based on revelation. It was rather a rational effort to adapt American forms of organization to the needs of the developing Cherokee society.

The Cherokees emerged by 1800 as the most cohesive of the Indian nations in the southeast. The Creek Confederacy had become fragmented into groups of towns hardly capable of concerted action in the face of the political crises of the times. Creeks submitted to the American Indian commissioner's efforts to organize them in new ways, but the new organization was not adapted to their needs and merely stimulated the growing internal differences. In contrast the Cherokees, after a period of disruption resulting from border warfare with the British and the Americans, began after 1795 to develop a new unity. They had renounced claim to hunting lands north of the Ohio and had been pushed southwestward by the settlers in eastern Tennessee. By 1800 their towns were concentrated east and north of the Creeks in south central Tennessee, northwestern Georgia, and northeastern Alabama. Here there were some 75 towns and villages.

In these settlements there were many mixed bloods resulting from the influx into Cherokee territory of Virginian settlers, British Tories, and itinerant peddlers from Germany. European missionaries had had almost no effect up to this time on the life of the Cherokees. The Creeks had permitted the Moravians to work among them as early as 1740 and the Presbyterians beginning in 1758, but there were very few converts. However, after 1800 missionary influences began to be important, chiefly through schools which the Cherokee leadership strongly insisted must be the major focus of missionary activity. A far-sighted group of leaders began after 1800 to lead the Cherokees into a cultural renaissance. This took place in the short space of about one generation, between 1800 and 1830.

The Cultural Renaissance. The renaissance came about in the midst of many pressures and was a response to these. The state of Georgia adopted a policy of eliminating all Indians, whether Creek or Cherokees, from their borders. Besides the casual murders and lawless seizure of land and livestock which had characterized the action of Georgians against the Creeks for nearly a century, there were also the relentless pressures from the northeast as the Cumberland area filled with settlers. The Georgians had ceded land in what became the state of Mississippi to the federal government in 1802, in return for which the government had agreed to extinguish Indian title to all land in the state of Georgia. The United States government thus became a party to the Georgians' program of Indian removal. The federal agent made constant efforts to get cessions of Cherokee territory, efforts attended with great success until 1819. Cessions made in 1804–05 and again in 1816–17 and 1818 resulted in compressing Cherokees ever southward and westward. The United States agent also worked effectively to stimulate changes in Cherokee economy, including home industry in weaving and improved agriculture. When Tecumseh's war in the north broke out in 1811 the Cherokees found themselves under pressure once again to go to war. They yielded to American influence, furnishing 800 men to help put down the Red Stick faction of the Creeks who fought under the aegis of the Tecumseh movement. In the midst of these pressures of war and for land cessions, the Cherokees struggled to re-cast their way of life.

One need which a majority of Cherokees felt was means for controlling persons within their own society who yielded to the pressures for ceding tribal lands. In 1817, for example, a minority of headmen signed a treaty to cede a large portion of

Cherokee territory for land on the Arkansas River beyond the Mississippi, and some 2,000 Cherokees went west to settle there. The great majority of Cherokees did not wish to go west and regarded this action as traitorous.

The leadership which succeeded in regenerating Cherokee life through secular reorganization took one reasoned step after another. They formed a political structure which was designed to enable the Cherokees to survive as Cherokees in what was left of the ancestral lands. This organization was built on, but constituted something new and different from, the system which they had developed along the lines of the Creek confederacy prior to the late 1700s. It bore no resemblance to the reorganization based on dominance of war leaders which McGillivray of the Creeks had tried to institute before 1790. A series of steps were taken beginning in 1802 which led during the next 25 years to a constitutional convention and a new form of government. The men who accomplished this were an old experienced "most beloved man," who had come up through the national council and had led negotiations with the British and the Americans in the border warfare of the late 1700s—Path Killer who remained throughout the period the Principal Chief of the Cherokees; Charles Hicks who had been converted by the Moravians in 1813, the second "most beloved man"; The Ridge who had no formal schooling and served as speaker of the Council; a young man named John Ross, the descendant on his father's side of a trading family of Scots who had had some schooling in Tennessee; and others of lesser importance and various backgrounds. It was not a revolution of young men, but a concerted action of elders and younger men, sometimes assisted by delegations of women whose place continued high in Cherokee affairs. They worked slowly, building along two lines: (1) pushing for schools which the missionaries ran and (2) working out innovations in their political and community organization.

They moved first in 1808 to write down the legislation of the national council and thus to develop a body of codified laws. The first law established "regulating companies" which were later called Light Horse Guards, for the maintenance of law and order in all parts of the Cherokee territory. In 1810, they legislated against the ancient tradition of clan revenge. They had already ruled that any killing which resulted from a Light Horse Guard's action in fulfilling his duty should not be avenged by relatives of the victim. Now they wrote off all standing clan grievances and prohibited further clan vengeance. This was followed in 1817 by the establishment of a bicameral legislature, consisting of a National Committee and the traditional National Council (modeled along Creek lines). The new Committee was given major responsibility for "national affairs," such as negotiating treaties and for regulating the payment of annuities for earlier land cessions. They were moved to do this because of the disorder and the activities of White land speculators at the annual national gatherings for annuity payments and by the fact that a minority of head men had in 1817 negotiated a land cession treaty for lands in the west.

In 1820 further measures for organizing the administration of justice were effected. The Cherokee territory was divided into eight districts, in each of which there would be a council house where a judge for the district would transact business of the court. Circuit judges were also provided for in a provision which linked districts in pairs. This legislation embodied a move toward geographical representation on the National Council, four representatives from each district to be elected for the term of a year. In 1822 the Council established a National Supreme Court, thus completing their judicial system, and also formally defined the offices of the national political structure with two "beloved men" at the top, a President of the National Committee and a Speaker of the Council. In 1825 the Council authorized and planned the building of a national capital at New Echota and the establishment of a national printing press. In 1827 a National Constitutional Convention was ordered by the Council to be composed of elected representatives, who then proceeded to draw up a constitution, which largely formalized what had already been developed. The constitution was prepared and, after some opposition by a leader named White Path, was approved in 1828. Thus the new state of the Cherokees grew during some twenty years, developing part by part out of the already existing national organization.

The other feature of the conscious program of the Cherokee

leadership consisted in the encouragement of formal education in the manner of the Americans. In this the National Council had to work with the missionaries, who increasingly after 1800 sought to evangelize the Indians. The Cherokees in general were little interested in accepting any of the denominational teachings. It seems doubtful that even after thirty years of work by the missionaries that there were as many as 3,000 converts, even though six different Protestant denominations were given freedom to pursue their efforts: the Moravians, the Baptists, the Methodists, and, under the auspices of the American Board of Commissioners for Foreign Missions, the Dutch Reformed, the Congregationalists, and the Presbyterians. From the first the Cherokee leaders insisted that each denominational group set up schools. When the missionaries were slow or when they seemed to emphasize evangelical work at the expense of schools, the Council put pressure on them to set up schools and generally the missionaries responded. By 1825 there were eight schools established by the American Board alone, and the Moravians and Baptists had perhaps another five schools in operation. Attendance at the schools was considerable, while interest in the churches was weak. The American Board also arranged for graduates of their schools, especially from the first established in 1817 at Brainerd in the Chickamauga country, to go on to more advanced work at Cornwall, Connecticut. Some ten young Cherokees, including a son of The Ridge and Buck Ooawatie (later known as Elias Boudinot), were trained at Cornwall and came back to take prominent roles in the Cherokee renaissance. Thus a leaven of formally trained young men and women began to play a part in the new orientation of the Cherokees, as a result of strong support by the Cherokee leadership.

A third important factor in the Cherokee development was wholly unplanned by the National Council. But this was of major importance nevertheless. Between 1809 and 1821 a Cherokee named Sequoyah, who also called himself Charles Gist, worked out a method for writing the Cherokee language. He was wholly without formal schooling, but was aware that the Americans wrote messages. He worked out a series of 85 symbols for the basic syllables of Cherokee, in the manner of the modern Japanese syllabary. A primer was prepared and the

American Board gave support for a press to publish a periodical in the new Cherokee writing. The New Testament was translated and printed in the syllabary. In 1828 a national press was established and Elias Boudinot was made editor of a national newspaper called the *Cherokee Phoenix*. In the space of a few years Cherokees generally became so interested that a great majority became literate. The stimulus to national growth was tremendous as the *Cherokee Phoenix* began to be published regularly. There was a convergence of the growth of a national leadership which combined experience in both American and Cherokee cultures, the development of ideas about the necessity for a new organization of the society as a whole, and a technological development in the form of writing for the Cherokee language, which stimulated and guided communication. These factors combined to produce the Cherokee renaissance.

The Cherokees and Andrew Jackson. Under these circumstances the Cherokees became the most influential Indian nation in the southeast. The Creeks had been in process of disintegration since the 1790s. They had been less able than the Cherokees to withstand the pressures to separate them from their land and had suffered increasingly from fraudulent land operations by the Americans. Their breakdown proceeded further when they split over the teaching of Tecumseh and Tenskwatawa in 1812. They divided sharply into two factions. One, the so-called Red Stick group, embraced much of Tecumseh's doctrine and when war broke out in the north after Tecumseh's return there, they initiated a rebellion against the Americans in their own country. General Andrew Jackson was able to persuade the Cherokees to give him support, and the Red Sticks were thoroughly defeated. Creek unity was broken and they steadily succumbed to the efforts of the Alabamans, supported by President Jackson, to get them out of Alabama and into the western country. The Choctaws, too, had disintegrated as a national group and like the Creeks found no means for resisting the American design for removing them. Only later after removal did the Creeks and the Choctaws reorganize themselves and when they did they took many leaves from the Cherokee book. Some Seminoles split from the Creeks and one faction, under the leadership of Osceola, retreated into the Florida Everglades where despite defeats they kept together and found in isolation some defense against the pressures of the Whites. The Chickasaws, depleted in population, and weary of fighting the Osages for the Spanish, were tending toward virtual absorption into the Choctaws.

Almost at the height of their new development, the Cherokees were cut down. In 1829, just as the Constitutional Convention had finished its work, and the *Cherokee Phoenix* was being avidly read each month by thousands of Cherokees, gold was discovered in the Cherokee country. All the old pressures were redoubled, with the traditional ruthlessness of the Georgians, for pushing the Cherokees out of their way and opening up Cherokee territory to White settlement. The Cherokee leaders brought to bear all their experience with their own government and that of the United States in a determined effort to maintain themselves in their homeland. They brought a suit in the United States Supreme Court against the State of Georgia, challenging the Georgians' right to remove them. The Cherokees won the case in 1831 with an historic decision by Chief Justice John Marshall. Their legal rights were recognized and established on paper, but President Jackson was determined, along with the Georgian governor, to make a clean sweep of the Indians from the southeast. (*See Document No. 22.*) He initiated a campaign of undercover persuasion and bribery of whatever Cherokees could be reached in an effort to get signatures to a treaty agreeing to removal. The campaign worked. The Ridge and Elias Boudinot, among others, signed such a treaty. It was clear that a minority of Cherokee leaders had been separated from prevailing Cherokee opinion. Meanwhile John Ross, representing the overwhelming majority, made every effort to persuade high level officials and the Congress in Washington, as well as the American public in general, that the main body of Cherokees had not consented and did not intend to consent to the removal efforts. The Cherokee National Council maintained a delegation in Washington for several years, fighting the trend so strongly supported by the president. But the Supreme Court decision, a considerable amount of public sympathy, and the high ability of the Cherokee delegation were of no avail. Like all the other nations in the southeast, in 1832 the Cherokees were ordered to move to Indian Territory. The Army was placed in charge of the operation, and the 16,000 Cherokees went west along the "Trail of Tears."

Cultural Pluralism in New Mexico. Indian life within the area of Spain's influence in the Southwest developed in a strikingly different way from that in the east. The three major modes of adaptation of the eastern Indians in this phase—religious revitalization, religious millenarianism, and political re-organization—made no appearance in New Mexico and Arizona. In this area Spain was without competition for power from other Europeans. The thrust of Spanish empire was strong at first, but by the late 1700s was very much on the wane. The frontier of New Spain steadily lost support from the weakening home country. Missionaries had increasing difficulty recruiting both funds and dedicated workers. Expenditures for maintaining the military posts declined, at the very time that the military power of the nomadic Indians was building to its peak. No mines of any importance had been discovered north of Chihuahua, and hence administrative interest in the area was weak.

Under these circumstances Spanish cultural influence was declining, in contrast with the vigorous growth of both military power and cultural influence of the British-Americans in the east. The town-dwelling Pueblos and the Piman-speaking villagers of New Mexico and Arizona, stimulated and changed by the earlier missionary and political influences, were entering a phase of greater political independence. This was accompanied by more freedom to integrate in their own ways what they had borrowed and what had been forced on them by the Spaniards. The nomadic tribes, so radically changed by the opportunities that Spanish weapons, animals, and settler communities offered them, had still not been subjected to full Spanish political control. Thus as Spanish controls declined, Indians found themselves with their cultures enriched and much freedom to make their own choices and develop further their own ways of life. This contrasted with the precisely opposite trend during the first half of the 1800s in the east, where Indians had become subject to greater and greater controls from the Europeans.

A European derived culture was nevertheless solidly implanted in New Mexico, where the first Spanish settlers had come. These well-established settlers did not withdraw with the decline in

Spanish political power and the reduction in number of officials and upper class residents of towns like Sante Fe. The Spanish-speaking settlers had developed their own distinctive way of life as they adapted to the New Mexican environment. They were in a sense cultural orphans increasingly cut off from contacts with their motherland. As they lost contact they became more deeply adjusted to the local scene. This involved close contacts with Pueblo Indians who were their neighbors. Inter-marriage and much cultural borrowing took place. Subsistence patterns and technology became similar. They fought side by side with the Pueblos to withstand the raids of the nomadic Indians, which became more intensive as the Spanish military weakened and as dependence on the Spanish and Pueblo settlements for horses, sheep, and other goods became greater.

The relationship between Spaniards and Indians was uncomplicated by either competition for land or political control. The population of the Spanish villages was nearly stable by 1800. No fresh increments of Spanish colonists came after the mid-1700s. With no aggressive additional immigration, relationships remained friendly from the late 1700s until 1848, when Americans began to come into the region. It was a period of relationships of equality between Indians and Europeans. The Pueblos learned to keep certain aspects of their ways hidden such as ceremonialism, but they and the Hispanos had much in common in Catholic ritual. We may speak of this situation as cultural pluralism characterized by an absence of pressures for dominance among either the Spanish-descended villagers or the long-time resident Indians.

CHAPTER 3

Dependent Domestic Nations, 1831-1898

After forcing the Mexicans from the Southwest in 1848, the Americans became the sole military power from the Atlantic to the Pacific. A transformation of Indian policy promptly began. From the explicit assertion by the United States Supreme Court in 1832 that the Indians had the right of self-government on lands guaranteed them by the United States, the Americans moved in 1898 to over-ride the right of even the highly organized "Five Civilized Tribes" to maintain their own local government.

The Supreme Court decided in 1831 (*see Document No. 11*), three years after the state of Georgia had passed legislation asserting Georgia's political jurisdiction in Cherokee country, that the Cherokees and other Indians were dependent domestic nations, that is, definable political entities within the United States. In 1832 the Court went on to make explicit the Cherokee right to self-government and to nullify the legislation which Georgia had passed over-riding that right. (*See Document No. 12.*) These decisions stemmed from the British policy of dealing with the Indians as nations possessed of rights to enter into treaties which both Europeans and Indians were obligated to honor. It was a part of the eighteenth-century conception of political rights on which the government of the United States itself had arisen. It was the basis on which the Cherokees, under the general protection of the United States government, had proceeded to build their national government.

The fact of military power in the hands of the United States government was working to bring about a wholly different conception of Indian-White relations. The American settlers throughout the west were finding an increasingly effective national military force on which they were able to call for controlling the Indians who stood in their way. The dominance of the settlers led steadily to the elimination of any conception of Indian political rights. A major step in the legal codification of

66

this view came in 1871 when the United States Congress acted to put an end to the making of treaties with any Indian group. This was the beginning of a formal repudiation of the position of the Supreme Court and signalized the new era in Indian affairs. The climax came in 1898 when Congress adopted the Curtis Act specifically dissolving the governments which the Five Civilized Tribes had maintained from the time of their removal to Indian Territory.

The Curtis Act was a response to resistance which the tribes in question made to carrying out certain other features of United States policy. During the 1870s and 1880s, as more and more western tribes were defeated and placed on reservations, strong public sentiment developed against the treatment of Indians. Various national associations were formed consisting exclusively of Whites, which took it on themselves to study the Indian situation. They found conditions which they urged the government to correct. They found bureaucratic corruption; unjust and arbitrary treatment of Indians which ignored bona fide treaties; and starving, ill-clothed, and hopeless Indians. A very influential book by Helen Hunt Jackson called *A Century of Dishonor,* published in 1881, recounted a long list of injustices, broken agreements, and disregard of Indian welfare. (*See Document No. 24.*) The organizations, such as the Indian Rights Association, persuaded Congress and the Secretary of the Interior, under whose jurisdiction the Bureau of Indian Affairs had been placed in 1849, to adopt a program designed to eliminate evils and provide for the bettering of conditions among the Indians.

Even though it stemmed from strong humanitarian sentiments, the program was itself an expression of the new dominant conception that Indians had no political rights comparable to those of the White society. It played moreover into the hands of members of Congress who represented persons interested in acquiring still more of the Indian-held land. The dominating view was that the Indian situation could be improved only if the Indians gave up their distinctive ways of life and were forced to adopt the dominant way. (*See Document No. 26.*) This, it was pointed out, would take place automatically if the Indian land were divided up and allotted to Indian family heads. The responsibility of owning and managing the individual allotments would turn Indians into self-sustaining citizens of American society. Incidentally, the "surplus" land left over after allotment could be opened for further White settlement. This plan, after some debate in Congress and out, was enacted in 1887 and became known as the General Allotment, or Dawes, Act.

The allotment of land to individual Indians was contrary to the traditional joint management system which all Indians practiced. It was assumed that there was no need to consult with Indians regarding this drastic change. Moreover the allotment program, it was decided by the Bureau of Indian Affairs, was to be accompanied by education of Indian children in boarding schools far from their homes where they would not be subject to the influence of their parents. This was to be carried out whether parents objected or not and resulted in much forced removal of children from their families. These measures were put into effect in conjunction with efforts to suppress Indian religions and by the institution of an authoritarian management of Indian communities by superintendents of the Bureau of Indian Affairs. In short, the trend toward denial of Indian political rights was only part of a general program instituted by the United States government for denial of Indian self-determination generally. Indian ways of life were regarded as a hindrance to improving Indian conditions and no discussion or consultation with Indians concerning changes was considered necessary.

During the sixty or more years following the crystallization of the removal idea for eastern Indians the framework of American political and cultural dominance closed in around all Indians in the United States. The ideas which defined the framework were linked on the one hand with sentiments about the supreme worth of the dominant American way of life and on the other hand with the growth of colonialism among Western nations. The United States by the 1880s had absorbed a large number of immigrants from northern and western Europe and the assimilation process was still in progress. The immigrants up to this time were basically similar in cultural background. No great problems had arisen in connection with the development of strong and unified national patterns. The idea of cultural assimilation dominated the view of those who made policy in connection with problems of Indian welfare. It did not occur to them that there might be serious obstacles when the cultural backgrounds were as sharply different as those of the Indians. That assimilation could be forced seems hardly to have been questioned. The forcing of different ways of life was part of the view which dominated the Western European nations in their nineteeth-century phase of colonial development. (*See Reading No. 27.*) Under the sway of this approach, Indian ways of life were hardly taken seriously. The idea that Indians were capable of participating in the process of deciding their future or that they had political and other institutions through which mutual adaptation might take place seems never to have been considered in the debates on the floors of Congress. The issues were seen only in terms of what the dominant society should do. (*See Document No. 28.*)

Indians nevertheless continued to exist as people and to try to make their own kinds of adaptation within the closing framework. Again, as in the adjustment to the looser conditions of the preceding period, the adaptations took several different forms. Religious messianism, religious revitalization, political re-organization, and more passive forms of adaptation appeared among various Indian groups. And again, among the tribes more newly confronted with domination, there was desperate military resistance.

The Five Civilized Tribes.   About the time they were forced to remove to Indian Territory the term "civilized" began to be applied to the Creeks, Cherokees, Choctaws, Chickasaws, and Seminoles. There was indeed a contrast between them and other Indians with whom they were thus thrown into contact. This was apparent in many aspects of their ways of life. The southeastern Indians had always been primarily agricultural in contrast with such tribes as the Comanches, Osages, Cheyennes, and others who relied on buffalo and other kinds of game for subsistence. This basic economic difference became associated with other traits which made it appear to the Americans that the southeastern Indians were in a special category. They had also adopted slavery, like the Whites, and took more than a thousand slaves with them to Indian Territory. Some of the prominent leaders among them tended to dress by this time like Americans and also to build houses in the American style, that is, log cabins or small frame houses. These features of their way of life were decisive in the American view and encouraged the distinction between "civilized" and "wild" tribes.

The Americans in general did not, however, realize that these traits were linked with devotion to their own languages, which in the case of Cherokees, Choctaws, and Creeks were becoming written languages with some literature of their own. It was further not generally realized that there was a developing new political life among all the five tribes. In the case of the Creeks at the time of arrival in the new lands, the evolution of the traditional government of the confederacy had not proceeded so far as had that of the Cherokees. But Creeks and Choctaws had both been moving in the same direction and continued to move along these lines after arrival in Indian Territory. The Creeks had begun to codify their legislation in written form, as had the Cherokees. In other ways the Creeks now began to adapt features of American representative government following the way pointed by the Cherokees. The new situation in Indian Territory gave impetus to this trend and the Choctaws and Chickasaws joined it. By the 1850s there was much convergence among these three tribes in political life. The Seminoles lagged.

This political development has often been disparaged by Americans as a poor "imitation" of the Whites. It is true that such features as bicameral government, constitutions, separation of judicial and executive branches, codified law, and annual elections with some form of geographical representation were borrowed, just as Americans had borrowed a legal system and bills of rights from the British. These were set, however, in a matrix of custom and procedure which gave much continuity with the Indian traditions. This was perhaps even more apparent in the case of the Creeks and Choctaws than the Cherokees, but even among the Cherokees, what was borrowed was adapted to their own needs, as new ideas and customs are always integrated with the old. In this sense a civilizing process had been accelerating among the five tribes for fifty years.

The Five Civilized Tribes were moved to Indian Territory

between 1831 and 1848. Indian Territory had been defined as all of modern Oklahoma except the panhandle. All arrived after struggles of greater or less intensity to hold on to their land in the east. Parts of each group had gone west earlier under pressure, imbued with the idea of putting distance between themselves and White men. The body of each tribe had remained in the east until the struggle seemed hopeless, when they had given in with a sense of defeat and irreparable loss. The Cherokee struggle resulted in deep factionalism. The Ridge family and Elias Boudinot, former editor of the *Cherokee Phoenix*, came to believe that opposition to President Jackson's policy was hopeless. They advocated acceptance of the inevitable and ultimately signed a removal agreement apart from John Ross and the majority of the National Council. Choctaws, Creeks, and Seminoles were also deeply split over the removal issue. In 1825 the Creeks, in accordance with their law, had executed William McIntosh, a leader who signed a land cession treaty without approval of the Creek National Council.

With arrival in the new lands, after the death of some 15,000 individuals under the terrible conditions of the migration, all the tribes began building anew, but not without opening new wounds. The Ridge and Elias Boudinot were assassinated within a year and this opened wider among the Cherokees the schism of the removal crisis years, which never healed completely. There developed a less clear division within all the five tribes. This was what came to be called the division between the "mixed bloods" and the "full bloods." The terms were misleading. Intermixture between Indians, Whites, and Negroes had taken place among all the tribes. The political divisions, or rather cultural tendencies, were not, however, along genetic or blood lines. The real division was between members of each tribe who tended to withdraw from further involvement with Whites and those who had accepted many White ways. This tended to create parties although alignment on this basis was never clear or consistent. There was moreover a unity among all in that no party or faction advocated the abandonment of the governmental autonomy which they had thus far developed.

The Creeks after Removal. The actions of the Creeks in the new setting were representative of what took place among all Five Civilized Tribes, although they were not identical by any means with developments among the Cherokees, Choctaws, Chickasaws, and Seminoles. The differences were greatly outweighed by the common features of organization and orientation. The Creeks were concerned immediately with two kinds of action. On the one hand they sought to continue the political development which had begun while they were still in the southeast, the codification of their law and the improvement of their political organization. On the other hand they sought to find and develop common cause with the other Civilized Tribes and with the tribes of prairies and plains with whom they found themselves in contact.

The objectives in internal policy were rather clearly formulated almost as soon as they arrived. These had to do with withstanding the pressures from the White society with which they were now thoroughly familiar. It was apparent during the 1850s that these pressures were not to be abated and that it would be necessary to combat the same White efforts that had been at work since the 1790s. Already by 1859 proposals were made by the Indian Bureau for survey of lands and allotment to individuals. Thus it was clear that the struggle for internal unity on land policy would have to be maintained.

The Creeks built a political organization which in some respects paralleled that of the Cherokees before them. It differed, however, in a few important ways. McIntosh, headman of the Lower Creek towns, had begun in 1817 the codification of the National Council's laws. This was continued and made easier by the development of an alphabet for writing Creek. A first constitution was written and adopted about 1858 which provided for a bicameral legislature, a House of Warriors and a House of Kings, based somewhat on the old peace (White) and war (Red) officials of the towns. The local town government itself persisted in main outline to a greater extent than among the Cherokees. Units of "lighthorsemen" (after the manner of the Cherokees) were set up for law and order and supreme and local courts established. A Criminal Code was adopted in 1861. In these respects the Creek trend followed the Cherokee. There were differences, however, which made it clear that the Creeks were developing their own ways. The Principal Chief operate more frequently outside the formal structure, calling informal councils of influential men whenever a serious issue arose, so that action was slower but more broadly based in common sentiment.

The growth of internal order and organization was interrupted by the Civil War, during which the Union government moved more slowly than the southern Confederacy in efforts to swing the tribes to their support. There was strong sentiment for the South among all the Five Civilized Tribes, many of the mixed blood leaders being slave owners. For three years the Creeks, like the others, appeared to embrace the Southern cause, making a treaty with the South which was more favorable so far as land guarantees and political autonomy went than any with the U.S. government. The Creeks were not unified in this alliance, however, nearly as many ultimately siding with the North as with the South. In 1864 the federal government took control again and the Creeks along with the other Civilized Tribes were penalized for joining the rebel cause by having half of Indian Territory removed from their jurisdiction.

Rebuilding both economically and politically was necessary again. It was not until 1875 that the first orderly election was held. Lochar Harjo was elected Principal Chief for a four year term. Now the special character of the Creek political structure became apparent. A "Full Blood" Party maintained as one of its tenets that its members had been loyal to the U.S. during the Civil War. It also stood more firmly than other groups on the old principle of no cession or alienation of Creek lands. Isparhecher, a non-English speaking Creek who had the support of the most traditional people emerged as leader of the "full bloods" who constituted perhaps a majority. There was a Muskogee Party which often elected Samuel Checote, a Methodist preacher and middle of the road leader, who utilized to the fullest the technique of wide consultation with influential elders. Another party, the Pins, with a secret organization was even less clear in its principles. Around the fringes of these parties were mixed bloods of ability, such as Pleasant Porter, who functioned in various important capacities in the Creek government.

The differences among these parties, except for the land issue, were as uncertain and shifting as in American political parties, but the parties became the vehicle for issues that did arise. One such arose in 1882 when the Green Peach War broke out. It was precipitated by efforts to neutralize the Isparhecher leadership which had refused to accept the selling of some Creek land to the Seminoles. The war lasted for a few months only and was settled in favor of the moderate leadership. The relatively non-violent character of the war and the compromise settlement revealed the flexible nature of Creek political ideology and the essentially unwarlike character of the Creeks. After 1883 there was less political conflict, but the finances of the government went from bad to worse.

The other side of Creek policy consisted in the effort to bring together for common action all the tribes which increasingly came to share the Indian territory with the Five Civilized Tribes. In this connection the Creeks played an interesting role, decribed by one historian as an "all embracing internationalism." Very soon after arrival in Indian Territory the Creeks called an intertribal council. The immediate motive was to stop the raiding of Pawnees and other tribes, not yet reduced to reservations, against newcomers like the Creeks to Indian Territory. Seventeen tribes attended including the Osages and the Kiowas. This was followed in 1843 by a more formally organized council presided over by John Ross of the Cherokees. An intertribal code was written based on the proposition that removal had changed the situation of all Indians. It included provision for naturalization procedures among tribes and asserted the principle of no land cessions by any tribe without consultation of all tribes. The Code remained a piece of paper, but it was clear that the Five Civilized Tribes with Creek and Cherokee leadership were seeking influence among all the tribes. In 1875 an intertribal constitution was promulgated at which 29 tribes participated. Creek and Cherokee activity in intertribal affairs continued into the very teeth of the American program in the 1880s for liquidating the Indian political systems. In 1887 and again in 1888 intertribal councils met, with as many as 29 tribes represented, to memorialize Congress against the General Allotment Act and to set up a committee to draft a plan for bringing all the tribes together under a common government, as an opposition measure to the Americans' program for ending tribal governments.

The acceptance of Christianity had proceeded rapidly after removal. The Creeks had remained opposed to evangelization, but like the Cherokees before them they encouraged Baptist, Methodist, and Moravian missionaries to establish schools. The programs of the churches involved the development of an Indian ministry, so that by 1873 there were some 23 Baptist and 32 Methodist Creek ministers in action. The Creeks and the other Five Civilized Tribes increasingly accepted Christian teaching and established their own local churches. The adaptation of belief and ritual proceeded rapidly in the hands of the native preachers and congregations, using translations of the New Testament into the Indian languages.

The Creeks, Choctaws, and Cherokees set up school systems of their own, utilizing the annuity payments for lands ceded to the U.S. government and also proceeds from taxation including taxes for cattle grazing and trading privileges.

White Pressures. The Creeks had learned by the early 1870s something of the nature of the political framework which enclosed them. They had become aware that the Bureau of Indian Affairs could not be entrusted with their interests as they saw them. Agents varied in honesty, efficiency, and energy. More often than not agents opposed the major Creek values—the maintenance of their title to what land was left and their form of government. They found it necessary to maintain representatives in Washington to keep watch on current legislation, so that the frequent bills which threatened Indian interests could be opposed. It became steadily clearer that the United States government was undependable with respect to their chief interests. It was increasingly responsive to the efforts of "boomers" intent on getting Indian land opened up for White settlement. Whites constantly entered Creek territory seeking footholds by any means. The machinery for enforcing the Indian Intercourse Acts, which restricted entry of Whites into Indian country, was too cumbersome to be effective, and often the Indian Bureau agent was himself a party to the intrusion. The Bureau of Indian Affairs not only failed to protect the territorial integrity of the Five Civilized Tribes, but also encouraged the view among

Washington officials that their governments were not working.

By the late 1880s the Five Civilized Tribes had demonstrated that they could adapt successfully to circumstances even as unstable and hostile to orderly government as those which had developed in the American west. They were economically self-sufficient, as they had always been, and generally speaking as well off as at the peak of their prosperity before removal. There was a range of wealth among them much like that in any rural region of the eastern United States. The school systems of the Choctaws, Creeks, and Cherokees were the best managed of any west of the Mississippi River. The Cherokee population was 90% or more literate in their own language, and literacy rates in English were high among the Five Tribes. Their systems of law and order, legislation, and local and national government were stable and probably as well-managed as those of most of the American states. These accomplishments had been achieved in the face of the bitter factionalism created by the removal crisis, complete uprooting, new divisive forces arising out of the Civil War, constant illegal interference by Whites in their local affairs, and the never-ending pressures of the frontiersmen to separate them from their land.

Their success was tacitly recognized in the provisions of the General Allotment Act of 1887. (*See Document No. 14.*) That act provided for the individual allotment of the land of all Indians except the Five Civilized Tribes. While it was provided that allotment was to take place among the other Indians whether they consented or not, the program was to be extended to the Five Civilized Tribes only with their consent. As allotment proceeded the Civilized Tribes made it clear that they were inalterably opposed. The Dawes Commission appointed to negotiate allotment took the position that there could be no compromise with the Indian desires. The Choctaws bowed to what they regarded as the inevitable, but the Creeks and Cherokees refused. The reply of the United States government was to pass the Curtis Act which provided for the dissolution of the governments of any tribes which rejected allotment, and this was accomplished in 1898. From this time the Five Civilized Tribes, like all other Indians in the United States, ceased to exist as recognized political entities. The era of domestic dependent nations was at an end.

Wanderers and Mercenaries of the Middle Border. The borderlands of settlement, conflict ridden and in flux, became a type of human environment to which some Indians made a specialized adaptation. Those who did so were chiefly the displaced Algonkians—the Delawares, Shawnees, Sac and Fox, Kickapoos, and a few others. Forced to move repeatedly, whenever it began to appear that a stable residence might be achieved, some lived a hundred-and-fifty-year odyssey. No generation experienced continuous residence in one place, and most went through several forced removals in less than twenty-five years. From the Atlantic Coast to the forests of the Great Lakes country, to the prairie lands of the midwest, to the prairies' edge in Kansas and Nebraska, to the Texas plains, even into the desert expanses of Coahuila in Mexico, and then sometimes back eastward to Indian Territory, Iowa, and Wisconsin, the route was a tortuous 2,000 miles. The Indian families learned to live and accept a life of frequent warfare and repeated movements. It was an adaptation forced not only by the loss of homelands, but also by determined devotion to their own ways of life. Algonkians found that by keeping out of the meshes of the settled life, where Americans dominated, they were able to pick and choose what they wanted to add to their way of life. At the beginning of their travels they were farming people, but not all remained so. Some underwent reverse evolution to hunting and the unsettled life.

The Delawares. The odyssey of the Delawares began before 1700 when the combined pressures of the Quakers and the Iroquois resulted in most Delawares moving to central Pennsylvania along the Susquehanna. Their traditional history told that they once had a homeland in the region of what became Indiana and had arrived on the Atlantic Coast not long before the coming of the Whites. Perhaps it began to appear to Delawares caught up in the next century and a half of forced wandering that they were continuing in their legendary tradition. Their odyssey cannot be said to have ended until 1867 when the main body of Delawares settled down beside the Cherokees in Indian Territory.

For 24 years following the Battle of Fallen Timbers the Delawares were in process of a gradual shift from eastern Ohio to Indiana. Some had come from Pennsylvania into Ohio in the mid-1700s, and, piecemeal, during the rest of the century

Delawares made the shift to the northwest, leaving Teedyuscung and others behind. About 1800 there were nine villages on White River in Indiana and some others in eastern Ohio. This period was one of turmoil in the northwest climaxing in Tecumseh's attempts to unite Indians of north and south. Most of the Delawares were a part of the Shawnee-led movement, but they seem not to have gained re-integration through it. Their villages in Indiana and Ohio were described by commentators of the time as badly disorganized and full of debauchery. There was factional strife among them. Some Delawares as early as 1789 had ignored the center of developing new Algonkian thought and pushed on west to Missouri and then southward to Texas.

In 1818 when the main body of Delawares ceded the last of their lands to the United States for new land in Missouri, there may have been about 1,500 of them. In 1820 it is recorded that 1,340 Delawares with 1,400 horses crossed the Mississippi River and headed for southwestern Missouri. Here for a brief period they tried to settle. It was an area under frequent attack from the Osages, who had for years been accustomed to raid the same area when it was Spanish frontier. Associated with some Shawnees and Kickapoos, the Delawares were again as they had been for the Iroquois against the British and for the Wabash against the Americans in a buffer position between contending nations. Dissatisfied with the land and the situation the Delawares agreed in 1829 to give up their land in Missouri for other land in northeastern Kansas near Fort Leavenworth. Here some 1,000 Delawares under the leadership of the elderly Captain Pipe settled down to farming and accepted American domination. For twenty years the greater number maintained the Kansas land as a base, built log cabins, and sent some children to school. At the same time they became well-known as far as the Rocky Mountains as traders and as far south as Florida as soldiers. A part of 800 Algonkians, including Delawares and Shawnees, was recruited by the United States Army to fight the Seminoles under Osceola during 1837.

Meanwhile some Delawares from Missouri had joined other Delawares and Shawnees in Texas, where during the 1820s they were allied with the Texans, some Kickapoos, and a small band of Cherokees under "Chief Bowles" against the Comanches.

The Texans, however, were undependable in their Indian alliances and some Delawares were driven out of Texas to settle on the edge of Creek Territory where again they were in a buffer position against the southern Plains tribes. In 1845 they fought with Texans against Comanches, and in 1854 along with Shawnees and Wichitas they were given a reservation by the Texans on the Brazos River. From this base they continued in alliance with Texas Rangers to fight the Comanches. They had given up farming and taken to the hunting of buffalo. When the Civil War broke out most decided to go north where they joined the Kansas Delawares, and 70 of them together now with their old enemies, the Osages, formed a regiment of the Union Army to fight in Indian Territory. At this time there were still about 1,500 Delawares, a few fighting with the Confederacy, but the majority recognizing the Kansas lands as their base. In 1866, after the Civil War, they yielded to American pressures again and allowed themselves to be sent to Indian Territory. The main body were given some land by the Cherokees where they settled down again, but a few joined the Wichitas around their agency west of the Cherokees and some associated with Chippewas and others became known as the Stockbridge Indians in Wisconsin.

The Kickapoos. The Kickapoos ranged even farther west and south than the Delawares, establishing in 1850 a community in the state of Coahuila, Mexico, which persists to the present. Rejecting American—and Mexican—cultural influences with great consistency, they maintained more than any other of the displaced Algonkians the tradition of the Shawnee Prophet. Already in 1819 when, like the Delawares they ceded their land in Indiana and Illinois to the United States, Kickapoos were living in places as widely separated as Texas and Prophet's Town in Indiana. In 1820 the main body of Kickapoos consisted of about 2,000 when they took up residence in southwestern Missouri on the Osage frontier. Several hundred refused to leave Illinois where they remained under the leadership of the prophet, Kennekuk. But in 1835 all the Kickapoos had crossed the Mississippi, some leaving Illinois in 1831 after joining Black Hawk, the Sac leader, in his last stand and the others of Kennekuk's group crossing in 1834. Like the Delawares, the Kickapoos who had tried to settle in Missouri, were dissatisfied, and together with Kennekuk's band made a treaty in 1832 with the United States. This resulted in about 800 settling in northeastern Kansas with Kennekuk and another 900 going to Indian Territory. A third group of 300 was already in Texas where a few Kickapoos had gone as early as the 1770s. The northern Kickapoos in Kansas along with several hundred Potawatomies accepted the Kennekuk religion and settled down to farming and peaceful existence, completely changing their way of life.

The Texas Kickapoos were settled on a land grant which had been given them by the Spaniards. Here they were joined by the Kickapoos who came south from Missouri. Texas in 1839, however, forced them into Indian Territory fearing that they might side with the Mexicans in the Texans' war with Mexico. They numbered more than 800 at this time, their population having been increased by the coming of a group from Kansas who had rejected the settled way of life encouraged by Kennekuk. Kickapoos had fought with the Texans against the Comanches, and even more than the Delawares had become known as great warriors in the constant warfare of the "Middle Border." In 1850 a delegation of southern Kickapoos under the leadership of Wild Cat, a Seminole, went to Mexico City to ask for land in Mexico. They were granted land in the state of Coahuila in return for which it was agreed that they would serve as protectors of the Mexican settlements against the raids of the Comanches and Lipan Apaches. They were given some help in setting up their settlements and were regarded by the government as citizens of Mexico. In 1852 along with Seminoles from Indian Territory they established themselves in the new location and engaged in some fighting against the southern Plains tribes. In 1859 they were persuaded by the United States government to return to the Indian Territory villages. However, in 1862 a group of 250 returned to Coahuila, seeking to avoid involvement in the Civil War and distrusting U.S. policy with respect to their Oklahoma land. Most of these resisted efforts by the United States government in the 1860s and 1870s to return them to Indian Territory and continued to live in their Coahuila community.

The Fox. Another Algonkian tribe, the Fox, was similarly forced to shift residence eight or nine times in the period of the nineteenth century and also like the other tribes considered were noted as fighting men. Their range was considerably smaller, however, than that of either the Delawares or the Kickapoos. Throughout the eighteenth century the Fox, who were living in the vicinity of what is now Green Bay, Wisconsin, when first encountered by Europeans, maintained hostility towards the French and so became the objects of efforts at extermination. They were not involved in any important way with the Tenskwatawa-Tecumseh movement. They did, however, have their own Prophet—Walokieshiek—who advocated maintaining the integrity of Algonkian culture. As the Delawares and the Shawnees seem inextricably inter-related in their history, so the Fox and the Sac, another Algonkian group, became closely associated for most of their wandering years. It was a Sac, Black Hawk, who made a last desperate effort to stand against removal west of the Mississippi, and Fox as well as other Algonkians including Kickapoos were part of the Black Hawk forces.

The wanderings of the Fox in the 19th century were forced by successive losses of land and followed a pattern like that of many other eastern Indians: ceding land in Illinois, accepting land in Missouri, ceding land in Missouri, accepting land in Iowa, ceding land in Iowa, accepting land in Kansas; but they withstood the usual last stage, namely, removal to Indian Territory. The Fox were unique in that they developed a determination to secure their own land quite independently of the United States government. Of all the land that they were pushed on to and off of only that in Iowa seemed really desirable. Hence as the pushing continued they bought 80 acres in Tama County, Iowa, twelve years after they had been removed from Iowa. They sold their horses in 1854 in order to do this. They were little interested in the land assigned them in Indian Territory and became angered against their associates the Sacs when they agreed to allotment of the land in 1858. From this time on all the Fox were focused on establishing themselves in Iowa. They slowly built up their land holdings there, buying more with an increase in annuity funds in 1867 and with money derived from the sale of allotments in Oklahoma they bought still more until they held some 3,000 acres. Before the end of the century then they were established as independent land-owners and entirely outside the federal system of management of Indian affairs. This did not mean that they had accepted the ways and values of the Americans, however. They resisted with determination interference in their local affairs. Through the 1890s they rejected schools and evangelization by the Americans and maintained their own traditional ways of socializing children and religious worship.

There were other wanderers, but these three Algonkian groups together are representative of some of the major adaptations which Indians chose under the special conditions of the frontier.

The Buffalo Hunters Give In. The great wedge of treeless land between the Great Lakes and the Mississippi Delta on the east and the Rocky Mountains on the west had been a region of changing life ways since the retreat of the glaciers from its northern margins 10,000 years before the coming of the Europeans. Its herds of bison which began to increase just after the beginning of the Christian era attracted people from the woodlands of the east, who continued their farming where possible as in the valleys of the Missouri and its tributaries, but adopted as an important addition to their subsistence the buffaloes they could hunt by stalking on foot. There were scatterings of such village clusters in the northern plains when Spanish horses began to be available in the late 1500s and early 1600s. Learning how to use horses brought a rapid transformation for many of the Plains Indians and a stimulation to others to move out from more sedentary ways, adopt the horse, and become hunting nomads. This latest transformation was still going on in the 1700s, as tribes moved from both the Great Lakes area and the central Rocky Mountains to adopt the nomad life of the plains. The European-introduced horses together with the guns supplied by the French and Spanish meant not only a new way of making a living, but also a general change in cultural orientation like that which characterized the Apaches farther south during the early 1700s. It led to the growth of war activities. Tribes raided each other for horses, and raiding became a way of life giving rise to a whole value system. Individuals and whole tribes or bands attained status and prestige through raiding and counting coup. Most of those affected had not been simple gathering tribes, but rather people with men's societies and other fairly complex forms of organization, with skin pictograph historical records (*see Document No. 3*), elaborate technology, and ceremonialism.

There was also some elaboration of political organization, far from rudimentary. Each group of associated bands, like the Sioux of the east or the Crow of the west or the Arapaho of the center, had its "Great Council" and its formal procedures for parley and for inter-tribal adjustments.

The Sioux in the Northern Plains. These tribes were from one to two centuries behind the other Indians of the United States in gaining experience of White men. Despite using European guns and horses in ways that had already altered their lives greatly by the early nineteenth century, they still had been able to maintain control of their own destiny. Some had contacts with Spaniards, who had got as far as Kansas even in 1540. Some knew the French, because during the eighteenth century the French penetrated either as explorers or as traders and trappers deeply into the plains country. Some had experienced pressure from the east during the 1700s and early 1800s, such as for example the Eastern Sioux who moved out of Minnesota into the eastern Dakotas or the Osages who retreated westward from Chickasaw and Kickapoo raids inspired by the French and Spanish. The Pawnees and the Otos also had been affected. None of these contacts, however, was intensive. The Plains tribes in the north were busy with developing their own new interests, while the Americans were achieving the role of dominant military power east of the Mississippi.

But when the Americans took over the Louisiana Purchase in 1807 the impact of intensifying settler invasion came suddenly to the northern Plains tribes. The two-centuries-long duel that had involved all the Indians east of the Mississippi was not to take place here. The many years of successes and false starts in adapting to the turmoil of European invasion which had been possible for the eastern Indians were compressed to barely 40 years. In the Southern Plains it was little longer. Here there was small chance to learn the game. The impact and the denouement were swift and definite.

By 1880 the Indians whom the French called Sioux (Nadowe-is-iw, a Chippewa term for these people meaning "Lesser Adders") had accomplished their new integration. They had begun to use horses about 1740 and fifty years later had guns. By the first decade of the nineteenth century they were settled on both sides of the Missouri River after a steady westward movement from Minnesota beginning about 1650. By 1750 their lives had become centered around buffalo hunting. During the last half of the 1700s they developed, like other Plains tribes, an intense interest in warfare and pushed such village-dwelling people as the Arikara out of their way northwestward. In 1805 they defeated bands of Kiowas from the south and Cheyennes to the northwest. In the early 1820s they successfully fought the Crows, thus extending their range as far as the Black Hills of South Dakota. In the 1830s and 40s they fought and pushed the Pawnees south. With the Pawnees they carried on a sort of religious war, first losing to them and then in 1843 retrieving some of their Sacred Arrows. This warfare with the northern Plains tribes was indicative of their full acceptance of the new way of life of the buffalo-hunting plains people. The Sioux had begun to dominate a fairly well-defined area extending over the modern states of North and South Dakota and parts of Nebraska and Wyoming. They had developed a method of historical record-keeping by means of paintings on deer skins called the Winter Count. They were traditionally divided into seven large groupings of independent bands and maintained the institution of an annual council called the Seven Council Fires. They had completed in 1814 a treaty with the Kiowas sanctioning a rough boundary between the tribes. They kept entirely clear of involvement in the British-French struggle over the fur trade.

Between 1851 and 1878 they did become involved with the Americans and in this short period of 27 years moved from the dominant position in their area to that of a defeated nation living on reservations established by the United States government. This crisis period in the life of the Sioux was touched off by the intensification of the settler invasion, the wagon trains moving west, and the Gold Rush for California. The invasion of their territory by the emigrants led the Sioux to attack party after party. The Americans, now capable of effective military action with no interference from other Europeans, initiated a program for control over the Sioux. They planned a series of forts scattered widely over the upper Missouri River area and began buying the old trading posts. The Sioux joined in "councils" with the American military and signed agreements, as at the Great Council called at Fort Laramie in 1851.

This theater of war was very different from those which had developed east of the Mississippi. Not only was there no complicating multiplicity of European nations, but also the Sioux Council Fires were much less centralized than even the Creek Confederacy or the League of the Iroquois. Their tradition of the Seven Fires was not a basis for concerted action. The four or five divisions of the tribe which existed in 1850 made an effort to meet annually in general council, but there was no control of war chiefs by the whole. Each operated on his own, except in very unusual circumstances. The Americans nevertheless persisted in believing that they could deal with a whole Sioux "nation" in groups assembled for treaty-making. The Indians assembled, but they went separate ways afterwards. The American efforts to engage and defeat the Indians intensified after 1854. In 1868 it appeared as if some general agreement had been attained. The U.S. in a somewhat conciliatory mood signed a treaty with Sioux under the leadership of Red Cloud of the Teton Dakota. Concluded at Ft. Laramie this new treaty made the usual American guarantee that Indian land would be entered only with Indian consent and affirmed that the Sioux would cease raiding. Red Cloud's reputation as a war chief was high, perhaps the highest of any Sioux. The territorial guarantees of the treaty were regarded by many Sioux as a great new Red Cloud exploit. But as usual neither side kept the treaty. The Americans continued to cross and settle in Sioux land. Rumors of gold in the Black Hills spread in 1876, prospectors invaded, and the U.S. chopped the Black Hills from Sioux country. The Custer massacre took place. Both sides had broken the treaty and total war was loosed. One by one the Sioux bands were defeated, Crazy Horse's Oglala band surrendering in 1877 and Gall and Sitting Bull of the Tetons in 1881. The Yankton band had been assigned a reservation in 1858 twenty years before. As the last fighting bands surrendered they were put on reservations in South Dakota, some on the Rosebud Reservation under Spotted Tail and the others at Pine Ridge under Red Cloud.

Red Cloud became widely known in the United States for his declarations urging the Sioux to a new and peaceful way of life. The reservation conditions which were instituted did not, however, follow his recommendations. The Sioux were given rations and over a 10 year period became dependent on them. White men's clothes were given out, some houses were built, hair was cut. Against Red Cloud's will, schools were set up. Red Cloud and other respected men were ignored, as the superintendent built his own power structure with Indian police. Then suddenly in 1889 rations were cut off in accordance with the treaty, and no adequate provision was made for food. Dissatisfaction was intense, and many were suffering. Young men broke away from the reservation, but the buffalo were extinct and hunting was no use. Red Cloud was famous but he was confused and all the old leadership had been undermined. The Sioux were ripe for a new religion which came in the form of the Ghost Dance.

The Comanches in the Southern Plains. The southern plains were dominated for a century by the Comanches who moved out of the Rocky Mountain country to embrace the buffalo-warfare way of life in much the manner of the Sioux. They were Shoshoni-speaking belonging to the far-flung Ute-Aztecan stock of Indian languages. In the early 1700s they already had horses and were raiding New Mexico. They drove various Apache groups southwestward during the 1700s. They made and broke treaties of peace with the Spaniards. On the east they prevented French traders from expanding to the southwest. On the west they maintained an unstable frontier with the Spaniards. The Spaniards made one unsuccessful effort in 1786 to reduce them to an agricultural way of life. This failed as did the Spanish attempt to do something similar with the Apaches. The Comanches maintained friendly relations with Caddo-speaking peoples such as the Pawnees.

In the 1830s they held sway over a vast territory extending from the Arkansas River on the north to Mexico and from Taos in New Mexico to the Cross Timbers of Texas and Indian Territory on the east. Thus when the U.S. created Indian Territory the Comanche eastern frontier was threatened. On the southwest they were in competition with the Texas settlers. They sought desperately for a boundary with the Texans, but the Texans would agree to nothing. In 1835 the Comanches agreed to share hunting rights, but not territory, with the eastern Indians settling Indian Territory. Fighting continued with the Texans who constantly refused to recognize Comanche land rights anywhere. In 1853 the Comanches with the help of some Apaches tried to wipe out the Indians settled in Indian Territory, but were defeated. They fought widely, but there was no organized unity. U.S. troops penetrated their whole area in 1858. A tract was set aside in the western Indian Territory at Anadarko for the Comanches, but they refused to settle down. More than half remained off reservation, raiding and trying to hunt the disappearing buffalo on through the 1860s and 1870s, their last raid off reservation being in 1879.

Meanwhile the usual division among the Indians first assigned to reservations appeared among the Comanches. In 1873 a Comanche claimed a revelation. His name was Ishatai, a medicine man who said he had talked with the Great Spirit and that he would bring back the dead. He predicted a comet and a drought, both of which materialized, the latter leading to serious suffering among the Comanches on the reservation. In 1874 a religious movement developed under Ishatai's influence. He preached against the sedentary life and urged a war of extermination against the Whites, in which there would be magical protection against White bullets. One large band refused to believe the prophet and left for Texas. Most of the others with some Kiowas, Arapahos, and Cheyennes, who had moved to Indian territory, listened to the teaching and joined in an effort to kill some Whites established at a place which had been a center of the last buffalo hunts— Adobe Walls. There was a fight. Ishatai's group was defeated and the little religious movement failed. The Comanches from this time on settled down to reservation life, although in 1881 they listened for a time to another man who said he had the power to make the buffaloes return.

The other Plains tribes presented about the same picture as either the Comanches or the Sioux: a twenty to twenty-five year period of intensive warfare both with other tribes and the Americans, a period of unsettled and sometimes desperate conditions as they were forced on to reservations and finally unhappy acceptance of the new way (*see Document No. 3*), usually with a ten or twenty year period of dependence on rations. The process of free selection of White ways changed to a process of forced acceptance of what the Whites restricted them to. The destructive effects of the new conditions unfolded in the next forty years.

New Messiahs. The kind of religious revelation which moved the Algonkians and gave a powerful ideology to Tecumseh's resistance movement in the early nineteenth century appeared again in the late 1800s among the plains and mountain people of the west. It arose under similar circumstances. The Algonkians had embraced their doctrine as they were faced with expulsion from their land and infiltration of their communities. They focused on holding what land remained at all costs, and the means for doing this was defined as rejection of the White way of life and return to the ways they had lost. This had led to war, although the doctrine itself did not emphasize war as a value. It was a religion of the oppressed, a religion of regeneration in the face of desperation. The viewpoint persisted, even after the societies were reduced to powerlessness, in the implacable resistance to White cultural domination by the Kickapoos and the Fox.

This cycle was repeated in the west. The causes were the same: the stark fact of loss of control over their land, as American settlement relentlessly continued; the less clear-cut loss of the old ways and of their identity as self-respecting people, as missionaries, Indian agents, settlers and the pressures of the White frontier surrounded them. Two major new religious movements began in widely separated places.

Smohalla. In Oregon Territory a prophet arose among the tiny Wanapum group of some 200 Indians in what is now Washington state. The prophet was called Smohalla. (*See Document No. 39.*) To the south in Nevada among the Walker River Paiutes, also a small band of a few hundred, a Messiah named Wovoka began somewhat later to preach a return of the old life. These two movements gained wide influence; the latter, called by the Whites the Ghost Dance, reached most of the tribes of the northern plains and Indian Territory by 1890. The Smohalla cult spread among the tribes of the northwest during the 1870s and 1880s and continued among many thereafter.

In 1855 some 3,000 Indians in the area of the Middle Columbia River signed a treaty with the U.S. government which ceded the lands on which they lived for small portions to be established as reservations where they were to be protected from White encroachment and receive certain services from the government such as schools, help with farming, and tools. The Indians included the Yakima, Cayuse, Wasco, Wishram and many others.

The treaty had come about not directly as a result of military defeat, but by common agreement in response to needs felt by the Indians. However, as usual no protection from encroaching Whites was given by the government and little help in making a living. The tribes were ones which had relied on hunting and fishing with no agriculture. About 1855 a man named Smohalla "returned from the dead" and began to preach. His return was actually from an extended journey after a fight with a rival medicine man. He traveled to the west coast, through southern California into Mexico, and through Arizona and Utah, being absent from Washington state for some four years. When he returned he began to preach concerning visions which he had had. Rapidly a following grew around him and a formal set of ceremonies under his guidance began to be carried out. These were based on a ceremonial called the Prophet Dance traditional in much of the region. There were also Catholic ritual elements such as the use of bells, the cross, and a flag which was Smohalla's special symbol. The Indians of the area were under great pressures from both missionaries and land-hungry settlers. Smohalla preached that pursuit of the new religion would result in the elimination of the White men. Smohalla taught also that the White man's way was undesirable, that agriculture ruined and defiled the Mother, earth. His preaching was an advocacy of the way of life which had formerly prevailed among the Indians and which was steadily becoming more and more difficult to maintain. It was not militant in the sense of inciting to war against the Whites, but it was implacably hostile to Christianity, to farming, and most other White ways. For more than twenty years Smohalla preached, and the religion spread widely to most of the Indians of eastern Washington and Oregon. On Smohalla's death the cult continued, as his son succeeded him and continued active on into the 1890s.

The teaching of Smohalla gained great notoriety in 1877 when Chief Joseph of the Nez Perce Indians became well-known over the United States. Joseph refused to be pushed from land on which his band lived. When Whites resorted to violence, killing a relative of Joseph, he and other Indians retaliated by killing 21 Whites. Then he conducted a remarkable 1,000 mile retreat in the face of U.S. troops. His dignity in retreat and in ultimate surrender and his feat of defying U.S. troops in the chase from Oregon to Wyoming caught the imagination of the American public. Interviews with him indicated that he and his followers had embraced the teaching of Smohalla. This gave publicity to the new religion. The religion influenced other new religions in the region such as the Indian Shaker Church founded about 1881 by John Slocum, a Squaxin Indian of Puget Sound.

Wovoka. Of far wider influence was what came to be called by the Whites the Ghost Dance religion. Its founder was a Paiute in Nevada named Wovoka (*see Document No. 41A*), who was known to local ranchers as Jack Wilson. Wovoka's doctrince derived from the teachings of his father Wodziwob who in 1870 had stirred Paiutes and others in the vicinity. This was an area inhabited by hunting and gathering tribes who had not developed farming and who belonged to the Uto-Aztecan language stock. By the 1870s they had begun to feel intensive pressures of White settlers. Living in very small communities in a difficult country, they found themselves increasingly dispossessed of their hunting grounds as Whites began to establish ranches. By the 1880s they had become dependent on what wage work was offered them in the White settlements. Wovoka was a ranch hand in the vicinity of Walker Lake. In 1885 in the tradition of his father he began to have visions, after having "died." His revelations were impressive to the neighboring Paiutes. He taught that there would be a natural catastrophe which would result in the extinction of the White men and the return of all the ancestors of the Indians. With this return would come restoration of the Indian lands and hunting grounds. It was necessary, in order to help bring this about, to pay attention to what Wovoka had been told to do in his talks with Christ, or God, in the spirit world. This consisted in a modification of a circle dance which was traditional among the Paiutes and many other Indians of the basin and range country and more widely in the west. A special set of songs which Wovoka learned in his encounters with the spirit world was to be sung while people gathered and danced in a circle through the night. The dance induced fainting spells among some of the dancers, who would fall out of the circle and thus come into communication with the dead ancestors. It was a dance of this type, which went by a wide variety of names among the Indians, which came to be called the Ghost Dance during the late 1880s.

The teaching of Wovoka, like that of other Indian prophets and messiahs, was entirely peaceful. Wovoka held that Indians should lead a better life, forgoing whiskey, treating everyone in kindly fashion. In some versions the new life was not to be wholly for Indians but would embrace Whites as well. Although warfare was not urged, it was nevertheless a teaching opposed to the acceptance of White values and way of life. It rested on the belief that the Indian ways were good and could be restored.

In 1885 when Wovoka had his first revelations, throughout the plains and much of the western mountain area the military campaigns of the U.S. troops had resulted in the placement of Indians on reservations. The buffalo had become extinct or nearly so. The new life on the reservations was restrictive and called for a sudden change of ways with great dependence on White men. The U.S. Bureau of Indian Affairs had begun a campaign for turning all the former hunting tribes into farmers and in the transition process had arranged to provide food and clothing to be rationed at regular intervals to the Indians. It was in this time of crisis in the lives of the western Indians that Wovoka began to preach. With great rapidity his name as a Messiah spread widely. The essential ritual built on traditional dance forms was immediately intelligible. As tribes through the west heard rumors, they sent delegations to visit the Messiah himself. Wovoka received one delegation after another, explained his teaching, and demonstrated the dance to them. (*See Document No. 41B.*) Kiowas, Cheyennes, Arapahos, and others who had been placed on reservations in Indian territory sent investigators. In many instances they themselves returned to preach. The Ghost Dance began to be performed in Indian Territory, especially among the Kiowas. Some tribes such as the Comanches, the Five Civilized Tribes, the Kickapoos, the Crows (who nevertheless had their own prophet of a different sort), and others remained uninterested even though they knew of the Messiah. In the northern Plains the Sioux began to show great interest.

In 1889 the Sioux were entering a period of very hard times. Crops failed in 1889 and the rations had been cut off. People

were starving and unrest was widespread on the Sioux reservations. In this crisis they sent a delegation to learn that Wovoka
was teaching. Short Bull and other Sioux medicine men were
deeply impressed and came back to instruct people in the dance
and the doctrine of the Paiute Messiah. The restless men and
women of the poverty-stricken Pine Ridge Sioux reservation began to gather in groups away from the agency for the Ghost
Dance. They began to make special "Ghost shirts" which according to their teaching could stop bullets. As they danced, dis-
satisfactions crystallized. An incompetent and fearful Indian
agent began to see the Sioux Ghost Dance as an Indian uprising.
He prohibited the dance, but was defied by the excited Indians
who were now deriving new hope from their religious activities.
Sioux leaders like Red Cloud found much that they liked in the
teaching and had not opposed it. The White fearfulness, however, increased danger of conflict. Red Cloud himself remained
of two minds, seeing no harm in what was going on but recognizing that misinterpretation by Whites could lead to serious trouble.

The trouble came in a way that affected the whole United
States. In 1890 as more Sioux at Pine Ridge began to accept
the new teaching, the Indian agent called for soldiers. They
came and, misinterpreting Indian actions, massacred a whole
encampment of Sioux at Wounded Knee Creek. The killing of
300 men, women, and children and leaving their bodies to freeze
on the plains for three days stirred the United States public. Investigation revealed that there was little in the way of threat,
that unintelligent opposition by the agent had fanned a religious
movement into a potential military action. The Sioux had indeed veered toward a more military-oriented movement than
had ever been intended by Wovoka, as might have been expected in view of the Sioux cultural background. Wovoka continued to insist that his teaching was not militant and was afterwards reluctant to receive delegations for fear of misinterpretation that would lead to tragic events like the massacre of Wounded
Knee.

In Indian Territory the Kiowas became for a time disillusioned
with the Ghost Dance, but after an interval resumed it as an
important ceremony which they retained into the 1890s. Elsewhere the Ghost Dance died out and the Indians who had em-

braced it returned to the hard realities of life on the reservations. The second surge of Indian prophecy in the service of a return to the old lifeways was over. The frustrated buffalo hunters had not achieved their new dispensation.

Transition to Reservations in the Southwest. New conditions of life came rapidly to the southwestern tribes after 1848. The peace of Guadeloupe Hidalgo between Mexico and the United States meant a new regime for the Pueblos, east and west, the Navajos and Apaches, and the Yuman and Piman speaking peoples of Arizona. Those who were to be most drastically changed by the appearance of new military power were the Athabascan-speaking Navajos and Apaches. As we have seen, their way of life had altered sharply as a result of the domestic animals introduced by the Spaniards and by the opportunities which faltering Spanish and Mexican control of the region opened up for exploitation of the settled peoples, both Indian and European. This herding and raiding existence dependent on the farming communities of others had become the way of life for the Athabascan-speaking peoples by 1848. Mexican control was weak, and the border had been unstable for nearly seventy years.

The expectation of the Apaches and Navajos was that they would and should have a freer hand in raiding the Mexican settlements. The Americans had not fought either the Apaches or Navajos. It was therefore inconceivable to the Indians that the Americans could regard their hunting and raiding ranges as United States territory. The Indians had never been conquered by the Mexicans and hence in the Indian view they still held their lands. It came as a shock to find that the Americans regarded their victory over the Mexicans as also a victory over the Indians of the region, especially when parleys indicated at the beginning that the Americans wished to prohibit raiding against the Indians' old enemies—the Mexicans. The first feelers with the American expeditionary leaders left no mistake about the American view. Apaches and Navajos knew from that point on that they had acquired new enemies, not new allies as they had hoped.

There was little actual change until after the Civil War, although several bands of both Navajos and Apaches made contact with Americans before 1860. But rapidly as troops came into the New Mexico territory toward the end of the Civil War, it became clear to the Indians that they were going to have to fight for their hunting ranges and for their independence. The Americans gathered a group of war leaders among the Navajos and executed a treaty at Bear Springs in 1864. They treated with Gila Apaches near the Santa Rita Mines in eastern New Mexico. As in the early days of contact with the Plains tribes it became apparent to Americans that treaties were not going to gain their ends, so long as there was no general authority among the tribes. The Navajos were stimulated to some unaccustomed unity by the building of Fort Defiance and other posts in the heart of their range in northeastern Arizona. There was some banding together of the many groups, not only war leaders and their supporters for offensive raids, but also peace leaders. No extensive unity was achieved, however, and the Navajos quickly found themselves fighting for very survival quite separate from one another in different parts of their large territory. One Navajo named Manuelito emerged as something of a general peace leader, but he achieved no wider unity than any single Sioux leader had been able to muster. The Americans, under the leadership of Kit Carson, organized a systematic scorched earth conquest. Large numbers of the sheep on which the Navajos had become heavily dependent were killed, and bands of Navajos were systematically pursued into the farthest hideouts such as Canyon de Chelly. At the end of 1865 the Navajos were largely without food and began to give in, band by band. Only a few hundred remained hidden, to escape the Americans.

The Americans immediately instituted a plan for converting the Navajos into farmers. Instead of leaving them within their range in New Mexico Territory, they forced the Indians to move en masse to Fort Sumner some 250 miles eastward on the edge of the Plains. This forced migration became known to the Navajos as the "Long Walk." They were placed, together with Apaches such as the Mescaleros who had also been rounded up, on a small fenced reservation. The American plan called for getting the Navajos to live in adobe houses, to farm, and to develop peaceful community life under the strict supervision of Army officers. The plan differed from that tried with the Plains Indians chiefly in that mutually hostile tribes were placed together and that the new location was at a great distance from their homeland.

The plan did not work. This became apparent within a year, and the Americans decided in 1868 to make a new treaty with the Navajos. (*See Document No. 13.*) This called for return to their old stamping grounds which were guaranteed to the Navajos free of trespass by Whites, the issue of sheep, attendance at schools with one teacher for every 30 Navajo children, and of course agreement by the Navajos to stop raiding and to remain at peace. With conclusion of the treaty the Navajos were faced with returning as best they could to their homeland—the second phase of the "Long Walk."

The incarceration at Fort Sumner had impressed the Navajos with the power of the Americans. It opened a new era in Navajo life. Their new reservation was large and was not yet attractive to Whites. The government began the issue of hundreds of sheep. The Navajos spread out again and began to develop their mixed herding-agricultural economy much as before but without reliance on raiding. The reservation was increased rather than reduced in size during the next thirty years and only a small part was subjected to allotment in the 1890s. Under these circumstances Navajo life blossomed. Their population began to increase. They developed not only the herding of sheep and horses but also blanket weaving which they had adapted from Pueblos and Spaniards.

The stay at Fort Sumner had resulted in some new tribal organization, or at least the dominance of Manuelito and several other peace leaders, so that foundations were laid for more unified political life. By the late 1890s they were one of the more prosperous of tribes under the reservation system. They were relatively little interfered with by Indian agents because of the great extent of their territory. They resisted sending their children to school. They were developing a new life which was rooted deeply in their two century adaptation of sheepherding. They were encouraged by the Bureau of Indian Affairs to develop an economy based on what they already knew. At the same time the Catholic Franciscans instituted missions which became an important source of contacts and the learning of some White ways, but only small numbers became Christians. So well adapted were they under the particular non-restrictive reservation situation that no Messiah arose among them. They rejected the Ghost Dance partly because its stress on the return of the dead conflicted with Navajo values, but also because they were not in desperate circumstances either with respect to economic conditions or loss of political autonomy.

In contrast, the transition for Apaches was more destructive, and solid foundations for a new peaceful life were not laid. The Apache lands were in the midst of mining and cattle developments in Arizona and New Mexico. The Jicarillas were rounded up quickly and isolated on a small reservation in northern New Mexico. The Chiricahua, the San Carlos, the White Mountain, the Tonto, and Gila Apaches did not experience such easy transition. Silver and gold mines were opened up in various parts of their range, and settlers moved into the relatively desirable valleys of the Arizona area. There were many Apache frontiers, and numerous massacres and conflicts. No one Army campaign was successful in starving them into submission. The Army was, in fact, in their rugged domain no match for the various hard-fighting Apache bands, until a campaign was designed to infiltrate their whole country with forts as bases for constantly active cavalry forces. The Army attempted to concentrate them in five different places, a major one being at San Carlos in central Arizona. For more than fifteen years the Army struggled to force the Apaches to remain on reservations. Able war leaders such as Cochise, appeared among them. It was not until 1887 that stability under Army control was finally established. Meanwhile one prophet, Nakai-doklini, arose in the White Mountains of Arizona and was promptly shot by U.S. Cavalry. After 1887 the Apaches were established on five reservations—San Carlos, Fort Apache, and Camp Verde in Arizona and Jicarilla and Mescalero in New Mexico. There had not developed among them any unifying leadership. Their subjugation under Army rule was complete in the 1890s. They settled down to a life of rations, as the Indian agents sought to encourage them to take up farming.

Atomization of the California Indians. One of the most densely populated regions of the United States where the Indians numbered 125,000, at the coming of the Europeans, California became during the 1800s the scene of the most complete destruction of native Indian life. Indian population declined to less than 25,000, and almost wherever Indians were to be found their tiny communities were in a state of disorganization and cultural breakdown. This came about chiefly during the period of American invasion between 1848 and the 1890s, although the trend in this direction set in during the period of Mexican control just prior to 1848.

There were many very small tribes or groups of Indians in California. They were hunters, gatherers, and fishers; not farmers. They had developed no confederations of tribes and seemed to lack interest in political organization, either before or after the coming of Europeans. The Spaniards had instituted large mission establishments among the Indians of southern California, where during the late eighteenth century bands were gathered together and converted to both farming and Christianity under tight control by the Franciscan missionaries. Perhaps 40,000 were so gathered at the time of the secularization of the missions in 1834 by the Mexicans. At this time the Mexican landholders instituted a type of peonage which left the Indians little control over their own lives. Some Indians, however, managed to continue farming on a small scale in some of the valleys of southern California. The Spaniards and Mexicans did not penetrate deeply into the interior valleys and mountains where the greater part of the large population of Indians lived. It remained for the Americans to break up these scattered small groups, as the miners of the 1849 Gold Rush and the waves of settlers moved into every corner of the state.

The process of dispossession and destruction of the California Indians was relatively easy for the invaders. Nowhere was there concerted resistance by the disparate bands. The Americans as frontiersmen had perhaps the freest hand here of anywhere in the United States. They murdered, ousted families and communities from their land, and turned the majority of Indians into dependent hangers-on at the edges of the rapidly growing White settlements. A first effort was made in 1850 to establish a policy by the federal government and plans for reservations were drawn up. Although some treaties were made, they remained unratified by Congress, forcing local authorities about 1870 to set up some fourteen reservations. The Indian population had dwindled by this time to less than 50,000 and was declining rapidly. The process of extinction and cultural breakdown continued unabated through the nineteenth century.

CHAPTER 4

The Colonial Pattern, 1871-1934

The wielding of the power over Indians which the United States had achieved through military conquest led to the self-consistent policy embodied in the General Allotment Act of 1887 (*see Document No. 14*) and auxiliary programs formulated in the Bureau of Indian Affairs. The policy came fully into operation in 1898 when the Dawes Commission acted to dissolve the governments of the Five Civilized Tribes. (*See Document No. 15.*) The position of the United States was now unmistakable. It had embarked on a program of forcing the Indians into the cultural mould of what was then the dominant set of values in the United States. The principle of Indian consent, embodied even in the Removal Act of 1830, had been discarded. The same policy now applied to all Indians regardless of their initiative and achievement in organizing themselves to cope with their changing situations. The Supreme Court gave sanction, reversing the position taken in the 1830s. (*See Document No. 16.*) Perhaps most remarkable, there had developed in support of the policy a near unanimity among members of Congress, the executive branch of the government, and those national associations which had collected the most information and held the most favorable and humanitarian views about Indians. In this respect it was clearly an expression of the unity of view in the Western world at this time concerning the right of powerful nations to dominate others politically and culturally.

There were nevertheless a few dissenters among the Americans, most notably a senator from Colorado and members of the National Indian Defense Association who were in close touch with Red Cloud of the Sioux. Senator Teller of Colorado predicted that the new policy would not work as the means for turning Indians into responsible farmers following the Anglo-American pattern of life. (*See Document No. 25.*) In the main the senator turned out to be right. The Indians who were already farmers, such as the Pueblos, the Five Civilized Tribes, the Pimas of

Arizona, and enclaves here and there elsewhere, continued to
farm to the extent that new losses of land or of water for irrigation permitted them to do so. In the plains some Sioux and
others became for a time moderately successful ranchers on their
allotments. But the expected cultural transformation of even
these farmers and ranchers did not take place. Forty years after
the Allotment Act there were as before striking and fundamental
cultural differences.

Moreover a host of new difficulties arose to complicate the
"Indian problem." By the middle of the 1920s it was widely
realized that Indians had lost to Whites most of the best land
which they had formerly possessed. Opportunities for economic
self-support had thus been drastically reduced. Indian farmers
and ranchers, usually on marginal land, were much poorer than
their White counterparts. These conditions and the multiplication
of the new category of "restricted" Indians, whose land and income were being managed by the Bureau of Indian Affairs, led
to a slowing down of the allotment program, so that much of the
large reservation areas in the Southwest was not allotted. The
boarding school program was seen to have given rise to a new
facet of the "Indian problem," namely the "return to the blanket"
—that is, Indians who found no use for the schooling they had
acquired and returned to the reservations as largely maladjusted
individuals to complicate the work of the government officials.
Even the missionary programs, which the government had encouraged strongly at first, were not bringing about new vigor
generally on the reservations, despite an increasing number of
church members. There was even the growth of a new religious
movement among the Oklahoma and Plains tribes, the Native
American Church, which seemed to the missionaries a diabolical
development.

In the late 1920s realization that the new policy had not
brought about the desired results was widespread. Several of
the national associations which had become advocates of the
Indians began to protest the government policy. A study of conditions on the reservations was carried through and resulted in
an influential set of recommendations for modifying government
policy. This report, known as the Meriam Survey (*see Document
No. 29*), was published in 1928 and immediately had an im-

pact on policy, resulting in many reforms in the Indian Bureau. The reforms were built nevertheless on the same foundation as the existing policy, namely, the assumption that the Indians were in a kind of wardship relationship to the United States government. This idea had been contained in one of John Marshall's decisions and, despite its inconsistency with the body of his views, had become dominant as justification for the colonial type policy of the early twentieth century.

The Decline of Local Government.   The placing of Indians on reservations was a form of Indian removal. By 1887 all the Indians west of the Mississippi had been, with the exception of most of the Papagos of southern Arizona, brought under the reservation system of control. The objective of the new policy as exemplified in the General Allotment Act was ultimately to eliminate reservations and merge Indians in the general population. Only in Oklahoma, however, did this take place during the 47 years that the policy operated. The number of reservations in the United States increased to more than 250 during the period, even though the amount of land under Indian occupation was reduced by two-thirds. In Oklahoma some thirty tribes ceased to live under the reservation system. But here it was soon apparent that a complex new involvement with the Bureau of Indian Affairs had developed, and the expectation of the Americans that the "Indian problem" would disappear was not realized.

The Reservation System.   The reservation system under which Indians continued to live influenced profoundly all aspects of Indian life, especially their social and political organization. The changes did not come about in precisely the same way on all reservations. Differences in administrative technique and differences in the nature of the varied Indian societies resulted in a remarkable variety of results. However, on the majority of reservations there was a basically similar pattern of action and response. The Pueblos, persisting in their well-organized towns, did not during this period follow the general pattern, nor did the Papagos of Arizona who were not brought under the reservation system until 1917 (*see Document No. 2*), nor did the Navajos whose scattered settlements enabled them to remain relatively free; but the majority were forced into a similar situation, which may be characterized as administrative domination with consequent paralysis of local governmental institutions.

This process reached a climax in the 1920s on most reservations. What happened generally may be understood from histories of a few selected tribes. Among them they illustrate typical developments during this period of loss of self-determination.

The San Carlos Apaches. The San Carlos Apaches who were placed on a reservation in central Arizona beginning in the 1870s constituted a mixed group of about 3,000. They were bands quite independent of one another formerly and included some so-called Mohave Apaches (actually Yavapais) who spoke a totally different language. They were concentrated into a single settlement in close proximity under direct Army supervision. The Army officers organized them into what were called "tag-bands" for purposes of taking a daily roll and issuing rations. They were prohibited from going to the mountains to hunt or gather wild foods. They lived under the rationing system until 1904, for some thirty years after the formation of the reservation.

Army control was slowly relaxed giving way to administration by a superintendent of the Bureau of Indian Affairs. The Army officers and later the Indian agent sought to encourage farming with some success. The Apaches had in fact been accustomed to raise corn and squash in clan-owned fields before the Americans arrived. The plan called for larger scale agriculture with irrigation water from the Gila River. The organization of the bands was ignored in all that the agent did. He appointed Apaches whom he knew and liked to serve as police and keep law and order. The agent also with a few selected older men set up a court in which to settle disputes. He selected the crops, planned the planting, and superintended the farming.

The superintendent here, as elsewhere on reservations, became increasingly powerful. Without consulting the Indians he decided to lease their excellent grazing lands to American cattlemen. Steadily the greater part of the reservation was leased, the proceeds from which were held in trust, like the land, by the Secretary of the Interior. The reservation community became a small dictatorship. The superintendent maintained law and order. He with his staff of paid employees managed the tribally owned resources with some help from Indians whom he selected. There was no machinery of local government either to check the superintendent's decisions or to bring about participation in decision-making on the part of the Apaches.

In 1922 the Apaches were in effect outsiders on their own land. The excellent grazing lands, some of the best in Arizona, were all under lease to Americans, who employed only a handful of Apaches as cowboys. The proceeds from the leases were being managed by government officials. The water which they had begun to use for irrigation was being diverted upstream on the Gila for the use of Mormon farmers. At this time the federal government decided to build a storage dam on the Gila River in such a way that it would flood the major Apache settlement. Meanwhile many Apaches had begun to work off the reservation as construction laborers in water projects of the U.S. Reclamation Service.

As the dam filled and Apaches moved into two new communities planned for them by the superintendent, there were some changes. The Bureau of Indian Affairs decided to bring the Apaches into the cattle business. The leases of the American cattlemen were not renewed. The superintendent and competent Bureau of Indian Affairs technicians and stockmen began to plan the development of an Apache-owned cattle industry. The pattern of agency planning for the Apaches was now well established. It was applied also to the development of land for "subsistence farms" at the new location. When the land was ready to be planted, Apaches were in doubt as to who now owned the land since they had taken no part in its preparation.

The band organization of pre-reservation days had decayed, and nothing of their own had been substituted for it. Fifty years of accepting the initiative of government officials had left a vacuum among the Indians. Rivalry for the favor of the superintendent and his staff constituted the only political life on the reservation. What had been a society vigorous as a number of self-sufficient bands had become an aggregate of heterogeneous Indians apathetic about community life, torn by family feuds and rivalries, and deeply dependent on American officials. Apache society had been undermined by the superintendency which had developed no leadership responsible to Apaches.

The Sioux. The San Carlos Apaches like other south-western tribes escaped the allotment program. However, what had been assigned them at first in the 1870s was reduced by nearly three-quarters as rich copper deposits were discovered in the eastern and western parts of the reservation. Nevertheless, the 1,500,000 acres remaining was some of the best cattle grazing land in Arizona. Indians on other reservations were less fortunate. Among these were the Sioux who not only lost very large portions of their original reservation assignments before 1887, but also continued to lose the greater part of what was left, as the General Allotment Act came into full operation.

A great transformation took place in Sioux life between 1879 and 1912. This transformation was begun by an Indian agent, who was determined to help the Indians by making cattlemen of them. But first he felt he had to establish his authority and therefore he entered into a struggle for power with the accepted leaders, the chiefs of council. As among the Apaches, but in a more open struggle, because the Sioux chiefs were stronger, the superintendent adopted methods for break-ing down the existing local government. He had two tools. On the one hand he had rations to give out at a time when the Sioux needed help to stay alive. On the other hand he had appointed Indian police to enforce his regulations and policies. He forbade the old councils and enforced the regulation with the Indian police. He steadily undermined the authority of the chiefs also by discouraging the old band encampments. The process was hastened by allotment, which began to take place even before the 1890s. Families were assigned their acreages and strongly urged, sometimes forced, to move on to them, a process which discouraged the continuation of the band grouping. Schools were inaugurated without discussion with and against the advice of such cooperative leaders as Red Cloud. Children were forced, when necessary by the withholding of rations, to attend schools. Thus the authority of parents was also undermined. The old great chief Red Cloud fought a long-standing battle with the agent, as did others like Luther Standing Bear, who finally left the reservation in frustration. Steadily Indian community organization broke down.

This process paralleled the rise to importance in Sioux life of the cattle industry. The reservation was thrown open to White settlement in 1890, so that Sioux holdings were checker-boarded with White ranches. The Sioux became superficially patterned in the mould of the individual American cattleman. Families scattered; the old institutions of tipi circle and band encampment were eliminated as the Indians yielded to acceptance of the agent's authority and the demands of the ranching system. Between 1885 and 1912 Sioux cattle herds increased fourfold. When full allotment was instituted in 1904 the separation of family groupings became more definite. By 1916 nearly all the land had been divided. The Sioux were becoming adjusted to the new life. Now, however, they were led to sell their herds because of high prices and intensifying pressure to lease their lands to White cattlemen. Between 1917 and 1921 a superintendent who favored leasing influenced the Indians to lease all their lands and the Indians were suddenly living as landlords without herds of their own. In 1921 the White lessees began to default as cattle prices went down. Indians were encouraged to sell their allotments. They continued to sell. By the early 1930s the selling of cattle, land, and finally horses led to the decline of Sioux prosperity, as the general U.S. depression set in.

The Sioux made a quick shift from buffalo-hunting to a new economy which appeared for a decade to be an effective adaptation. Local group and tribal, and to some extent traditional family, organization had been discarded. The only substitute was the authority of the superintendent and perhaps school teachers who were not responsible to nor conversant with the viewpoints of Sioux family heads. Participation in White local government did not take place.

Something like the Apache or the Sioux experience characterized most of the reservations. The institution of the superintendency sapped the Indian capacity for community organization and initiative. Wherever the superintendency was able to reach into the Indian communities, it undermined rather than built independence.

A similar result, but through a different process, was taking place in the areas where reservations were dissolved, as for example in Oklahoma. Here vigorous efforts were immediately focused on allotment of Indian lands. What happened however was not a prompt disappearance of government supervision of Indians, but rather a peculiar intensification of it, with a fundamental change in character. The chief new development was the "restricted Indian," that is to say, the Indian individual who now had a land assignment, but who could not deal with this new possession until the federal government declared him "competent." The territory of the reservation as the administrative social unit no longer existed. The new relationship between government and Indians had become individual to individual. A 25-year trust period had been seen as necessary to prevent Indians from losing the new allotments. Thus, the Bureau of Indian Affairs undertook to manage the land or to decide which Indians were ready to manage themselves. Indians became subject to government determination of their competency.

The Five Civilized Tribes. Among the Five Civilized Tribes there was immediate reaction to the loss of the autonomy which they had achieved through their 19th-century form of local and national government. The tribal organizations were permitted to exist only as legal entities for the purposes of federal liquidation of group assets. The United States government appointed "Principal Chiefs" of the various tribes for purposes of such business. Appointment was necessary because there was no longer any legally constituted electorate. Under these circumstances, some Creeks made an effort to resist allotment. The great majority of Creeks were opposed to allotment, as they had been to removal. (*See Document No. 42.*) A movement developed under the leadership of a man named "Snake" (Chitto Harjo). (*See Document No. 5.*) In 1904 he attempted to form a new government based on old treaties. His associates were jailed promptly and what came to be known as the Crazy Snake Rebellion was over.

Under the pressures for allotment in the 1890s and before, Cherokees were stimulated to a peaceful kind of nativism. Based on an earlier secret society, called the Keetoowah, a tribe-wide interest in revival of certain older Cherokee symbols and rituals spread rapidly in 1902. What were called *gadhiyos,* or "fires," were set up under the leadership of a man named Redbird Smith. A fire was a sort of local chapter of those interested in the revival movement. It maintained a set of officers, a treasury, and a dance ground. Twenty or more local groups had sprung up before 1920. Redbird Smith and associated leaders got in touch with Iroquois in an effort to learn about and restore traditional Cherokee-Iroquois rituals. The movement was conducted in the traditional Cherokee manner of committee planning and peaceable conference. It had no Messiah, and no ideology of a millenium, but it was a vehicle through its ceremonialism for the expression of the sentiments which a large number of Cherokees felt about themselves in the changing world of complete White domination. (*See Document No. 43.*) Other Cherokees, so-called mixed bloods, opposed the Redbird Smith movement and began slowly to participate in the county and state government system of Oklahoma. In general what happened where the administrative unit of the reservation, or the "nation" (such as the Five Civilized Tribes had) was dissolved was an immediate throwing of government officials more intimately into the affairs of individual Indians, the infiltration of Whites in great numbers into Indian communities, the emergence of a class of relatively prosperous "mixed-bloods," and withdrawal to the more remote and poorer areas by other Indians. For the first fifteen years after allotment in Oklahoma about one-third of the Indian land remained in the "restricted" category. Thirty-five years after allotment, local government of all the counties in what had been the Five Civilized Nations was being conducted by a predominantly White population. Mixed blood Indians were participating prominently, holding office as well as voting. Every county of eastern Oklahoma had its minority of "full-bloods," gathered in the more hilly country around Baptist or Methodist churches, with a "Fire" and a dance ground nearby, where the language of the home was Indian and participation in county government was the exception rather than the rule.

There were regions of the United States where neither the reservation nor the allotment system brought about great changes in Indian government. These involved a minority of Indians, but some of the groups had, beginning in the 1920s, rapid population increases. The Pueblos of both New Mexico and Arizona maintained their traditional village organizations, the Rio Grande Pueblos having integrated a few Spanish features and the Hopis of Arizona having a politico-ceremonial system altered in no significant way from pre-Spanish times. The Indian superintendents were frequently baffled as to how they could get rid of or basically change these well-organized towns. But they and their staff were not permitted by the Indians to live in their towns; consequently both because of the disadvantage at which the Indians kept the agents and because of the ability of the Indian organizations to meet the Pueblos' needs, interference was at a minimum. Chiefly because of the scarcity of Whites, in the absence of allotment of land, and because of the great distance that could be maintained from superintendents, the Navajos and the Papagos on their large reservations during this period escaped intensive disruption of local government. However, in the 1920s among the Navajos an enterprising agent stimulated an adaptation of existing Navajo local government— the "chapter"—which was to become important in the next phase of Navajo life.

The Growth of Heterogeneity. In 1830 barely two years after the inauguration of the *Cherokee Phoenix,* Elias Boudinot the well-educated Cherokee editor of the new newspaper resigned. He differed with Principal Chief John Ross over editorial policy. He held that there were two sides to the removal question and thought they should both be discussed in the *Phoenix.* John Ross thought differently and put a new editor in charge. John Ross adhered to the position that the Cherokee National Council had taken that there should be no more cession on Cherokee lands. It was this policy that he maintained without swerving for as long as it was possible to resist the pressure and the maneuvering of United States officials and the Congress. He refused to allow free discussion managed by an individual who in conjunction with another Cherokee leader, The Ridge, were known to favor compromise with the position of the Cherokee majority.

White Pressures. Difference of opinion among import leaders in Indian societies did not suddenly erupt at the time of removal. One of the earliest sources of instability in Indian-White relations had been differential influence of Europeans on Indian leaders. This was not always a result of bribery and unscrupulous methods. There were Indian leaders who were short-sighted and acted in accordance with White rather than long-term Indian interests. There were some who came to the honest conclusion that White power could not be resisted, while other leaders of the same tribes felt they could take no other course but resistance. The Creek Confederacy was always plagued with independently acting town leaders who behaved in ways that the National Council regarded as inimical to Creek interests. The Cherokees were early split by second generation backlash against policies favored by earlier leaders. Thus Dragging Canoe of the Cherokees, son of the head man, Attacullakulla who had been very amenable to British suggestions, became strongly anti-British, as did Massasoit's son, "King Philip." Dragging Canoe fought further cooperation and made the Chickamauga towns of the Cherokees a distinct faction, "hostiles" from the White viewpoint, within Cherokee society. The Iroquois were frequently split after 1700 between following the lead of French or British, and within each Iroquois nation factions resulted from different views and sentiments before, but especially at the time of, the American Revolution.

The case of Elias Boudinot in 1830 is merely one example, at a time of intense crisis in Cherokee affairs, of a process general among all Indians who made contact with Whites. The European influences stimulated a greater heterogeneity, making impossible the unanimity which had been the ideal, if not the actuality. Almost immediately on accepting reservation conditions the Sioux experienced such results of intensive contact. Red Cloud, the hardly disputed war leader of all the Sioux began to act in ways that puzzled Indians and Whites alike, and probably surprised himself, under the conditions of trying to live peacefully with both his people and Bureau of Indian Affairs agents. The dispute among Whites as to whether Red Cloud accepted the Ghost Dance continues to the present. The fact probably is that he accepted it in the context of Sioux thought but knew that it would be misunderstood by the Whites about whose limitations he had come to know something.

To Whites intent on programs of cultural assimilation all growth of heterogeneity tended to be interpreted in terms of "progressivism" and "traditionalism," but this was an extreme oversimplification.

The growth of different viewpoints within any tribal group was not a single process. Under the conditions of the new policy between 1887 and 1934 the various processes were intensified because the superintendency and associated activities now became an institutionalized, focused means for bringing American influences to bear on Indian life.

Internal Issues. It would be a mistake, however, to assume that all issues which arose had their origin in the pressures of the superintendency. There continued to be internal issues, which were merely somewhat complicated by the intensive new pressures. In 1906 one of the Hopi towns in northeastern Arizona split apart, a disaffected faction establishing a new town of its own. Hopi local government had probably changed less than that of any other Indians during the 350 years of the European invasion. The tribe had thought it necessary in 1700 to massacre one of their own villages in order to keep out Spanish missionary influences. From that time they had been successful in maintaining their cultural independence, until the 1870s when the Bureau of Indian Affairs established an agent in their country. For 25 years there was increasing influence from the Americans, especially through the boarding school program. Hopis resisted the kidnapping of children for the schools, not only hiding children but even physically resisting the officials who came to find them. There were some differences of opinion about the desirability of schooling among Hopi leaders. One clan leader of the important town of Oraibi, Yokioma, made a trip to Washington and became more inclined toward acceptance of friendly relations with Americans. His successor as ceremonial head of Oraibi was of the same inclination. In 1906 long standing friction came to a climax in Oraibi over certain details and the right to leadership of important clan ceremonies. The dispute erupted into violence, but was settled in the traditional non-violent way by a tug-of-war. The losers in this case refused to accept the winners as rightful leaders, picked up their belongings, and set up a new town a few miles away. The conflict was a serious one and had repercussions in Hopi religious life for the next 60 years. The pattern, however, was not wholly new. Hopi villages had split over such matters long before the coming of the Spaniards.

Although a traditional type of factionalism, the Hopi division was nevertheless influenced by the current pressures. The dispute over leadership was affected by the favorable view of the established leader of old Oraibi toward American influences, including schooling. However, after the split he became strongly opposed to Christian proselytizing and refused to allow any church within the site of the old town. He also became opposed, although less violently, to schooling for Hopi children at boarding schools. His attitudes were a result of the fact that he was sent, immediately following the dispute, to an American boarding school by the Bureau of Indian Affairs officials. His stay in the school had the reverse effect from that expected by the officials. At the same time the newly established community, while unswerving in regard to traditional Hopi religion and in fact devoting itself to a sort of revival or intensification of a selection of the most distinctive Hopi beliefs (*see Document No. 46*), became increasingly favorable toward the use of many tools and house furnishings of the American type. In fact, by the 1930s it was physically one of the more Americanized Hopi towns. The Oraibi developments of the early twentieth century indicated clearly the intertwining of issues around traditional, as well as introduced sources of difference.

Mixed Bloods and Full Bloods. Elsewhere the major source of differentiation was a result of varying receptivity to features of White civilization. But where this developed it was by no means a split between generations as White policy-makers seemed to expect. Splits along such lines were spoken of as between "mixed bloods" and "full bloods," which was a misnomer. There were persons of mixed ancestry in both kinds of factions. Physical appearance in, for example, eastern Oklahoma was no guide at all for identifying either a "pure blood" or a "mixed blood." The lines of cleavage were not biological, but cultural. The "mixed bloods" were those who tended to accept White customs more extensively, to speak English, adopt American house types and attitudes toward work and money-making. As a result of speaking English children of "mixed blood" parents frequently gained more schooling than children of "full blood." Widely among the Plains Indians, the Five Civilized Tribes, the

Indians of the Great Lakes and the Northwest a distinction between "full bloods" and "mixed bloods" became common.

Religious Differences. A third important form of differentiation was along religious lines, particularly between Protestants
and Catholics, but also on some reservations between Christians
and "pagans." The Papagos were an example in one part of
their reservation of a vigorous growth of the first kind. Here
during the first two decades of the 1900s both Catholics and
Presbyterians gained converts in the same villages. By 1917
when the reservation was instituted there was sharp hostility and
refusal to cooperate between Protestant and Catholic communicants in the villages. Such differences with social consequences
appeared also among Apaches, Sioux, Chippewa, and many
others.

The reservation system of administrative control stimulated
the growth of political issues, but suppressed the means for
settling them. Political power for decision-making remained in
the hands of the superintendent. Lacking mechanisms for re-
solving differences, the Indian communities became pervaded
with factional strife under the surface of imposed order.

The Procrustean Bed. The American program for changing the Indians had rather well-defined goals, even though the
means for attaining these had been considered only in a general
way and in the absence of any real knowledge of cultural
processes among Indians. The goals were seen in terms of values
current in the dominant American society, at least that part
of the society from which government policy-makers came. The
values emphasized were those expressed in the more individualistic aspects of American culture—individual landholding, individual economic achievement through public schooling, individual seeking of salvation through Christian revelatioi, the
small nuclear family with an individual head.

The means for accomplishing the transformation of Indians
consisted of replacing all the collectivities then existing among
Indians, specifically, tribal land management, tribal government
both in its wider and local manifestations, tribal religions, and
extended families, especially as educational units. The transition
was to be brought about without consultation and community

interaction, but through paid government employees who were to assume authority over Indians generally and work in various ways with individuals whom they could persuade or, when necessary, force. The process seems to have been seen as an individual-to-individual operation. The ultimate result was viewed as individualized persons identifying with the United States as a whole, individuals who would, after schooling, found new families the continuity of which with former generations would have been effectively severed.

There was some conception of a master process which, once set in motion, would bring about all the rest. This was the growth of individual economic responsibility to be encouraged by independence on the land. For nearly fifty years efforts to bring this process into operation constituted a major influence on the lives of the Indians. Not all parts of the program were applied with the same intensity among all Indians, but in greater or less degree different parts came into operation wherever Indians lived.

Effects of Land Allotments. The results of this concerted effort by Americans were not what the most vocal advocates of the policy seemed to expect. It must be recognized, however, that strong supporters of the General Allotment Act included persons who wanted to acquire Indian land for their own purposes. The acquisition of land by Whites was rapidly achieved. Even by 1900, less than fifteen years after the Act of 1887, Indian land holdings had been reduced by nearly half. This was a result of two features of the legislation: (1) the opening to White settlement of large areas declared "surplus" after allotments of 160 acres had been made to Indian family heads and smaller allotments to others and (2) the loss of allotments which Indians sold or were cheated out of in a variety of ways devised by Whites. In this sense of achieving results favoring individual American interests the new policy was precisely what some of its proponents wanted and expected. Nearly 60,000,000 acres of land changed hands from Indians to Whites in the space of 13 years. Moreover this land loss by Indians continued until 1934, although it somewhat decelerated after 1921.

Those Americans who were honestly interested in Indian

welfare had no such objective in pushing the Allotment Act. For them almost from the beginning of the new policy there was dismay. Its application did not bring about a favorable transformation of Indian life, nor even begin to establish a clear trend toward improvement. The loss of hundreds of thousands of acres through all sorts of American schemes took place despite the inclusion in the act of a twenty-five year trust period for each allottee. In 1906 the Secretary of the Interior was authorized to remove the trust arrangement whenever he should decide that an "Indian allottee is competent." This placed judgment of "competency" in the hands of Bureau of Indian Affairs officials. The category of "restricted Indian," individually subject to federal government controls, was created. Millions of acres had been lost before the creation of the restricted Indian. Once he came into existence the process of creating landless Indians was accelerated and at the same time "restricted Indians" complicated the federal government-Indian relationship.

In general the results of the allotment program in the 54 years between 1881 (allotment had begun before the general act of 1887) and 1934, when federal policy changed again, may be summed up in the following way. During the fifty-year period the amount of land held by Indians declined from 155,000,000 acres to 70,000,000 acres, or that is, by considerably more than one half. Of the 70,000,000 acres about 30,000,000 were retained under general tribal title, or that is in the manner that prevailed before the allotment program began. Most of this land was in the Southwest, where lived some of the largest tribes, such as the Navajo. By 1933 allotment had barely begun in this region and relatively little land was ever allotted. The allotment program had, as a matter of fact, bogged down. It had turned out to have reverse effects from those desired, namely, the creation of many new trust responsibilities which the federal government felt it necessary to assume in order to prevent complete disaster for Indians. It was complex, requiring additional new staff for the Bureau of Indian Affairs as it went into the business of trust management of individual property. It had not indeed demonstrated itself as successful with regard to the ends set, and general skepticism and outright opposition had set in in the 1920s. As the program bogged down, some 100,000 Indians in the Southwest and here and there elsewhere in the United States escaped its effects and continued to live on collectively owned land. This was about one-third of all the Indians in the United States at that time.

In 1933 the Bureau of Indian Affairs reported that some 40,000,000 acres which had been allotted through the years was still in Indian hands. Thus somewhat more acreage was held by Indians as individuals than by tribal collectivities. Of this amount 23,000,000 acres were reported as "alienated," that is, presumably held in full title without any restrictions by Indian owners, while 17,000,000 acres which had been allotted were held in trust by the federal government for the Indian allottees.

It is a curious fact that no acceptable statistics were ever compiled translating these figures on acreages in terms of the human beings involved. How many Indians became successful independent farmers? If there were 23,000,000 acres in individuals' hands in 1933, did that mean that there were some 120,000 Indian farmers and ranchers? If the original assignments of 160 acres per family head were still held by these allottees that would be the figure. This would mean that more than one-third of the Indians had become individual landholders. No such figure can be accepted, however, because of the complexities of inheritance and other factors. The fact is that the success of the program has never been measured or assessed with reference specifically to how many Indians became independent farmers.

The Meriam Survey in 1928 described in general terms the state of the Indian farmers and cattlemen as one of almost unrelieved poverty and cited certain reasons. One was landlessness resulting from the allotment act and subsequent policies of land leasing pushed by the Bureau of Indian Affairs. Another was the marginal character of the land which Indians retained, whether as individual allottees or as tribes. One estimate in 1933 held that 20,000,000 acres of the total held by Indians was nonproductive semi-desert, mountain, or swamp land. Rather general assessments of this sort were being made in the 1920s and leading to drastic reconsideration of Indian policy. It seems that only a very small proportion of Indians had become effective ranchers or farmers.

Restricted Indians. An unanticipated result of the policy was the closer interweaving of Indian affairs with the federal bureaucracy. The trust function was no longer the relatively simple one of administering tribal annuities as it had been for decades, or even of the handling of funds on a tribal basis from other than land sources, which had been developing. The effort to protect individual Indians from the effects of the allotment policy had led to direct trust functions for individual Indians. This meant detailed administration of small accounts by the federal government, which called for a considerable increase in the number of Bureau of Indian Affairs employees. It meant the placing of judgment about an individual's "competency" in the hands of relatively low level government employees. In this respect the policy had in fact resulted in precisely the opposite effect from that expected. It had created new conditions favoring dependency and loss of initiative. Again no records have ever been compiled which tell us reliably how large this unanticipated result of allotment was. If 17,000,000 acres were in the hands of allotted, but restricted, Indians in 1933, then we might guess that approximately 95,000 were in these circumstances. This estimate is based on the assumption that each allottee held 160 acre assignments, but that cannot be accepted, because the Dawes Act originally provided for allotments to others besides heads of families. Moreover subsequent sale and inheritance had led to almost infinite complexities in individual holdings. We are led to speculate that more than 100,000 Indians were in restricted status.

In the absence of reliable data to make a good assessment, we might suggest that something like this had resulted from the allotment program. One-third of all Indians remained as before under the tribal trust system of land management, although corresponding tribal governmental systems had been eliminated. One-third of all Indians were in a new relationship of social dependency on government employees so far as their economic affairs were concerned. Another third had become independent land owners, but their condition was not that of self-sufficient and prosperous farmers. A variety of circumstances led to the very great majority living at a level regarded as poverty-stricken by most Americans, on marginal land the value of which was decreasing. Some few were leasing to others, a few were farming or running stock of their own. Land allotment had forced two-thirds of the Indians into situations of poverty and economic dependency.

The Boarding School System. Americans had hoped also of course that Indians taking their places in American society would be aided by schooling. The approach aimed at transforming the Indians through "education" had become important before the 1880s. (*See Document No. 40.*) Churches had worked hard at putting their kinds of schools at the disposal of Indians and some had, as among the Cherokees in Georgia, accepted Indian policy regarding these. The federal government in its 1868 treaty with the Navajos had required the Navajos to agree to send 30 children for each teacher to government-provided schools. However, there was wide variation among Indians by 1890 regarding acceptance of schools. The Five Civilized Tribes had almost uniformly adopted a variant of the American school system but had managed the schools themselves, paying to a large extent with annuity money derived from sales of land. The Navajos strongly resisted the first schools when they returned to their reservation from incarceration in New Mexico. (*See Document No. 4.*) The largest scale approach to schools for the 125,000 Indian children was that adopted by the government about the time that extensive land allotment began. This approach ecbodied the boarding school program which called for establishing schools in eastern United States and elsewhere distant from reservations. It was conceived in terms of driving a wedge between children and parents and thus hastening the process of cultural assimilation. Between 1880 and 1930 some 50,000 Indian youths were taken, by force when necessary if parents resisted, from various reservations and sent to the Pennsylvania, Virginia, and other schools. In Oklahoma it was proposed to dissolve the school systems which the Indians had built and to set up entirely new ones without the benefit of Indian planning. This was systematically carried though against bitter resistance by Choctaws and Cherokees. Schools which had been Indian-managed became government-managed. Here and there as on the Gila Pima reservation in Arizona, local boarding schools which had profound effects were set up by churches. Some tribes gradually accepted the boarding school systems. A majority of most Indian tribes had their children in federal, mission, or public schools by about 1920. Some continued to resist on into the 1930s. Probably most obstructive to accomplishing the objectives of the Americans was a declining interest by Congress in Indian schooling. Thus, by 1930 only a small minority of Navajo children were in schools largely because the Congress had not provided the necessary funds.

Like the allotment program, the compulsory school program for Indians had extensive effects. It was not, however, until 1927 that a serious effort was made to determine the nature of these effects. One finding of the Meriam Survey was that information was not available for assessing the results of schooling. It was perfectly clear, however, that Indian children had been gotten into schools. In 1926, 69,892, or 82.7%, of the known total of school age Indians were in schools. No one knew precisely, however, how many school age children there actually were. A little more than half of these were in public schools and two-fifths were in government schools. The others were in private schools, chiefly mission. The greatest success in getting Indian children into school took place after 1912. The percentage of Indian children in schools, if the doubtful figure of 69,892 is accepted, was only 8% below that for the general population. There was no doubt that these figures, however imperfect and incomplete, indicated a high degree of realization of the plan for reaching Indians with schools.

Measuring the effects in terms of the aim of bringing Indians "into the mainstream of American life" was a different matter. Literacy among Indians had certainly increased. Only 3.4% of Indians in South Dakota were illiterate and there were comparable figures for other states. However, the range was very great, reflecting in large part the recency of getting schools established in areas like the Southwest. Thus in Arizona 52.5% of Indians were illiterate, as compared with 20.4% illiterates for the state as a whole. The figures indicated that literacy was very likely to increase steadily as the 82% figure of Indians in school was maintained or increased. The question remained as to what these increases in literacy and in school attendance meant with reference to "entering the mainstream."

The Meriam Survey was not able to offer even a very general finding to the effect that schooling had increased the capacity of Indians to live in the manner of Americans. On the contrary, it heavily emphasized that schooling had been accompanied by an increasing difference between Indians and Americans. This was spoken of in connection with poverty, for example. The great majority of Indians were living in a state of poverty, by American standards. Whatever the total set of causes, there was no indication that schooling had brought about better adjustment of Indians generally in the American economic system. The burden of the Meriam Survey was that the school program of the government was almost wholly inadequate to the task of educating Indians for participation in American life on a level with the majority of other Americans. This persistent condition was attributed to a whole series of weaknesses in the government school system, ranging from poorly trained teachers and school administrators through ineffective teaching methods to maladaptation of curriculum to the realities of the situations in which graduates of the schools had to live. Thus, while precise information was lacking because of complete failure to evaluate what was being done, the survey concluded that success in getting Indians into schools had not resulted, during a period of more than forty years, in consistent moving of Indians towards the educational level of Americans generally. This contrasted with the progress in education made in the Five Civilized Tribes in comparable or shorter periods of time in the preceding phase of Indian history. It was now the case that the rate of literacy among the Cherokees, for example, had drastically declined. There was nowhere in the United States any longer an Indian school board, and "full-blood" Cherokees, Creeks, and Choctaws were increasingly ceasing to attend schools of any kind.

White Churches. The churches had begun in a favored position for achieving their objective of making Christians out of Indians. Cherokees, for example, accepted missionaries and gave them great freedom so long as they kept schools going. Eventually all the Civilized Tribes did the same. The federal government had been especially impressed with the aims and work of the Quakers during the 1860s at the time of Grant's Peace Policy and tended to accept their advice. In the 1870's and 80s the federal government adopted a policy of assigning different reservations to different church groups. For a time the government even gave responsibility for schools to the various churches. This conflicted, however, with American values and by 1894, the government had accepted schools as its own responsibility. Before the 1890s churches were established on all reservations, and everywhere the Indians joined them. By 1930 there were some 150,000 Indians reported to be communicants of various Christian demoninations. The Catholics reported 61,456 adherents, the Protestants 80,000. Protestant missions among Indians reported a total of 26 sects and 32,164 Indians involved in these missions. Ordained Indian ministers numbered 86 among Southern Baptists, 36 Methodist, 75 Presbyterian, and 36 Episcopalian. It would appear that at least one-half of the Indians had by this time been reached and that most of these counted themselves communicants of one or another Christian denomination. Many also participated in one or another of the native ceremonies. Thus the Pueblos and the Papagos were accounted Catholics, but actually their religious life involved both native and Christian traditions. This was less true of Protestant adherents.

This condition had come about at the same time that the Bureau of Indian Affairs exerted pressure to suppress Indian religious life. Thus the Sun Dance of the Plains Indians was prohibited, and there was a systematic effort to destroy the Native American Church with its use of peyote. The BIA tried also in the 1920s to suppress Pueblo religion. These efforts had the effect of driving many ceremonies underground.

There was no mention of political development in the Meriam report, and consequently no assessment of the extent to which Indians had been brought into the American political system. This was probably the clearest indication that Indians were faced during this period with a colonial pattern of thought and action on the part of dominant Americans.

The Native American Church. Despite the determined efforts to bring about replacement of Indian cultures, the more usual process of fusion of Western and Indian tradition continued to take place. A religion of a new sort combining Christian and traditional Indian elements originated and spread rapidly during the colonial phase of Indian history. It was a religion of much wider scope and appeal than the earlier fusional Handsome Lake religion, which remained confined almost entirely to a single tribal tradition. This new religion was called the Native American Church. It was opposed vigorously by Whites, especially Protestant missionaries and ministers. It therefore necessarily grew up outside the framework of control which the Americans had established in religion, schooling, and economic life. Between about 1880 and 1930 the Native American Church spread to most of the tribes of the United States. Several tribes rejected it, namely, the Navajos, all but one of the Pueblos, and Papagos, Pimas, and other smaller tribes of the Southwest. It was to spread later among the Navajos. In the whole of Oklahoma, the Plains and the Great Lakes, and here and there in the Northwest the new religion diffused during the same 50 years that Christianity was making its way in the hands of paid missionaries.

To one careful and well-informed White observer the period of the final capitulation of the buffalo-hunting peoples resembled the 1st century A.D. when there were a host of new religious revelations in tiny conquered Palestine. Among the tribes of the plains just after they had been conquered and placed on reservations a dozen or more new religions arose among them. One was the Ghost Dance religion which died out completely within a few years after the massacre of Wounded Knee. Others were of even lesser duration, such as the Kiowa "Sons of the Sun" and the strange sword prophet among the Crow Indians. Their quick demise indicates that they were highly specialized expressions of reaction to the most severe deprivations of early reservation life. They could have no function after those extreme conditions ended. The Native American Church was of a different, more universal order. It grew around customs involving the use of a cactus fruit—peyote—which induces visions and meditative states. The use of peyote was widespread aboriginally among Indians in northwestern Mexico and had been adopted by such groups as the Caddo-speaking peoples of Texas before 1860. Beginning perhaps in the 1880s Indians at the Kiowa-Comanche-Wichita Agency in western Oklahoma began to develop new rituals employing peyote. During the 1890s the new rituals spread among the Cheyenne, the Osage, the Arapaho, the Poncas, and the Pawnees in Oklahoma and the Fox in Iowa. During the first decade of the 20th century (or earlier) the use of peyote in religious rites diffused widely among the northern Plains Indians, such as the Sioux, the Omaha, and the Arikara and in the Great Lakes region among Winnebagos, Menominee and Chippewas.

The new religion combined elements from Christianity and the Indian religions. The use of peyote became a collective rite in contrast with its earlier use as an individual vision inducer. As it came widely into use many varieties of ritual and belief developed. No creed became general; the religion rested not on specific theological beliefs, but rather on group ceremonials. Among the varieties which developed there were some common elements. These included beliefs in a Great Spirit, often identified with the Christian God or with Jesus. Visions received during the ceremony were sometimes interpreted as coming from Jesus. The use of rosaries or crucifixes was present in some form. The central rite was fairly well standardized. An altar was set up in a tipi, or house, which consisted of a peyote plant, called Great Peyote or Peyote Chief, near a fire built in V-form in the center of the floor. Around this "fire" the communicants gathered in a circle and passed from hand to hand a water drum and rattle as each individual sang special peyote songs. Both the words and the musical forms showed White influences. A peyote chief, a drummer, and other officials constituted the group organization. The rite lasted all night and was capped by a special form of communion called the Peyote Breakfast of fruit, corn, and game flesh. The devotees formed groups with permanent organization and began eventually to call themselves churches. This synthesis of Indian with Christian ceremony appealed chiefly to young persons who had much experience with White ways and who were in need of some personal reorganization in their efforts to find linkage between their Indian and White experiences of life. It was thus a regenerative movement. It was in no way militant as the Ghost Dance had become among the Sioux.

The Native American Church involved, like the Handsome

Lake religion, a new morality which included rejection of alcohol and sometimes tobacco. It emphasized brotherly love and family responsibilities. It was inter-tribal in outlook, unlike the Iroquois religion, and became even more so as it developed. Clearly it filled a need which a great many Indians felt as a result of common disruptive encounters in relations with Whites.

It was regarded as dangerous by Christian missionaries who held that it made conversion to Christianity difficult or impossible. The missionaries opposed the new religion vigorously and persuaded the Bureau of Indian Affairs to attack it. Between 1910 and 1918 the attack grew more determined, and efforts were made to outlaw the peyote plant. No federal legislation was secured, however, because there was no medical proof of any harmful or addictive effects of peyote. As efforts to suppress peyotism grew stronger, the religion itself grew stronger. Indian leaders sought to prevent the suppression by various means. They hired lawyers and in the name of freedom of religion gained some favorable decisions. They also sought protection from interference through legal means.

In 1918 a group of Indians in Oklahoma formed a corporation. The incorporators were Cheyenne, Oto, Ponca, Comanche, Kiowa, and Kiowa Apache. The first president of the newly formed Native American Church was a Ponca named Frank Eagle. Important leaders were Quanah Parker (Comanche) and Alfred Wilson (Delaware). A similar group called the First Born Church had been incorporated earlier in 1914. By 1944 the organization had changed its name to the Native American Church of North America (*see Document No. 44*) and had organizations in some six states besides Oklahoma.

The Native American Church was never accepted by Christian church groups and was opposed frequently by Christian Indians. Its communicants, however, insisted that it was as much a religion as any other. They emphasized its Christian elements. The problems of its growth illustrate the difficulties which any new development faced in this period if it did not spring from the dominant society.

CHAPTER 5

American Citizens, 1924-1968

Chief Justice John Marshall's decision in 1832 did not settle to the satisfaction of all Americans the legal status of Indians. A century later the issues with which Marshall had dealt were still live ones. To some extent they reflected broader questions with which the whole population was concerned, such as the relations between Negroes and Whites, between Jews and Christians, and between European and Oriental immigrants. The terms in which Americans thought about such ethnic relations were sometimes invoked in seeking solutions for "the Indian problem." How‹ ever, the situation of the Indians, as neither voluntary nor involuntary migrants to the United States, but rather as conquered people with whom treaties had been made until 1871 and whom the Supreme Court had ruled to be domestic nations, was sharply distinct. Moreover the behavior of Indians in their centuries of resistance to White domination had caught the imagination of Americans and inspired sentiments which led to the Indians' occupying a wholly unique place in American literature and public conscience. The national Congress by the middle of the 20th century had demonstrated that it was inclined to shift its position periodically on the issues which lay at the roots of Indian-White relations, thereby revealing the continuing uncertainty and ambivalence of Americans generally.

Indeed by the 1960s it was clear that a fairly regular cycle of action and reaction had begun to characterize congressional behavior. The underlying issues were not often clearly defined, but there appeared to be two basic ones. The first, around which public discussion and feeling often centered, was the question of whether or not there ought to be any special kind of relationship between the federal government and the Indians, different from any maintained with other residents of the United States. This issue was not to be ignored (*see Document No. 19*), for in fact there had been special relationships from the beginning of the republic. A special relationship was a fact of life in the

United States, and yet the increasingly dominant value orientation with respect to racial and cultural minorities was that there should be no differences, whether of rights to participate in all citizenship privileges or of freedom from interference by federal agencies in local government. There was, in short, as it appeared to many, a continuing inconsistency in the relationship between government and Indians and the trend in American life toward sanctions against all forms of discrimination among ethnic groups.

The other issue was whether or not Indians should conform to the cultural norms of Anglo-Americans. This, however, was a delicate issue concerning which public discussion was often confused, for the dominant value orientation held that everyone in the United States had a right to choose his own way of life. Therefore many Whites were not inclined to take public positions advocating Anglo conformity, and yet as members of the dominant society whose experience was bounded by the Anglo norms they regarded cultural assimilation to those norms as "inevitable." Few were well enough acquainted with the facts to know that there was no accelerating trend among Indians toward loss of distinctive identity. Thus there existed an inconsistency which was internal in the dominant White world view, not external as in the case of the special federal relationship. Whites tended to believe at one and the same time in the necessity of Anglo conformity and the desirability of freedom of cultural choice. The ambivalence of Whites was such that the Anglo conformity position was not explicitly expressed in Congressional legislation after 1887–98. Nevertheless sentiments focused around this issue, pro and con, influenced the positions taken in Congress on Indian legislation and were especially influential on the administrative policies of the Bureau of Indian Affairs.

During the century from the 1860s to the 1960s there were two peaks in Congressional action based on dominance of the view that the special governmental relationship should be severed. There were also two peaks based on the opposing view that it should continue. Reaction against the effects of the General Allotment Act led to the first important legislation favoring and defining the continuing special federal relationships. This counter trend to the Dawes Act became clear in 1910, continued through 1924, and reached a culmination in 1934. In 1910 the Congress recognized the chaos in Indian affairs which had been brought about by allotment. The result was a spelling out of new federal trust responsibilities with respect to individual Indian property and definition of trust responsibility for tribal lands. In 1924 the Congress passed an act which granted full citizenship to Indians. This was especially significant because the act was an explicit rejection of the principle underlying the General Allotment Act, namely, that citizenship for Indians should be contingent on individual ownership of land; being born in the United States was now sufficient and conformity to Anglo custom was, implicitly, irrelevant. The process of reversal of national Indian policy culminated in the Indian Reorganization Act of 1934. (*See Document No. 17.*) This not only prohibited further individual allotment and provided for acquisition of more tribal land, but also affirmed the right of Indians to local self-government based on, if Indians so desired, Indian customary law. This was a position consistent with John Marshall's decisions of 1831–32. It involved recognition of the destructive effects on Indian community life of the superintendency and sought to correct the blind spot in federal policy with reference to Indian political existence. Specifically the Indian Reorganization Act provided for voluntary adoption of a tribal council system of representative, constitutional government and for the organization of tribes as business corporations to manage the development of Indian-owned resources. (*See Document No. 30.*)

Within a decade a reaction set in against the newly defined relationship between Indian communities and the nation. The administration of Commissioner of Indian Affairs John Collier was accused of "re-Indianizing the Indians," despite the fact that the tribal council and corporate forms of organization introduced on reservations were basically of the Anglo-American type and not at all like the loose confederacies which had characterized Indian political organization. Slogans such as "Set the Indian Free" began to be heard in Congress and in popular writing. The Bureau of Indian Affairs in 1949 formulated a plan for progressive severing of relations between the Bureau and

the tribes in accordance with an "index of acculturation" prepared by the Bureau as a measure of readiness. By 1954, 20
years after the IRA, this approach to Indian affairs had become
dominant again among officials of the federal government. It
was essentially that of the Dawes Act era, emphasizing again
the withdrawal of the federal government. The major difference
now was that some effort was being made to secure real information about the condition of the various tribes. It was this increased respect for information which led to the proposal
that withdrawal be phased rather than immediately applied to
all tribes alike. The legislation embodying the dominance of this
approach consisted chiefly in House Concurrent Resolution 108,
passed in 1954, which provided for the assumption of responsibility for law and order on reservations by the several states
and for "termination" of federal relations with tribes which
should vote for termination. (*See Document No. 18.*) The
Bureau of Indian Affairs, taking the Congressional mandate,
proceeded to apply pressures to two tribes which had long been
involved in profitable lumber industries—the Menominee of
Wisconsin and the Klamath of Oregon. As termination was
carried through for these tribes, an immediate reaction set in
against the new-old policy.

Indians, with some individual exceptions, wherever they lived
opposed the policy. They were backed by Whites in various
national organizations and especially by those who lived in
the vicinity of the terminated tribes, who faced new economic
and political complexities. The result was a steady swing of the
pendulum in the direction of de-emphasizing the termination of
the federal relationship. (*See Document No. 31.*) At the same
time support grew for taking some of the services to Indians
out of the hands of the Bureau of Indian Affairs. In 1956 the
United States Public Health Service took over health and
medical services. By the late 1960s the trend was towards increasing involvement of various federal agencies in Indian
affairs. The agencies newly involved, such as the USPHS and the
Office of Economic Opportunity, adopted an approach which
emphasized participation of Indian local communities in their
programs. The pendulum was swinging (*see Document No. 20*),
but by 1968 there was no new legislation specific to Indians

clearly defining the trend. In 1967, however, a so-called Indian Omnibus Bill was proposed. The bill was submitted first to all tribal councils for discussion and emendation, a development which in itself indicated the nature of the trend towards recognizing the existence of Indian communities as political entities.

The years following the granting of citizenship in 1924 were marked not only by a shifting of the governmental framework regarding Indian affairs, but also by the assumption of active new roles on the part of Indians in national, as well as local, political life. Most notable was the formation of an all-Indian national association in 1944, called the National Congress of American Indians. It represented the emergence of a leadership among Indians which was no longer content to permit organizations founded by Whites, such as the Association on American Indian Affairs and the Indian Rights Association to stand as spokesmen for Indians. This trend continued vigorously through the 1960s, resulting in a variety of organizations and national conferences representing Indian interests in which Indians from various tribes in the United States assumed active leadership.

Emergent Societies. Indian life was by no means moving along the same lines everywhere in the United States by the middle of the 20th century. At least four different kinds of development could be distinguished. Which of these characterized a given tribe depended on combinations of several factors. An important influence was the nature of the resources which remained to the group, whether usable farm or range land had been included in their reservations, whether there were timber or mineral resources, or whether the reservation was in the path of urban growth. Another factor of great importance consisted in the degree to which interference in community adaptation by the administration of the Bureau of Indian Affairs had fostered attitudes of dependency and paralyzed local initiative. These factors were of basic importance and influenced the spirit and the cohesiveness of each group, but often it was impossible to explain fully by reference to either of these the kind of adaptation being carried on by a given tribe. The crystallization of a given world view under the particular circumstances of one phase of relations with frontier Whites, as among the Kickapoo or the Fox, sometimes played a major role. The nature of Indian social and religious organization, as among the Pueblos, seemed in some instances to transcend the effects of the various contacts with Whites. And, of course, the different demographic conditions of small or large population at the beginning of contact or of declining or increasing population in the course of contact played their part. The outstanding fact with regard to 20th-century Indian life was that it was developing along a number of different lines.

The Navajos. One striking development was the emergence of some tribes as subsocieties within the whole of the United States with not only a strong sense of distinct identity but also a capacity for collective action in meeting their problems of continuing adaptation. The Navajos in the Four Corners region of Arizona, New Mexico, Colorado, and Utah were the most striking example of this kind of growth. By the 1960s the Navajos were by far the largest tribe in the United States. From about 8,000, when they had been incarcerated at Fort Sumner, New Mexico, in 1864, they increased to at least 125,000 during the following 100 years. In a treaty of 1868 they had been guaranteed 3,500,000 acres in their former homeland, and this had been periodically expanded until their land holdings were the largest—15,000,000 acres—of any Indians. The mineral and range resources of this area did not become of interest to Whites until well after firm protective measures had been taken by the government.

On their return from the "Long Walk," where they acquired new conceptions of both tribal consciousness and the power of the United States government, the Navajos spread out over the great extent of their reservation. They were immensely aided by the issue of sheep by the Bureau of Indian Affairs. The land was well adapted to sheep raising and the Navajos had behind them two centuries of experience as stock raisers. Encouraged at every point to develop their flocks, they soon began to produce blankets for sale widely in the United States. The extent of the reservation was such that Indian agents could not maintain very close supervision. Encroachment by Whites was inhibited by the relatively undesirable nature of the grazing lands, so that at only a few points did their boundaries have to be protected and only on the east were some allotments carried out. They thus had by the 1920s something of an economic foundation.

In the 1920s and 1930s they were encouraged by the BIA to develop some forms of internal organization, most notably at first "chapters" or territorial administrative units, and later an overall organization called a "business committee" for legal dealings with Whites. In the 1930s the committee became an increasingly effective political organization with a representative basis. This council was in existence before the Bureau of Indian Affairs under the IRA instituted its efforts to stimulate tribes to organize Tribal Councils. It continued to operate without a formal constitution into the 1960s and to stimulate Navajo leadership. Both the council and the chapter organization were weakened during the late 1930s as the BIA imposed a program for stock reduction which experts claimed was necessary if the Navajo range was to be saved. Stock reduction gave rise to bitter opposition, but the council survived and later instituted its own grazing restrictions, so that stock raising continued to be an important part of the economy of the Navajos. The council, working closely with a very active tribal attorney, undertook the development of the resources of the reservation. (*See Document No. 47.*) These efforts included the establishment of a tribal sawmill and development of oil, gas, and other mineral resources. In 1957 the Navajo Tribe, organized as a business corporation, had an annual income of nearly $35,000,000 from oil and gas leases and royalties. This and other income was used for further development, and $10,000,000 was set aside in 1959 as a trust fund for scholarships for Navajos for higher education. The U.S. government assisted with road building and other development programs and with redoubled efforts for schools. Thus by 1960 the Navajo Tribe, operating with both tribal and federal funds, was integrated into American society as a recognized political unit.

Meanwhile the Navajo language was generally used by most people on the reservation. It had become a written language through the efforts of the Bureau of Indian Affairs in the 1930s and 40s, and Navajo was even taught to government employees. Election regulations, a Navajo newspaper, and historical studies were prepared in the Navajo language. (*See Document No. 4.*) However, by 1960 the tribal newspaper was published exclusively in English and the Navajo language paper was discontinued. The Tribe organized a bureau of historical studies and a museum and park system.

Religious life was varied. Catholic missions and schools of the Franciscan Fathers were strong; in 1950 about 12,000 Navajos were baptized Catholics. More than 15 Protestant denominations maintained active mission programs among Navajos. An estimated 14% of all Navajos were communicants of the Native American Church which had gained adherents rapidly after 1940. Regardless of Christian or Native Church affiliation, there was strong participation in native ceremonials, such as Blessing Way, which were not only religious in significance but also regarded as therapeutic and accepted as such by some White physicians. There was thus low emphasis on religious exclusivism as between Indian and Christian religious life.

The sense of Navajo identity was vigorous, fostered by a relative geographical isolation and by the existence of modified native institutions such as the chapter house districts and the tribal council. It was also fostered by intertribal ceremonials such as those held annually in the Navajo Tribal Fair. Radio broadcasting in the Navajo language was well established by stations in the vicinity.

The Navajo emergence as a vigorous and distinctive people was the product of initial isolation and the beginning of intensive contact at a time when federal policy had taken a turn toward active encouragement of Indian initiative.

The Pueblos. The Pueblos of the Southwest were at least equally distinctive. Like the Navajos they maintained their own clothing and hair styles, house types, and religious and other cultural characteristics. The story of their emergence in the welter of U.S. life is quite different, however, from that of the Navajos. Their adaptation to the changing circumstances of contact was guided by a highly selective conservatism in contrast with the free borrowing of the Navajos. The fact that they were settled agricultural people with tightly integrated religious organization made the difference. In the 17th and 18th centuries they modified their town organization along lines required by

the Spaniards, but retained their basic cultural orientations.
When the IRA was introduced, they responded conservatively.
Not until the 1950s did two of the Pueblos—Santa Clara and
Isleta—adopt the tribal council form of organization. In the
60s others were tending in the new direction under the encouragement of the BIA. There were many fusions of Spanish and
Indian elements of culture in their arts and religion as well
as town organization, yet the guiding principles of Pueblo integration were unmistakable. Insistence that the Catholic churches
were built on their land and therefore did not belong to the
Catholic Church indicated the nature of the Pueblo tradition of
independence and local autonomy. At the same time each
Pueblo insisted on a high degree of cultural conformity among
all residents. They, along with other Southwestern Indians, contributed to the growth of a distinctive school of water color
painting which took its place as a part of the fine arts tradition
of the United States generally.

In Oklahoma the only reservation left was the Osage on
which rich oil deposits had been discovered about 1906. Living
in house types ranging from that of country squires to tipis, the
Osages were individually the wealthiest Indians of the United
States. They functioned under direct government supervision
rather than through tribal council or Indian business corporation and maintained no tribal resources. They were thoroughly
individualized. Yet it was clear that their sense of Indian
identity was very strong and was maintained through other than
political or economic organization. They were well-known at
intertribal gatherings in Oklahoma and elsewhere and under
such stimulus continued to develop their tribal dances and
ceremonials.

The Iroquois. In other ways Indians in the United States
emerged, but not as societies bounded by reservation territori-
ality, even though they retained a reservation as a land base.
Their daily lives centered in the larger society where they made
their livings. One such group, widely known to other Americans,
were Iroquois. These were mostly Mohawks, who had been
given land in Ontario, Canada, as a reward for remaining
loyal to Britain during the American Revolution. There they
maintained themselves as a group of some 3,000 during the 19th

century. While farming a little they gradually found better opportunities away from the reservation. By the 1940s they had become well established as a specialist group in the making of steel frames for buildings and bridges. They steadily adapted themselves to this kind of work until they were in considerable demand, their ability in "high-steel" work being widely recognized especially by bridge contractors. Their high-steel specialization began in the 1880s with the building of the Canadian Pacific railroad bridge across the St. Lawrence. Some 1,000 Mohawks based themselves in Brooklyn, New York, others in Buffalo and Detroit, but without giving up their rights to land in Ontario. The Brooklyn Mohawks numbered between 400 and 500. Here their families lived, periodically accompanying the workers on their jobs. Here they were for the most part Catholics and Presbyterians. A Presbyterian minister who worked with them found it worthwhile to learn Mohawk and to make some use of the language in sermons and parish work. The Mohawk high steel workers usually went back to their reservation on retirement, but their primary adjustment was off the reservation. They were a persisting enclave having found their particular occupational niche in American life.

Other Iroquois integrated in various ways into American life as residents of reservations in western New York and northern Pennsylvania where there were in 1950 some 3,000 Senecas. Some were professionals, some were skilled workers, some were practitioners of no special trade, but their center remained the reservations where they combined wage work of some sort with income from tribal properties on which Whites had settled in the Kinzua basin. Here in 1956 the recurrent attack on Indian local government was renewed when a large project for flood control and water development was proposed. The heart of the proposal was the Kinzua Dam which was to flood much useful Indian land. The Senecas of the reservations fought the proposal by hiring their own engineers who took an opposing position to the Army Engineers and took the case to court. The case centered around the Pickering Treaty (*see Document No. 48*) of 1896 which had guaranteed land and local government rights to the Senecas. The Indians lost the legal battle as the U.S. overrode the treaty, but much public sentiment was roused in their favor. The controversy showed that the Senecas had learned something about U.S. Courts and, like the Cherokees a century and a half before, could make a legal case. It also, of course, showed the continuing dominance of the integrationist approach to ethnic group differences in the United States. The crisis also demonstrated the existence of a Seneca political community in New York State.

The Senecas who carried through this court struggle were for the most part devotees of the Handsome Lake, or Longhouse, religion as it was now called. They maintained in modified form the institutions of the hereditary chiefs which, although primarily with ceremonial functions, were capable of a kind of political solidarity in the face of outside threat.

Other Tribes. Utes in Utah, Jicarilla Apaches in New Mexico, Wasco and Wishram in Oregon, Crows in Montana, and others also developed a political existence in their respective areas. In each there was the usual factionalism which made political action sometimes tense and difficult, but there was some resolution of such factionalism. The Crows developed a buffer sort of tribal council which kept the Bureau of Indian Affairs' staff at arm's length and made for a semi-independent development of decision making and political action. Wherever these conditions existed there was also a politically inert segment of the reservation which did not participate, but either withdrew or adopted the individualistic Anglo approach to problems.

It was impossible to say what the future would hold, but for the time being at least there were societies of Indians which were political entities capable of action on a range of issues. They were frequently split, as for example when the Indian Claims Commission set up by the U.S. Congress in 1946 made judgments of large sums of money in their favor. In connection with these sums there developed issues over per capita payments versus tribal management of the money awarded.

It must be emphasized that for every tribe which was achieving some emergent vigor, there were half a dozen which continued to live in the social limbo of inhibited local initiative created by the long, interfering arm of bureaucracy.

Submerged People. In 1960 nearly half the Indians in the United States lived outside of federal reservations. Precise figures regarding the numbers were not known, but various surveys indicated that at least 200,000 of the 500,000 to 600,000 identified as Indians were not reservation residents. Most of these, moreover, were not affiliated in any way with tribes which possessed reservation land. Their relation to land was like that of other citizens of the United States; they either were landless, possessed home sites or farmland which they had bought, or held land allotted to them as individual owners. Indians lived in this way in all parts of the country, but the great majority were concentrated in four regions—the Atlantic coastal area especially in the southeastern states; the Great Lakes area, especially in Michigan and Wisconsin; in Oklahoma; and in California and Nevada. Their history in each of the major areas of concentration was strikingly different.

Eastern Tribes. East of the Mississippi the 90,000 to 100,000 non-reservation Indians were people whom the sweep of conquest had failed to obliterate as social groups. They had escaped in one way or another the great removal program instituted in the 1830s, usually because they had already lost control of land which the Whites wanted and therefore were passed by. As a consequence neither the federal nor the state governments set aside reservations for them. Thus they had lived continuously outside the 17 federal reservations (chiefly in the Great Lakes area) and the 18 small state reservations (chiefly in New York, Connecticut, Maine, Pennsylvania, and Virginia) and had no experience of the special relationships with government agencies which reservation life involved.

The nearly 100 communities of Indians scattered from Maine to Mississippi were nevertheless places where people had maintained a sense of Indian identity. This was rarely accompanied by any very distinctive customs or beliefs, for everywhere there had been adoption of the dress, house types, ways of making a living, and religious customs and beliefs of the surrounding people. They had often lost their Indian languages and more often than not the name of the tribes from which they had descended. Some retained their tribal names, such as the 700 Passamaquoddies of Maine, the 395 Nanticokes of Delaware, the 500 Creeks of Alabama, the 700 Miamis of Indiana, the more than 6,000 Ottowas and Ojibwas of Michigan, and the 1,500 Winnebagos of

Wisconsin. But many traced their common identity back to no tribal group and had come to refer to themselves by the name of some locality with which they had been associated, or even as the Indians of such and such a county. A few sought to revive tribal names which had been lost, such as the Narragansetts of Rhode Island and the Lumbees of North Carolina, sometimes as in the case of the Lumbees of doubtful authenticity.

The communities in which the non-reservation Indians lived in eastern United States were varied in size and characteristics. The largest single group consisted of the Lumbees. They numbered perhaps 30,000 in southeastern North Carolina, and an offspring urban community of 2,000 had grown up in Baltimore, Maryland. They struggled through more than a hundred years to gain official recognition of their ethnic existence as separate from either Whites or Negroes and ultimately in 1953 succeeded in having the legislature of the state of North Carolina declare that they were officially "Lumbee Indians." Five years later the Lumbees came to national attention when they scared off an organized demonstration of the Ku Klux Klan aimed at keeping the Indians "in their place." Most communities were small, ranging from less than 100 to 300 or 400, and most were much concerned with their Indian identification, partly as a result of the tendency of Whites in their vicinity to segregate them in school and church life.

Oklahoma Tribes. In Oklahoma the Indians without reservations were by no means people whom the invaders had passed by and more or less forgotten. The majority here were descendants of the Five Civilized Tribes who had been removed from the southeast and then dissolved as political units by act of the national government. No longer owners of the whole eastern half of Oklahoma as a result of the allotment program, individuals retained of their allotments about 1,250,000 acres. Much of this was poorer grade land, such as the many individual holdings of the Cherokees in the hill country of eastern Oklahoma. Estimates of the numbers of persons descended from the Five Civilized Tribes in eastern Oklahoma in 1960 ranged as high as 150,000. Such a figure is dubious and represents an effort to include all persons of any known degree of Indian "blood." A reliable figure for the number of persons actually participating in the persisting Indian societies was 30,500 for all five tribes. There were many other non-reservation Indians in Oklahoma, but we shall consider only the best known of the Five Civilized Tribes—the Cherokees—of whom there were about 10,000 in 1965.

The Cherokees lived chiefly in small rural settlements of not more than 300 inhabitants. They farmed land on a small scale and chiefly on a subsistence basis. They had adopted the technology of the Whites of rural Oklahoma and were scarcely distinguishable in material culture from the poorer farming population around them. In this respect they were like the Indians of the eastern United States, but in one very important respect they were different in that they used Cherokee as the language of the home. Cherokee of course had become a written language since the days of the Cherokee Phoenix. The Cherokees differed sharply from Whites in that their family life was not focused around the couple with children; rather there was a broad co-operating group of kinfolk. This larger family group made for flexibility in the adjustment to making a living, permitting adults to leave the Cherokee country for wage work more readily. The majority were members of the Baptist and Methodist churches and community life centered around the local church. There was also a traditional Cherokee religion, stemming out of the Redbird Smith movement of the early 1900s. The "stomp ground" was the center of such religious groups and played a comparable part to the church in the lives of the non-Christians. The Cherokees did not participate, as a rule, in the county and state governmental system, but remained withdrawn from it. There existed a superstructure of appointed Cherokee officials which represented the nation in legal dealings with the federal government, left over still from the unfinished business of the General Allotment Act.

Cherokee society was in general, like that of the other Five Civilized Tribes, a result of withdrawal from contact with the larger society following the forced dissolution of the national Cherokee government in 1898. Its boundaries were fairly clear, not geographically, but in terms of social participation. It constantly lost members as a result of the cultural assimilation of individuals raised in Cherokee families who were attracted into the general Anglo society. However, there was some return of such individuals, and it appeared that Cherokee society was growing in numbers rather than declining. This was assisted in some degree by the considerable diversity of occupational adjustment which characterized Cherokee life and which had resulted in Cherokees living and working temporarily in all parts of the U.S.

California Indians. In California and the West Coast non-reservation Indians had a still different situation and history. A few very small reservations had been established by the federal government by treaty or by executive order. The state of California had purchased homesites for landless Indians under a special program and had thus set up the so-called "rancheria" system of reserved lands. On such reservations or rancherias of very small size some 7,000 Indians lived in 1960. However, in the state of California at this time there were at least in addition 65,000 Indians. About half of these, perhaps 33,000 were native California Indians, the other half being from a great number of different states. The Indians of non-California origin were almost all in urban areas, 20,000 in Los Angeles and 15,000 in the San Francisco area. Some 9,000 California Indians also lived in urban areas. Thus the California region differed from the other two major areas of non-reservation Indian concentration in that large numbers of Indians converged there from many different parts of the United States and in that they were heavily concentrated in urban rather than rural communities. In these respects the Indian population was following trends parallel with those of the rest of the population of the United States.

The urban Indians in California were most often migrants from larger reservations, such as the Navajo and the Sioux. They constituted distinct ethnic groups in the urban mass although not often living contiguously. The different tribal groups knew each others' whereabouts and maintained communications and cooperative relations. There were also Indian centers where members of all groups came together for social and ceremonial purposes and where intertribal contacts were stimulated. These urban communities were not stable in population, however, but appeared to be for the most part composed of a shifting population members of which were constantly returning to reservations or rural areas.

The rural native California Indians were highly atomized, having come from originally separate, rather small band and village communities. They lived for the most part at the edge of the reservation areas and rancherias. They were probably less completely culturally assimilated than the eastern non-reservation Indians, but nevertheless did not constitute cohesive social units with distinctive institutional organization. Their income level was extremely low relative to other Californians. Their condition generally reflected the extreme conditions of subordination and infiltration which had followed on the Gold Rush of 1849 and subsequent rapid settlement of California.

The non-reservation Indians of the United States could be regarded as submerged peoples for the following reasons. Wherever they lived they had not merged with Anglo-American or other ethnic groups. Despite different histories of contact they had maintained in various ways their sense of Indian identity. This had happened in the face of a high degree of acceptance of specific cultural ways from members of the dominant society. It had continued despite a constant contribution of persons to the larger society through the assimilation of individuals. The Indian communities persisted as distinct social entities, occasionally increasing their population during different phases of their history, but more often seeming to remain rather constant in numbers. They were by no means extremely isolated from American society generally, but had adapted to that society by means of a varied occupational adjustment and through the maintenance of functioning kin groups larger than the nuclear family. They could be regarded as submerged in the sense that they tended to live at a local level of social integration, disengaged from the national political and social structure. They were distinct subsocieties with a sufficient number of distinctive cultural orientations and symbols of Indian identity to make it clear that there were real boundaries between them and the many other ethnic groups of the United States.

In the general ideology of the dominant society it was assumed that such Indian groups represented the last stage before final assimilation into the "melting pot." The history of the various groups seemed, however, to offer little evidence for the validity of such a belief. Rather their persistence seemed to call for drastic modification of the prevailing views concerning the nature of cultural assimilation in the United States.

Terminated Tribes. Indian self-sufficiency within American society had been proclaimed as the objective of the General Allotment Act. It was also held to be the aim of the Indian Reorganization Act of 1934. Yet this goal, certainly generally agreed on by the formulators of federal Indian policy, seemed to be elusive. Neither the Dawes Act nor the IRA had, by the 1950s, brought about the generally desired condition. There seemed to be two horns of the dilemma. On the one hand, there was apparent need for special assistance to Indians in learning the ways of White society. This seemed to call for basic schooling, for experience in the American type of political action, for understanding something of the legal system in which Indian affairs were enmeshed, and for the development of ability in management of individual and tribal resources. The IRA sought to meet these needs in a manner in sharp contrast with the forcing technique adopted in the 1880s. It assumed that the federal government could play an important part in providing this kind of technical assistance and rested on the ground that special relationships between Indians and the government were a necessity of the situation. On the other hand, there was the second horn of the dilemma. The continued helping hand of the federal government led quite obviously to the growth of dependence on the part of Indians on the special institutional framework developed by the Bureau of Indian Affairs. The heart of the dilemma, from the White point of view, was the question how self-sufficiency of Indian societies could develop without governmental assistance and at the same time how it could develop in the constant presence of a governmental bureau.

Federal Withdrawal. In the late 1940s, after the resignation of Commissioner John Collier, attention began to focus again in Congress and in the Bureau of Indian Affairs on eliminating the special federal relationship. In 1946 the Congress created the Indian Claims Commission which was designed to provide a means for eliminating once and for all the claims of Indians against the United States for losses of land. If carried through, it was held, this would finally fulfill a basic obligation of the government to Indians. In 1949 a commission under the chairmanship of ex-President Hoover completed investigations into the situation of the Indians and recommended in favor of terminating special administrative relationships. By 1953 the view had become dominant in Congress that the second horn of the dilemma, namely, the severance of government supervision in Indian affairs must take priority in Congressional considerations.

The result was the affirmation of a policy of withdrawal by the federal government. This was expressed in House Concurrent Resolution No. 108 which stated that Indians should be made subject to the same laws as other citizens of the United States as rapidly as possible. It also declared that nine specifically designated groups of Indians and their individual members should be "freed" at the earliest possible time from federal supervision and control and called on the Secretary of the Interior to submit recommendations for bringing this about. The same Congress in 1953 passed Public Law 280 which authorized states to assume responsibility for law and order in Indian areas. In none of the Congressional Acts was mention made of any need for securing Indian consent. The mood of Congress was like that in the 1890s which led to the dissolution of the governments of the Five Civilized Tribes. In effect what was being authorized was a policy directly opposed to that which had guided the legislation of the Indian Reorganization Act.

These Acts of Congress led to further legislation specifically providing for the termination of federal relationship with the nine tribes mentioned in House Concurrent Resolution No. 108. Public Law 587, providing for the termination of the federal trusteeship over the Klamath tribe in Oregon, was passed in 1954, as were similar laws applying to the Alabama-Coushatta of Texas, the Menominee of Wisconsin, and the California Indians. The transfer of federal responsibilities to the state of Texas for the 394 Alabama-Coushatta was desired by the Indians and was quickly accomplished. In the other cases it was not so simple, but the termination action was carried through over a period of three or more years.

The Klamaths. The case of the Klamath illustrated very clearly the complexities which had developed as a result of the nature of federal programs up to this time. The 2,000 Klamath enrolled as members of the tribe were all English-speaking. They had instituted a tribal council long before the IRA and since 1913 had developed the timber resources on their reservation. In the 1950s private companies were cutting the timber on a sustained yield basis and the Klamaths were receiving about $2,000,000 annually which was distributed on a per capita basis, resulting in yearly incomes of from $3,000–$4,000 per family. Because of such facts as these the Klamath appeared to government officials to be one of the most suitable candidates for the Congressional effort to bring about termination.

Under the surface of the figures regarding extent of cultural assimilation, family income, and the existence of working political organization was a condition of deep cleavage within the Klamath tribe, a history of fruitless efforts to reach agreement concerning tribal management of the rich timber resources, and uncertainty and distrust of the federal government. Although all administrative expenses of the agency for the tribe were paid out of tribal resources, there had been no participation of the Klamaths themselves in the management of their timber resources. A tribal corporation had been proposed and rejected in 1929, a tribal cooperative plan was rejected in 1933. A proposal for liquidation of the tribal holdings was opposed in 1947. The Klamath Termination Bill of 1954 proposed final closure of the tribal roll in six months, the adoption of a management plan for the timber resources at the end of 18 months, and complete termination of federal trusteeship within three years. The two authorized delegates of the tribe who appeared at the hearing on the bill opposed the termination, and the tribal chairman held to the position that the tribe was not ready for federal withdrawal. It was clear, however, that there was strong sentiment among tribal members opposing this position. Various studies revealed that confusion and lack of understanding were rampant. A choice was finally presented as between withdrawing from the tribe and forming a tribal corporation for management of tribal assets. In 1958 more than 70% voted to withdraw, only 5%

voted to maintain and operate a tribal corporation, and 20%
were so confused or uninterested that they did not vote. The
division of the timber resources on a per capita basis led to a
storm of protest on the part of the surrounding Whites who
feared adverse effects on the local timber market.

The ultimate result was indeed a withdrawal of the federal
government from Klamath affairs, but the government nevertheless was forced to buy the Klamath forest resources. Nearly 65%
of the Klamaths simply moved from federal trusteeship to
private trusteeship as the government declared some 48% not
competent to manage their affairs and another 13.5% voluntarily
sought a trust relationship. The U.S. National Bank assumed
that trust relationship. Only about 15% were declared competent and continued to live on what had been the reservation
among the Whites who were already settled there. The tribe and
the reservation status had been liquidated, but again the condition of general self-sufficiency had not been achieved. It was
obvious that the lesson of the General Allotment Act had not been
learned.

Indian Nationalism. While federal Indian programs were
major determinants in the lives of considerably more than half
the Indians of the United States in the period following the
granting of citizenship, it was not true that Indian life consisted
merely of reactions to the actions of the government. In the midst
of the most repressive period of governmental interference, there
were new cultural syntheses such as the Native American Church.
The federal government did not control Indians, however much
it might interfere or help in community development. Indians
working along their own lines during the period of the shift to the
IRA policy and after came increasingly to influence life in the
United States, their own and that of others, in a number of
different ways. There were indeed two levels of influence. One
was regional and the influence here was chiefly on the arts and the
daily life of Americans. The other operated at the national level,
chiefly on the political and ethical life of the country. Both kinds
of influence were a result of the collective impact of Indians as
Indians rather than as members of particular tribes, although the
influences of particular tribes such as the Navajo and the eastern
Cherokee were not absent.

As we have seen, Indians from the very beginning of contact

with Whites were stimulated to form confederacies, to unite and confront the Europeans collectively. We have seen that the movement of the Five Civilized Tribes to Oklahoma led to efforts to form confederacies as a basis for resistance to White pressures that were felt to be coming. At first such movements, like Tecumseh's, were often militant resistance movements to oppose further White encroachment. Later in Indian Territory they were resistance movements also but they no longer looked to military means. Tendencies toward Indian unification of this sort were seriously interfered with by the direct attack of the United States on Indian political life in the 1890s. They were in fact effectively stopped for a time. But at least one concerted resistance movement took form during the 1920s when the land of the Pueblos of New Mexico was suddenly in jeopardy during the corrupt Harding administration. The All Pueblo Council was formed and not only succeeded in getting sufficient national support to stop the efforts to get the Pueblo lands, but also through Anna Wilmarth Ickes, Mary Austin, John Collier, and others who came to know the Pueblos, exerted some intellectual and moral influence on the United States as a whole. Thus by the 1920s the Pueblos were influencing as well as being influenced by general American life.

National Congress of American Indians. On a broader scale this kind of impact began to be exerted much more systematically after the 1930s. The influence of John Collier, who did not forget his Pueblo experience, was important in this new development, for as Commissioner of Indian Affairs he encouraged it. In 1944 Indians from various parts of the United States, but at first chiefly from Oklahoma and the Plains, organized a national association called the National Congress of American Indians. (*See Reading No. 45.*) It was the first such non-religious, national political organization of Indians. Organized as an exclusively Indian membership association, it was in part a reaction against the various White associations which had assumed for themselves the role of spokesmen for Indians. The first president of the NCAI was Judge N. B. Johnson, a "mixed blood" Cherokee from eastern Oklahoma who served for eight terms. Later presidents and important officers came from among Plains tribes, Pueblos, Western Apaches, and others. The NCAI had a number of aims, but chief among them were keeping an eye on legislation before the Congress and disseminating more realistic information about Indians. The first of these led to a lobbying organization in Washington which effectively worked against legislation harmful to Indian interests, as conceived by the NCAI, and for favorable legislation. The second objective led to the publication of a regular periodical which not only served to provide more accurate information but also became a forum for Indians all over the country and thus became a means of increasing Indian interaction and solidarity. The NCAI continued as an active organization and became increasingly influential as spokesman for an important segment at least of the Indian population. Its influence was considerable through an especially able succession of executive directors, such as Ruth Muskrat Bronson, Helen Peterson, and Vine Deloria. By the 1960s, it had become an important political influence nationally on Indian affairs.

By the same time there had begun to grow, inevitably, some dissatisfaction with the NCAI. Younger Indians sometimes held that it was dominated by "mixed bloods" and felt that other viewpoints needed expression. In 1961 a National Indian Youth Council was organized in which younger Indians began to exert influence at the national level in the manner of the NCAI. The NIYC was influenced by the rising tide of popular movements of the times and in 1964 became active in a demonstration in the northwest known as a "fish-in" which sought to remind the country that Indians had prior rights in important fishing streams. It also published a journal and made an effort to pay special attention to educational problems of Indian youth. These two organizations were indicative of the increasingly effective participation of Indians in national politics and public education. They were supra-tribal. They expressed a solidarity which had been forced on Indians by the long period of identical pressures applied to all Indians alike. Tribal differences were merged in the national interest of Indians under pressure. Both organizations by the 1960s were vigorous in their affirmation of certain values which they defined as Indian and in which they expressed pride. They constantly attacked the belief that Anglo conformity was inevitable. They adopted a program of needling the complacency of the dominant society about Anglo-American cultural values which they rated as inferior to Indian values. (*See Document No. 49.*)

Pan-Indianism. These two organizations were major expressions of what may be called a nationalistic movement among Indians. Indians had developed a common consciousness as an ethnic group, in part goaded by actions of the United States government. They were actively at work to combat those actions and to gain practical advantages through the usual political means in the United States, but also to affirm and make clear to the rest of the country the Indians' right to choose their own ways of life. (*See Document No. 50.*) Below the level of such national action and affirmation, there were more localized movements of particular tribal groups. For action at the national level did not mean that there had taken place any general mergence of separate tribal identities. On the contrary, everywhere in the United States there were strong resurgences or continuities in tribal consciousness. Among the eastern Cherokees under their tribal council system an historical pageant "Unto These Hills" was instituted which became a major summer festival for many thousands of Indians and non-Indians. The pageant was merely one of many indicators of the growth of tribal pride in what had been for many years a submerged people in North Carolina. In New York State there was similar growth during the 1950s of a nationalistic spirit among the Senecas. Navajo, Sioux, Hopi, Fox, Ute, and many others were moving along the same path. They were asserting themselves in various ways, stimulated by the changing national conception of Indians assisted by the national organizations and also by the post-1934 approach of the Bureau of Indian Affairs and other government agencies.

These political expressions of Indian life rested in part on cultural developments of many years standing, on what had been labelled Pan-Indianism. This term had been applied to the sharing of common interests by Indians of many tribes in certain dances, ceremonials, and music of the Plains and Oklahoma tribes. In different parts of the country, most notably in Oklahoma where many different tribes had been thrown together, but also in the northern plains and the Great Lakes area, annual "powwows" and similar gatherings brought together Indians of various tribal origins. During the 1940s and 1950s the scope of such gatherings widened and they increased greatly in numbers. They stimulated interchange of costumes, dances, songs, and ceremonial paraphernalia. By the 1960s the whole of the United States was linked by a system of annual summer powwows or "ceremonials." The common experience of Indians as reservation dwellers and as persons of Indian cultural heritage was pooled. To some extent the situation was contributed to by the fact that the boarding schools had also brought Indians of different tribes together, often with resulting intertribal marriages. There was thus a growing common pool of selected Indian cultural elements and interests. "Pan-Indianism" was undoubtedly one important basis for the Indian political consciousness which expressed itself in the national organizations.

Part I1
DOCUMENTS

Indian History as Seen by Indians

There is some record of Indian history as Indians wrote or spoke it. Some tribes had traditional methods for record-making although none had any form of writing before contact with Europeans; some rapidly developed written records after learning to write their own language from missionaries. Beginning in the 18th century there were many recorded speeches of Indian leaders participating in councils and conferences with Whites. By the 19th century autobiographies by Indians, such as Black Hawk's, were recorded to enrich the historical sources. The Cherokees inaugurated the keeping of full records of political and other proceedings in their own language. Such records in an Indian language or in English are now the rule. These varied sources await the dedicated student who, if he devoted himself to discovering and presenting the Indian points of view from such records, would produce a very different history from the present one.

The Walam Olum of the Delawares*

This fragment was attached to the long traditional history of the Delawares—the Walam Olum—painted on bark and found in an Indiana village of the Delawares about the time of their forced departure for Missouri. The fragment deals in very brief fashion with the period of European contact, beginning about 1600 when the Walam Olum proper ends and carrying the story to about 1818.

FRAGMENT

On the History of the Linapis since abt 1600
when the *Wallamolum* closes.

Translated from the Linapi—By John Burns

1. Halas, halas! we know now who they are; these Wapsinis (White men) who then came out of the Sea to rob us of our land; starving wretches! with smiles they came, but soon became Snakes or foes.

2. The Wallamolum was written by *Lekhibit* (the writer) to record our glory. Shall I write another to record our fall? No! our foes have taken care to do it; but I shall speak to thee what they know not or conceal.

3. We have had many Kings since that unhappy time. They were 3 till the friend *Mikwon* (Penn) came. *Mattanikum* when the *Winakoli* (Swedes) came to *Winaki* (Pensylv.)—2 *Nahumen* (Raccoon) when the *Senalwi* (Dutch) came—3 Ikwahon (Sharp-fighter for Women) when the *Yankwis* (English) came with Mikwon soon after and his friends.

4. They were all well received and fed with Corn; but no land was ever sold, we never sold any. They were all allowed to live with us, to build houses and plant Corn, as our friends and allies. Because they were hungry, and thought children of Sunland and not Snakes or children of Snakes.

5. And they were traders, bringing fine new tools and weapons and cloth and beads, for which we exchanged Skins and wampuns. And we liked them and their things because we thought they were good, and made by children of Sunland.

6. But alas they brought also Fireguns & Fire Water, which burned & killed. Also baubles & trinkets of no use: since we had better ones.

* *Walam Olum or Red Score. The Migration Legend of the Lenni Lenape or Delaware Indians, A New Translation . . . ,* Indiana Historical Society, Indianapolis, 1954, pp. 209–215.

7. And after *Mikwon* came the children of Dolojo Sakima (king George) who said more land more land we must have, and no limits could be put to their steps and increase.

8. But in the North were the children of *Lowi Sakima* (King Louis) and they were our good friends, allies of our allies, foes of our foes; yet Dolojo always wanted to war with them.

9. We had 3 kings after Mikwon. *Skalichi* or (Last Tamenend), 2 *Sasunam Wikwikhon* (Our Uncle builder) and 3 *Tatami* (Beaver taker). This last was killed by a *Yankwako* English Snake, and we vowed revenge.

10. Netawatwis (first renewed being) became king of all the Nations in the West, again at *Talligewink* (Ohio) on the R. Cayahaga, with our old allies the Talamatans (Hurons or Guyandots) and calls all from the East.

11. But Tadeskung was king in the East at Mahoning and bribed by the Yankwis; there he was burnt in his house, and many of our people massacred at Hickory (Lancaster) by the Land robbers yankwis.

12. Then we joined our friend Lowi in war against the Yankwis; but they were strong and they took Lowanaki (North land) from Lowi; and came to us in Talegawink when peace was made; and we called them Bigknives, *Kichikani*.

13. Then Alimi (Whiteyes) and Gelelenund (Buck-killer) were chiefs, and all the Nations near us were allies under us or our grand children again—When the Eastern fires began to resist Dolojo, they said we should be another fire with them.

14. But they killed our chiefs *Unamiwi* (turtling) & our brothers on Muskingum, and Hopokan of the Wolf tribe was made king and made war on the Kichikami Yankwis rather choosing Dolojo for ally as he was so strong.

15. But the Eastern fires were stronger, they did not take Lowanaki, but became free from Dolojo. We went to Wapahani (White R) to be further from them; but they follow every where & we made war on them, till they sent *Makhiakho* (Black Snake, Genl. Wayne) who made strong war.

16. We made peace & settle limits, and our next King was Hakhing-pomskan (hard walker) who was good, and peaceful. He would not join our Brothers Shawanis & Ottawas nor Dolojo in the new war.

17. After the last peace, the Yankwis come in crowds all around us, and they want again our lands of Wapahani: it was useless to resist, because they are getting stronger and stronger, by increasing their United Fires.

18. Kithtilhund & Lapanibi (White Water) were the chiefs of our 2 tribes, when we resolved to exchange our lands and return at last beyond the Masispek (muddy water or Mississipi) near to our ancient Seat.

19. We shall be near our foes the Wakon (Ozages) but they are better than the *Yankwiakon* (English Snakers) who want to possess the whole Big Island.

20. Shall we be free and happy there? at the New Wapahani, We want rest and peace and wisdom.

DOCUMENT NO. 2

A Papago Calendar Stick*

Papagos and Pimas of Arizona maintained a tradition of record-ing events by means of marks carved on wooden sticks. Each in-dividual recorder had his own symbols which jogged his memory. Thus he could give orally a chronological account with his stick in hand. The following are excerpts from such a record taken down by an anthropologist. "The Enemy" referred to are Apaches, with whom the Papagos were at war in the 19th century.

1857–58—The Whites and the People together started taming the Enemy.

1858–59—The prayerstick festival was held at the Narrow Place. Some of the People went to get corn from Mexico and, coming back, they camped on the other side of the Rotten Ground. Early next morning, a few of them started before the rest. The Enemy were watching from a mountain top, and as the People were passing among some trees, where they could not see them, the Enemy rushed down and attacked. One of the People was killed.

1859–60—At the drinking ceremony at Burnt Seeds, two evil medicine men were killed. It was a good medicine man who in-formed about them. This good man had been called in to treat a sick man and found that he was bewitched. So he told the man's relatives and told who the sorcerer was. They waited until the drink-ing ceremony, got the sorcerer drunk and killed him. His brother, who was also a medicine man, was looking for him. He met the band of killers and, when they found who he was, they killed him also.

1860–61—A White man came to Dead Cottonwood and started a ranch, but the chiefs of the People got together and ordered him out. He asked for three days to make ready and they consented. On the third day he started. When he came to Pond in a Gully, the Enemy saw him from the hilltop where they were watching. They left their moccasins and water jugs on a little hill and ran through the trees to head him off. When he saw them coming, he let his cattle loose and he and his peons hid under the wagon, with their guns between the wheel spokes. The Enemy shot at him from trees and one nearly got him. But the White man saw that Enemy peeping out and he shot him through the forehead, so the bullet came out the back of his head. Another Enemy was badly wounded and then the Enemies ran away.

* Ruth M. Underhill, *A Papago Calendar Record.* The University of New Mexico Bulletin, Anthropological Series, Vol. 2, No. 5, Albuquerque, 1938, pp. 26–43.

The People heard about this and they went to enjoy the dead Enemies. They danced around the bodies and called them names and from those names, they got nicknames themselves. One man laughed at the ribs of the dead Enemy and said they were big so they called that man Ribs. Another said the dead man's head was smooth like a gourd so ever after he was called Gourd Head.

During that same time, another band of the People, from Coyote Sitting saw the Enemy tracks and trailed them. When they camped that night, their medicine man "looked" to see what was ahead, and reported: "Ahead, it is all dark, nothing happens. But, behind, there are Enemies. They fall when we look at them." So the People turned around and went back to Coyote Sitting and there they heard the news. They went to see the dead Enemies but they did not joke, for the first party was there waiting to give them nicknames and these people did not want them.

1861–62—The White people at the Hollow Place had made soldiers and stationed down near the border, on this side, to watch the White people's horses. Enemies came and stole the horses but no one went after them.

1862–63—The prayerstick festival was held at the Narrow Place. When it was over, the Burnt Seeds went to the Narrow Place to sing, and then the Narrow Place sang for the Burnt Seeds. At the Narrow Place there was a great runner, champion at kickball for the Narrow Place, Willows, and Mouth of the Gap. This man had been trained by a famous medicine man who could shoot at a rainbow, cut off a piece and put it on the runner's shoulder, so that he kept ahead of his opponents as a rainbow is always ahead. His name was Champion Man. At Mesquite Root, there was a clever medicine man called Something-Laid-There-Loose and he understood where the Champion Man got his power. The Mesquite Root people wanted this man to train one of their boys to race against the Champion Man but he did not dare. "My power," he said, "is only from Elder Brother, but that of the other trainer comes from the Morning Star." So Mesquite Root sent no runners at all and Champion Man won all the races.

1863–64—Some of the People were behind Turkey Neck Mountain (near San Xavier), roasting mescal. There they met the Enemy and had a big fight. Two Enemies and one of the People were killed. The People burned their slain warrior as must always be done with any one touched by the enemy, and then they burned all the mescal, saving only enough to eat until they got to the Rotten Ground. There they picked more and roasted it and took it home.

1864–65—The prayerstick festival was held at the Narrow Place and after it there was racing. Champion Man was still the winner. This man used to go alone every morning to practice running on a cleared track in the desert. One day, as he was starting, he heard the sound of something falling and he saw a man standing there, waiting to run with him. That man was an eagle in human form and the eagle is the fastest of all the birds. The champion ran with the man-eagle to the end of the track and back and then the stranger walked away.

This happened four times and the last time the stranger came in eagle form with his wings spread. He said to the champion: "You will be like me, a killer and a runner." Then he took small feathers from his breast and thrust them into the skin of the champion, above the wrists. After a while, feathers began to grow on his arms, almost like wings. So he was the fastest runner among all the People. But, at the command of the eagle, he never told about his vision until he was an old man and could run no longer; nor did he boast of his power, for people might have found out whence it came, and might have destroyed it. . . .

1871–72—A little before winter, word came from Little Springs that the People were wanted there for court. They spread the news and people went from all the Desert and River villages. The White people took them. All the Enemy were gathered there too and they stood on one side of the room, while the People stood on the other. The chief of the Enemy was seated by the agency man, then the chief of the People and then their agent. The Enemy chief said: "You have destroyed many people." The Mexicans said "Why did you kill two of ours. We avenged it." Then he advised the Enemy to stop warring. But the Enemy chief said it had been given him from the beginning, he could not change his ways. Then the agent for the People said: "You should be friendly with the People, they are peaceful."

But the Enemy was still determined. He said it had been so since creation. He said the Enemy had been the first to speak, the first to drink cold water. That is why they are so fierce. That chief had a rock as big as his fist. He slammed it on the table and said he would not change. The agent said: "If you disobey the law, the law will kill off the Enemy. Soldiers will come. The other Indians will help." The Enemy chief said: "If you'll give me food and all I ask, I'll stop."

The White man agreed. He promised a wagon and horses to the chief, and food and clothes for all the tribe. That was why the Enemy got so much. Every time the government delayed the gifts, the Enemy went on the warpath.

After the court, the Enemy chief and the chief of the People shook hands. Four Indians were appointed to go to Washington and to tell the government there would be no more war. They were two Enemies, one Desert Man, one River Man. Each of them was given a medal and then they were sent home by sea to California and overland to Yuma at the Red River. The agent took the mail buggy and went to Yuma to meet them, changing horses at every station. He took them to Maricopa and there the Pima got off to walk to his village Vahki (Sacred House). Then at Black Tips (on the road to Tucson) the Enemy got off to walk to their country. Only the Desert man was left and he was driven to the Foot of the Black Hill, and then to the Hollow Place, while the agent went on to where he was stationed.

1872–73—Many Dresses, who had been made chief of chiefs by the Whites, died at the Narrow Place and the same year his messenger died too. The son of Many Dresses, who was called the Player, took his place. . . .

1876–77—There had been no prayerstick festival for ten years because there had been no rain, and no crops. But this year the festival was held at the Narrow Place and one of the images was that of a black water monster. It was made by a man who had long since dreamed a song about it and thought the people should know.

1877–78—There was a disease called Chills which would make people shiver even when they sat by the fire on a summer day. Many died at the Hollow Place, and the people sang to "step down" the sickness as Elder Brother had told them they should do. The Keeper of the Meeting summoned old men to sing in the council house, and, meantime, the medicine man went to every house where there were sick people. He carried with him a branch of white thorned cholla (Opuntia Bigelovii) to which everything sticks. He sucked and blew on the sick people and then he spat on the cholla branch and waved it so that it gathered up the disease. Then he went far to the north of the town, while the men were still singing and he dug a hole and buried the cholla. Above it he placed a stake of ironwood to hold it down. That is called sinking the sickness.

1878–79—The prayerstick festival was held again at the Narrow Place. The image of the black water monster was shown again, and with it was an image of a white water monster, dreamed by another man. That dreamer knew the noise which is made by the white monster and he made it in his song.

1879–80—The railroad came to the Foot of the Black Hill from the Red River.

1880–81—Many Desert people went to Yellow to work for the Mexicans and eat corn.

The Calendar History of the Kiowa*

Like the Papagos various Plains Indians kept records of events, but by means of paintings on skins. In the 1890s James Mooney took down from a Kiowa a long calendar history, of which the following are a few excerpts.

SUMMER 1882

This summer Dohásän, whose hereditary duty it was to supply the buffalo for the sun dance, failed to find even one, and in consequence there was no dance. For this summer the Anko calendar notes the death of Pätso'gáte, "Looking-alike," a daughter of Stumbling-bear, noted for her beauty. In accordance with the tribal custom in regard to speaking of the dead, Anko for a long time refused to mention her name. The incident is indicated by the figure of a woman where the medicine pole is usually pictured.

The Set-t'an calendar notes the excitement caused by the efforts of Dátekâñ, or Pá-tépte, to bring back the buffalo, also noted by Anko in the preceding winter season. The figure represents the medicine-man seated in his sacred lodge, wearing his ceremonial red blanket trimmed with eagle feathers, and with a buffalo beside him.

The buffalo had now disappeared, and with it the old Indian life, the sacred sun dance, and all else that they most cherished threatened also to pass away. According to Kiowa mythology, the buffalo originally lived in a cave underground, from which they had been released by their great hero *Sinti* and scattered over the prairies for the benefit of his children, the Indians. Somewhat similar beliefs are entertained by other tribes. As the buffalo had disappeared with the coming of the white man, who, by reason of his superior knowledge, was rapidly dispossessing the Indian, the native tribes almost universally believed, not that the buffalo had been exterminated—a calamity too terrible for their comprehension —but that it had been shut up again underground by their enemy, the white man, in order more easily to accomplish their subjection. It was believed that by prayer and sacred ceremonial the buffalo might again be released to furnish food and life for the Indian, and in every tribe there sprang up medicine-men who undertook to effect the restoration.

Among the Kiowa this task was adventured by a young man named Dátekâñ, "Keeps-his-name-always," who announced early in 1882

* James Mooney, *Calendar History of the Kiowa Indians.* 17th Annual Report of the Bureau of American Ethnology, 1895–96. Part I. Government Printing Office, Washington, 1898, pp. 349–353.

that he had had a vision in which he received a mission to bring back the buffalo. Accordingly, he began to make medicine and assumed the name of Pá-tépte, "Buffalo-bull-coming-out," in token of his new powers. He was already noted in other directions as a medicine-man, and had been the winner in the great *dó-á* contest mentioned in the calendar of the preceding winter. It is possible that his success on that occasion encouraged him to this attempt, as he began his buffalo medicine immediately afterward. He erected a medicine tipi, in front of which he set up a pole with a buffalo skin upon it, and prepared for himself a medicine shirt ornamented with blue beads, over which he threw a red blanket trimmed with eagle feathers. Thus attired, and carrying a sacred pipe in his hand, he began his mystic ceremonies within the tipi, and from time to time announced the results to the people, most of whom believed all he said and manifested their faith by gifts of blankets, money, and other property; they were further commanded to obey him implicitly, on pain of failure of the medicine in case of disobedience. His pretensions were opposed by the younger men among the returned prisoners from the east, who used all their influence against him, but with little effect. After nearly a year of medicine-making, being unsuccessful, he announced that some one had violated some of the innumerable regulations, and that in consequence his medicine was broken for the time and they must wait five years longer, when he would begin again. Before that time had elapsed, however, he died, but his claims and prophecies were revived and amplified five years later by Pá-iñgya (see summer 1888).

WINTER 1882–83

For this winter the Set-t'an calendar records the death of a woman named Bot-édalte, "Big-Stomach," indicated by the figure of a woman with an abnormal abdomen above the winter mark.

The Anko calendar notes that the Indian police camped this winter on *Dónä'i P'a,* "Pecan creek" (Elk creek of North fork of Red river), indicated, as in 1877–78, by the figure of a pecan nut below the winter mark. The Texas cattle trail crossed at that point and the police were stationed there to keep the cattle off the reservation. Quanah, chief of the Comanche, was there also in the interest of the cattlemen, and it was through his persuasion that the allied tribes finally agreed to lease their grass lands.

Anko notes also that the Indians now "began to talk about grass leases," but that as yet there was no grass money paid. It is indicated on the calendar by three circles for dollars below the winter mark, with a +, intended for a picture of the Indian gesture sign for "cut off" or "stop," made by bringing the extended right hand downward in front of the other, as if cutting a rope with a knife-stroke.

On this subject the agent says, under date of August 17, 1883:

The grass question seems to be the most difficult thing I have to contend with. I find it impossible to keep trespassing cattle entirely off the reservation, and we are now crowded on all sides. It seems to do very little good to put them off, for it is found that cattle that have just been driven off will come back on the reservation as soon as the police force advances. Our Indians are not disposed to rent the grass, yet if it is used it seems they should be paid for it. . . . The grass should be utilized in some way that will benefit the Indians, and if it is not possible to supply them with herds sufficient to consume it, it does seem as if the grass should be rented and the Indians receive the money for it (*Report, 102*).

The final result was the establishment of the system of grass leases.

SUMMER 1883

Â'dalk'atói K'ádó, "Nez Percé sun dance," so called on account of a visit from the Nez Percés, called by the Kiowa the "people with hair cut off across the forehead." The figure above the medicine pole on the Anko calendar is intended to represent a man in the act of cutting off his front hair. The Set-t'an calendar has beside the medicine lodge the figure of a man wearing the peculiar striped blanket of the Nez Percés. This sun dance is sometimes known as *Máp'ódal K'ádó,* "Split-nose sun dance," because held on the Washita on pasture lands inclosed by a cattle man known to the Indians by that name.

On account of difficulties with the whites, the Nez Percés of Chief Joseph's band had left their homes in eastern Oregon in the summer of 1877, and after a retreat of a thousand miles were intercepted in Montana by General Miles, when within a few miles of the British border, and compelled to surrender. They were brought as prisoners to Fort Leavenworth, and thence removed, in July, 1878, to a reservation assigned to them in Indian Territory. The climate and surroundings proving entirely unsuited to them, they were returned to reservations in Washington and Idaho in 1885, their numbers in the meantime having been reduced from about four hundred and fifty to three hundred and one, about one-third of their whole number having died. It was while domiciled in Indian Territory that they visited the Kiowa and other tribes, dancing with the Kiowa and Apache at the head of *Sémät P'a,* "Apache creek" (upper Cache creek), and attending the Kiowa sun dance, which was held on the north side of the Washita, about ten miles above Rainy-mountain creek, near where now is Cloud Chief. This was the first time the Kiowa had ever seen the Nez Percés, although they had a dim traditional memory of them in their old northern home.

In the spring of this year the keeper of the *taíme* medicine, Set-dayá-ite, "Many-bears," died, and the image was taken by Taímete, "*Taíme*-man," who continued to hold it until his death in 1894.

WINTER 1883–84

For this winter the Set-t'an calendar has the picture of a house with smoking chimney beside a tipi. It appears to be a canvas house, such as those Indians in a transition state sometimes use. Set-t'an explains it to mean that Big-tree was given a stove by the government and put it into a large tipi which he occupied; but Scott's informant, who is corroborated by Anko and others, explains it as meaning that Gákiñäte, "Ten," the brother of Lone-wolf, built a house this fall on the south side of the Washita, about opposite Cobb creek. Stumbling-bear says that he himself had received a stove as far back as 1875, two years before the government built his house.

The Anko calendar records the taking of a large number of children to the Chilocco Indian school, near Arkansas City, Kansas. The heavy drafts made during the term to furnish children for Chilocco and other schools very considerably reduced the number of pupils in attendance at the reservation schools; according to the agent's statement, seventy were thus taken at one time (*Report, 103*). The figure below the winter mark is intended to represent two wagons filled with children.

Anko notes also that a party of Dakota came down to dance with the Kiowa, indicated by the feather dance-wand at the side of the winter mark.

SUMMER 1884

There was no sun dance this summer, and the Set-t'an calendar has only the figure of a tree to indicate summer, with a figure below intended to represent an inclosed field, inmplying that the owner stayed at home. Concerning this the agent says, under date of August 28:

> The Kiowas have danced less this year than usual, and they seem to have given up their annual medicine dance, for as yet they have said nothing about it. The holding of this dance has always been a great occasion and considered one of their most important ceremonies, for they have believed it absolutely necessary to secure their health and success in all their undertakings, either at war or in the chase. They have generally gone out on the plains from 40 to 60 miles from the agency and been absent from five to six weeks. On several occasions since the buffalo disappeared, they have suffered very much with hunger while out, and I hope we have heard the last of the dance (*Report, 104*).

The calendar of Anko for this summer notes the hauling of government freight by the Kiowa, including himself, indicated by a figure of a wagon where the medicine pole would otherwise be. This was in agreement with a plan inaugurated several years before, by which those Indians who had suitable teams and wagons—the latter furnished by the government—were permitted to haul supplies for the agency and were paid for their labor as an inducement to get them to adopt the white man's industries. As there was no railroad near at that time, most of the freight had to be hauled overland from Caldwell, Kansas, a distance of 150 miles. For such labor during this year the Indians received nearly $8,000, and performed the work cheerfully and in a satisfactory manner (*Report, 105*).

WINTER 1884–85

The Set-t'an calendar has a house above the winter mark, which is interpreted to mean that the Kiowa camped all winter on the Washita near Set-k'opte's house, just above the agency. This was the fact, but another informant suggests that the original intention was to record the event that the Kiowa about this time began to build houses for themselves. On this subject the agent says at this time:

These Indians retain much of their roving disposition, and except during the cropping season do not camp long in one place, but do not go far from their fields. Few of the Kiowas, Comanches, and Apaches have houses, and most of them live in tents. This will probably be the last of their savage customs to be abandoned (*Report, 106*).

In 1886 it is officially stated that only nine Kiowa families were living in houses, all the rest being in tipis (*Report, 107*).

The Anko calendar records the stealing of another man's wife by Tón-ak'á, "Notched-tail," i.e. "Water-turtle," a noted medicine-man, for which the woman was whipped and a number of Tón-ak'á's horses were killed by the injured husband. The turtle below the winter mark indicates the event.

The Trouble at Round Rock*

by the Nephew of Former Big Man

The Bureau of Indian Affairs in the 1940s assigned a trained linguist to the job of helping Navajos develop a literature in their own language. A transcription was devised and publication of a monthly newspaper and a series of historical narratives begun. The following was recorded in Navajo, translated into English, and published in both languages in 1952 along with other accounts by eye-witnesses of the same events.

In the Fort Sumner Treaty we were told to place our children in school. So when we got back policemen were sent from Fort Defiance down toward Round Rock to carry out this provision. To get all of the children they went from hogan to hogan.

The leader of one of the parties was a man named Charlie. Others in this party were one called Bobbed Hair, one by the name of Bead Clan Gambler, another called Slender Silver Maker, and the one who was known as The Interpreter (Chee Dodge), as well as several others.

For a long time the men and womenfolk had held back their children. So on the dates set for bringing the children to Round Rock, very few were brought in. When the children were taken there a man by the name of Black Horse said, "No," and stood against the children being taken away to school. There was one man by the name of Limper, who may still be hunched with old age (still alive). There was one called Slow One, and there were Canyon De Chelly Man, Tall Bitter Water Clansman, Ugly Knife, Sucker, Weela, and Gray Haired Man. All of these said, "No," and stood against the proposal. And then many young men joined with them. All of these men are now perhaps dead.

Here at this meeting to get children together for school the man known as Black Horse stubbornly balked on it. "What the devil, you can jerk our children away from us if you want to. If you want trouble over this matter go to it," he shouted. Several others who were of like mind were behind him. In fact, they had probably conspired with him.

The one called Little Chief (Shipley) came also. He was the Agent. But when a hot argument got under way in the meeting, the

* Left-Handed Mexican Clansman *et al., The Trouble at Round Rock.* Navajo Historical Series: 2, United States Indian Service, Phoenix, Arizona, 1952, pp. 34–35.

Navajos threw the Agent out. Then things really happened. The man called Bead Clan Gambler got the Agent back from those who had laid hands on him. This Bead Clan Gambler was a husky man. As the mob made away with the Agent he dashed in among them and grabbed the Agent up under one arm (like a football). When the mobsters would have jumped him he straight-armed them and bowled them over backward, and running hard he beat them to a flour storage room. When he had gotten the Agent in there he piled things against the door from within, and the mob was frustrated. The Interpreter (Chee Dodge) also took refuge in the flour storage room. It was said that they stayed inside for several days without going outside. And while they were in there they dirtied the flour.

The news of this trouble spread all about, even up into the Monument Valley. Everyone said, "They're not going to take our children away, that's all there is to it." People were ready to fight. Some said that no soldiers had come to the scene of the trouble. Some said that bear hunters had been brought to the rescue, but the truth is that it wasn't these. That was just a tale. Soldiers came from Fort Defiance. They were sent for from there, and those who came moved up on top of Row of Willows (near Wheatfields). At that time there was a beautiful meadow there. There was not a single wash at that time. There they were encamped. When they moved again they went to the burned trading post at Black Rock Spring (near Tsailee). After camping there for two days they moved on. They moved down to Blue Clay Point (near Round Rock).

This was not the only time a school party went out. They went out many times. Summer and winter they would go about telling the people to place their children in school.

When the soldiers who were sent for arrived to fight, my older sister, who was the wife of Weela, acted as a peacemaker. Here she acted as go-between to restore the peace. One man took credit for restoring peace. He was a man called White Man. I heard him saying that he was the one who restored the peace. I told him, "You are a liar. You just made that story up. It was my sister who restored the peace. I know it. I am sure of it." So that is how Black Horse made trouble by holding back the children.

Now school is a wonderful thing. They had no reason for keeping us out of school, I'm convinced of that. School is not a thing of no value. It is something to be longed for and sought after. Had I gone to school I wonder how I would be today. By school we mean an endless learning. It's a means for accomplishment without end.

People who have children, and who put them in school, are right in so doing. I think they are indeed lucky children. I was one of those who spoke in favor of schools in days gone by. Not long ago a paper was brought up before us in a meeting. They said, "Here's a list of the men who asked for education, and here's one of the men. These men knew the advantages of schooling." They said this, mentioning my part in it. When they mentioned me in this connection

I almost wept. I was right when I took that stand. Had I gone to school I often wonder how good a leader I might have become.

Long ago our forbears went after one another with weapons over this question of schooling. On account of differences over education they threw out an Agent. It nearly brought tragedy. When people were about to come to blows my sister restored the peace. These things happened just about the time when my mind had become mature enough to reason and remember, so I know whereof I speak. And to many things which occured I was a witness, while in others I took an active part. So the people nearly came to blows over schools. But now education is, without doubt, the right thing. So go on children Go to school. Study hard. In the future you will profit by it.

The Plea of Crazy Snake*

This view of Creek history was presented in 1906 in the Creek language by Crazy Snake (Wilson Jones) to a Congressional Committee holding hearings regarding the admission of Oklahoma to statehood.

I will begin with a recital of the relations of the Creeks with the Government of the United States from 1861 and I will explain it so you will understand it. I look to that time—to the treaties of the Creek Nation with the United States—and I abide by the provisions of the treaty made by the Creek Nation with the Government in 1861. I would like to enquire what had become of the relations between the Indians and the white people from 1492 down to 1861?

My ancestors and my people were the inhabitants of this great country from 1492. I mean by that from the time the white man first came to this country until now. It was my home and the home of my people from time immemorial and is today, I think, the home of my people. Away back in that time—in 1492—there was man by the name of Columbus came from across the great ocean and he discovered this country for the white man—this country which was at that time the home of my people. What did he find when he first arrived here? Did he find a white man standing on this continent then or did he find a black man standing here? Did he find either a black man or a white man standing on this continent? I stood here first and Columbus first discovered me.

I want to know what did he say to the red man at that time? He was on one of the great four roads that led to light. At that time Columbus received the information that was given to him by my people. My ancestor informed him that he was ready to accept this light he proposed to give him and walk these four roads of light and have his children under his direction. He told him it was all right. He told him, "The land is all yours; the law is all yours." He said it is all right. He told him, "I will always take care of you. If your people meet with any troubles, I will take these troubles away. I will stand before you and behind you and on each side of you and your people, and if any people come into your country I will take them away and you shall live in peace under me. My arms" he said, "are very long." He told him to come within his protecting arms and he said, "If anything comes against you for your ruin I will stand by you and preserve you and defend and protect you."

* *Chronicles of Oklahoma*, Vol. XI, No. 3, 1933, pp. 899–911.

"There is a law," he said at that time, "that is above every other law and that is away up yonder—high up—for," said he, "if any other town or nation or any other tribe come against you I will see through that law that you are protected. It does not make any difference to you," he said, "if as many as twelve other nations come against you or twelve other tribes come against you it will not make any difference for I will combine with you and protect you and overthrow them all. I will protect you in all things and take care of everything about your existence so you will live in this land that is yours and your fathers' without fear." That is what he said and we agreed upon those terms. He told me that as long as the sun shone and the sky is up yonder these agreements shall be kept. This was the first agreement that we had with the white man. He said as long as the sun rises it shall last; as long as the waters run it shall last; as long as the grass grows it shall last. That was what it was to be and we agreed upon those terms. That was what the agreement was and we signed our names to that agreement and to those terms. He said, "Just as long as you see light here; just as long as you see this light glimmering over us, shall these agreements be kept and not until all these things shall cease and pass away shall our agreement pass away." That is what he said and we believed it. I think there is nothing that has been done by the people should abrogate them. We have kept every term of that agreement. The grass is growing, the waters run, the sun shines, the light is with us and the agreement is with us yet for the God that is above us all witnessed that agreement. He said to me that whoever did anything against me was doing it against him and against the agreement and he said if anyone attempted to do anything against me, to notify him for whatever was done against me was against him and therefore against the agreement. He said that he would send good men amongst us to teach us about his God and to treat them good for they were his representatives and to listen to them and if anyone attempted to molest us to tell them (the missionaries) and they would tell him. He told me that he would protect me in all ways; that he would take care of my people and look after them; that he would succor them if they needed succor and be their support at all times and I told him it was all right and he wrote the agreement that way.

Now coming down to 1832 and referring to the agreements between the Creek people and the Government of the United States; what has occurred since 1832 until today? It seems that some people forget what has occurred. After all, we are all one blood; we have the one God and we live in the same land. I had always lived back yonder in what is now the State of Alabama. We had our homes back there; my people had their homes back there. We had our troubles back there and we had no one to defend us. At that time when I had these troubles, it was to take my country away from me.

I had no other troubles. The troubles were always about taking my country from me. I could live in peace with all else, but they wanted my country and I was in trouble defending it. It was no use. They were bound to take my country away from me. It may have been that my country had to be taken away from me but it was not justice. I have always been asking for justice. I never had justice. First, it was this and then it was something else that was taken away from me and my people, so we couldn't stay there any more. It was not because a man had to stand on the outside of what was right that brought the troubles. What was to be done was all set out yonder in the light and all men knew what the law and the agreement was. It was a treaty—a solemn treaty—but what difference did that make? I want to say this to you today, because I don't want these ancient agreements between the Indian and the white man violated and I went as far as Washington and had them sustained and made treaties about it. We made terms of peace, for it had been war, but we made new terms of peace and made new treaties. Then it was the overtures of the Government to my people to leave their land, the home of their fathers, the land that they loved. He said, "It will be better for you to do as I want, for these old treaties cannot be kept any longer." He said, "You look away off to the West, away over backward and there you will see a great river called the Mississippi River and away over beyond that is another river called the Arkansas River." And he said, "You go way out there and you will find a land that is fair to look upon and is fertile, and you go there with your people and I will give that country to you and your people forever." He said, "Go way out there beyond these two rivers; away out the direction of it—and I will locate you and your people there and I will give you that land forever and I will protect you and your children in it forever." That was the agreement and the treaty and I and my people came out here and settled on this land and I carried out these agreements and treaties in all points and violated none. I came over and located here.

What took place in 1861? I had made my home here with my people and I was living well out here with my people. We were all prospering. We had a great deal of property here, all over this country. We had come here and taken possession of it under our treaty. We had laws that were living laws and I was living here under the laws. You are my fathers and I tell you that in 1861, I was living here in peace and plenty with my people and we were happy; and then my white fathers rose in arms against each other to fight each other. They did fight each other. At that day Abraham Lincoln was President of the United States and our Great Father. He was in Washington and I was away off down here. My white brothers divided into factions and went to war. When the white people raised in arms and tried to destroy one another; it was not for the purpose of destroying my people at all. It was not for the purpose of destroying treaties with the Indians. They did not think of that and the Indian was not the cause of that great war at all. The cause of that war was because there was a people that were all black in skin and color who had always been in slavery. In my old home in Alabama and all through the south part of the Nation and out in this country, these black people were held in slavery and up in the North there were no slaves. The people of that part of the United States determined to set the black man free and the people in the South determined that they should not and they went to war about it. In that war the Indians had not any part. It was not their war at all. The purpose of the war was to set these black people at liberty and I had nothing to do with it. He told me to come out here and have my laws back, and I came out here with my people and had my own laws and was living under them. On account of some of your own sons—the ancient brothers of mine—they came over here and caused me to enroll along with my people on your side. I left my home and my country and everything I had in the world and went rolling on toward the Federal Army. I left my laws and my government; I left everything and went with the Federal Army for my father in Washington. I left them in order to stand by my treaties. I left everything and I arrived in Kansas—I mean it was at Leavenworth to do what I could for my father's country and stand by my treaties. There at Fort Leavenworth was the orator of the Federal Army and I went and fell before the orator of the Federal Army. It was terrible hard times with me then. In that day I was under the sons of my father in Washington. I was with the Federal soldiers.

I am speaking now of this orator in the Federal Army. I went and fell before him and I and my people joined the Federal Army because we wanted to keep our treaties with the father in Washington. Things should not have been that way but that is the way they were. The father at Washington was not able to keep his treaty with me and I had to leave my country, as I have stated, and go into the Federal Army. I went in as a Union soldier. When I took the oath, I raised my hand and called God to witness that I was ready to die in the cause that was right and to help my father defend his treaties. All this time the fire was going on and the war and the battles were going on, and today I have conquered all and regained these treaties that I have with the Government. I believe that everything wholly and fully came back to me on account of the position I took in that war. I think that. I thought then and I think today that is the way to do—to stand up and be a man that keeps his word all the time and under all circumstances. That is what I did and I know that in doing so I regained again all my old treaties for the father at Washington conquered in that war and he promised me that if I was faithful to my treaties, I should have them all back again. I was faithful to my treaties and I got them all back again and today I am living under them and with them. I

never agreed to the exchanging of lands and I never agreed to the
allotting of my lands. I knew it would never do for my people and
I never could say a b c so far as that is concerned. I never knew anything about English. I can't speak the tongue. I can't read it. I
can't write it. I and my people, great masses of them, are un-
enlightened and uneducated. I am notifying you of these things because your Government officials have told me and my people that
they would take care of my relation with the Government and I
think they ought to be taking care of them as they promised. He said
that if anyone trespassed on my rights or questioned them to let
him know and he would take care of them and protect them. I always thought that this would be done. I believe yet it will be done.
I don't know what the trouble is now, I don't know anything about
it. I think my lands are all cut up. I have never asked that be done
but I understand it has been done. I don't know why it was done.
My treaty said that it never would be done unless I wanted it done.
That anything I did not want to be done contrary to that treaty
would not be done. I never made these requests. I went through
death for this cause and I now hold the release this Government
gave me. I served the father faithfully and as a reward, I regained
my country back again and I and my children will remain on it and
live upon it as we did in the old time. I believe it. I know it is
right. I know it is justice.

I hear the Government is cutting up my land and is giving it
away to black people. I want to know if this is so. It can't be so for
it is not in the treaty. These black people, who are they? They
are negroes who came in here as slaves. They have no right to this
land. It never was given to them. It was given to me and my people
and we paid for it with our land back in Alabama. The black people
have no right to it. Then can it be that the Government is giving it
—my land—to the negro? I hear it is and they are selling it. This can't
be so. It wouldn't be justice. I am informed and believe it to be
true that some citizens of the United States have title to land that
was given to my fathers and my people by the Government. If it
was given to me, what right has the United States to take it from
me without first asking my consent? That I would like to know.
There are many things that I don't know and can't understand but
I want to understand them if I can. I believe the officers of the
United States ought to take care of the rights of me and my people
first and then afterwards look out for their own interests. I have reason to believe and I do believe that they are more concerned in
their own welfare than the welfare of rights of the Indian—lots of
them are. I believe some of them are honest men, but not many. A
man ought first to dispossess himself of all thought or wish to do
me or my country wrong. He should never think of doing wrong to
this country or to the rights of my people. After he has done that,
then maybe he can do something for himself in that regard; but

first he must protect the Indians and their rights in this country. He is the servant of the Government and he is sent here to do that and he should not be permitted to do anything else.

All that I am begging of you, Honorable Senators, is that these ancient agreements and treaties wherein you promised to take care of me and my people, be fulfilled and that you will remove all the difficulties that have been raised in reference to my people and their country and I ask you to see that these promises are faithfully kept. I understand you are the representatives of the Government sent here to look into these things and I hope you will relieve us. That is all I desire to say.

White Policy

The legal framework which now is a major influence on the lives of Indians grew slowly and not always consistently out of Spanish, French, British, and finally American ideas about what the relations between Indians and Whites should be. Proclamations, resolutions, legislation, court decisions, and executive orders have contributed to this still developing body of "Indian law."

Francisco de Vitoria's Principles*

The first of the European nations to consider seriously the ethical issues involved in the domination of the Indians, Spain set its theologians, scholars, and philosophers, as well as statesmen to work on the problems. The scholar Francisco de Vitoria delivered two lectures in 1532 at the University of Salamanca which expressed the ideas underlying Spain's later legislation regarding Indians. Following is a summary of Vitoria's lectures.

1. Since unbelief does not preclude ownership of property, the Indians are not precluded from owning property, and they are therefore the true owners of the New World, as they were before the advent of the Spaniards.

2. The Emperor is not the lord of the whole world, and, even if he were, he would not therefore be entitled to seize the provinces of the Indians, to put down their lords, to raise up new ones, and to levy taxes.

3. Neither is the Pope the civil or temporal lord of the whole world. He has no secular power except in so far as it subserves things spiritual. He can have no power over the dominions of unbelievers and therefore cannot give such dominions to secular princes. A refusal on the part of the aborigines to recognize the power of the Pope cannot therefore be regarded as a reason for making war upon them and seizing their goods. If the Christian religion had been expounded to the Indians with never so much sufficiency of proof, and they still refused to accept it, this would not render it lawful to make war upon them and despoil them of their possessions.

4. The Spaniards, on the other hand, have the right to go to the lands of the Indians, dwell there and carry on trade, so long as they do no harm, and they may not be prevented by the Indians from so doing. If the Spaniards have diligently informed the Indians that they have not come to interfere in any way with the peace and welfare of the Indians, and if the Indians still show hostility toward them and attempt to destroy them, then, and only then, will it be lawful to make war upon the Indians. In the event of war the Indians may be despoiled of their goods and reduced to slavery, because in the law of nations whatever we take from the enemy becomes ours at once, and so true is this that men may be brought into slavery to us.

* Lesley Byrd Simpson, *The Encomienda in New Spain.* Univ. of Calif. Press, Berkeley & Los Angeles, 1966, pp. 127–128.

5. The Christians have the right to preach the Gospel among the barbarians. The Pope has the right to entrust the conversion of the Indians to the Spaniards alone and to forbid all other nations to preach or trade among them, if the propagation of the Faith would thus be furthered. If the Indians do not hinder the preaching of the Gospel they may not be subjected by war, whether they accept it or not.

Rules for the Praying Indians*

The Praying Indians were those Indians of the Massachusetts Colony converted by the Puritans who then took up residence in villages separate from both Whites and other Indians.

Conclusions and Orders made and agreed upon by divers Sachims and other principall men amongst the Indians at Concord, *in the end of the eleventh moneth, An. 1646.*

1. That everyone that shall abuse themselves with wine or strong liquors, shall pay for every time so abusing themselves, 20 s.
2. That there shall be no more *Pawwowing* amongst the *Indians.* And if any shall hereafter *Pawwow,*[1] both he that shall *Powwow,* & he that shall procure him to *Powwow,* shall pay 20 s apeece.
3. They doe desire that they may be stirred up to seek after God.
4. They desire they may understand the wiles of Satan, and grow out of love with his suggestions, and temptations.
5. That they may fall upon some better course to improve their time, then formerly.
6. That they may be brought to the sight of the sinne of lying, and whosoever shall be found faulty herein shall pay for the first offence 5 s. the second 10 s. the third 20 s.
7. Whosoever shall steale any thing from another, shall restore fourfold.
8. They desire that no *Indian* hereafter shall have any more but one wife.
9. They desire to prevent falling out of *Indians* one with another, and that they may live quietly one by another.
10. That they may labour after humility, and not be proud.
11. That when *Indians* doe wrong one to another, they may be lyable to censure by *fine* or the like, as the *English* are.
12. That they pay their debts to the *English.*
13. That they doe observe the Lords-Day, and whosoever shall prophane it shall pay 20 s.
14. That there shall not be allowance to *pick lice,* as formerly, and eate them, and whosoever shall offend in this case shall pay for every louse a penny.

* *Rules for the Praying Indians at Concord, Massachusetts, January 1647. Collections of the Massachusetts Historical Society,* Vol. IV of the third series, Cambridge: Charles Folsom, 1834, pp. 39–40.
[1] Pawwows are Witches or Sorcerers that cure by help of the devil.

15. They weill weare their *haire* comely, as the *English* do, and whosoever shall offend herein shall pay 5 s.
16. They intend to reforme themselves, in their former greasing themselves, under the Penalty of 5 s. for every default.
17. They doe all resolve to set up prayer in their *wigwams,* and to seek to God both before and after meate.
18. If any commit the sinne of fornication, being single persons, the man shall pay 20 s and the woman 10 s.
19. If any man lie with a beast he shall die.
20. Whosoever shall play at their former games shall pay 10 s.
21. Whosoever shall commit adultery shall be put to death.
22. Wilfull murder shall be punished with death.
23. They shall not disguise themselves in their mournings, as formerly, nor shall they keep a great noyse by howling.
24. The old Ceremony of the Maide walking alone and living apart so many dayes 20 s.
25. No *Indian* shall take an English mans *Canooe* without leave under the penaltie of 5 s.
26. No *Indian* shall come into any *English* mans house except he first knock: and this they expect from the *English.*
27. Whosoever beats his wife shall pay 20 s.
28. If any *Indian* shall fall out with, and beate another *Indian,* he shall pay 20 s.
29. They desire they may bee a towne, and either to dwell on this side the *Beare Swamp,* or at the east side of Mr. *Flints Pond.*

Commission for Government of French Possessions*

French policy was based on the concept of absolute power in all matters residing in the monarch, as detailed in this commission to the Marquis de Tracy authorizing him to assume the government of the French possessions in the Americas in 1663.

These and other considerations Us moving, We have constituted, ordained and established, and by these Presents signed by our hands, do constitute, ordain and establish the said Sieur de Prouville Tracy Our Lieutenant General in the entire extent of territory under Our obedience situate in South and North America, the continent and islands, rivers, ports, harbors and coasts discovered and to be discovered by Our subjects, for, and in the absence of, said Count D'Estrades, Viceroy, to have command over all the Governors, Lieutenant Generals by Us established, in all the said Islands, Continent of Canada, Acadie, Newfoundland, the Antilles etc. likewise, over all the Officers and Sovereign Councils established in all the said Islands and over the French Vessels which will sail to the said Country, whether of War to Us belonging, or of Merchants, to tender a new oath of fidelity as well to the Governors and Sovereign Councils as to the three orders of the said Islands; enjoining said Governors, Officers and Sovereign Councils and others to recognize the said Sieur de Prouville Tracy and to obey him in all that he shall order them; to assemble the commonalty when necessary; cause them to take up arms; to take cognizance of, settle and arrange all differences which have arisen or may arise in the said Country, either between Seigniors and their Superiors, or between private inhabitants; to besiege and capture places and castles according to the necessity of the case; to cause pieces of artillery to be dispatched and discharged against them; to establish garrisons where the importance of the place shall demand them; to conclude peace or truces according to circumstances either with other Nations of Europe established in said Country, or with the barbarians; to invade either the continent or the Islands for the purpose of seizing New Countries or establishing New Colonies, and for this purpose to give battle and make use of other means he shall deem proper for such undertaking; to command the people of said Country as well as all our

* *New York Colonial Documents,* vol. ix, p. 18. Quoted in Cyrus Thomas, *Indian Land Cessions in the United States.* Bureau of American Ethnology, 18th Annual Report, Part 2, Washington, 1902, p. 547.

other Subjects, Ecclesiastics, Nobles, Military and others of what condition soever there residing; to cause our boundaries and our name to be extended as far as he can, with full power to establish our authority there, to subdue, subject and exact obedience from all the people of said Countries, inviting them by all the most lenient means possible to the knowledge of God, and the light of the Faith and of the Catholic Apostolic and Roman Religion, and to establish its exercise to the exclusion of all others; to defend the said Countries with all his power; to maintain and preserve the said people in peace, repose and tranquility, and to command both on sea and land; to order and cause to be executed all that he, or those he will appoint, shall judge fit and proper to be done, to extend and preserve said places under Our authority and obedience.

DOCUMENT NO. 8B

French Policy Regarding
Settler-Indian Relations*

Cultural assimilation, one of the stated aims of French rule, was guided by ideas advocating the intermingling of Frenchmen and Indians, in such letters as those written by Charles Colbert, the French statesman. The following are from letters dated respectively 1666, 1667, and 1681.

In order to strengthen the Colony in the manner you propose, by bringing the isolated settlements into parishes, it appears to me, without waiting to depend on the new colonists who may be sent from France, nothing would contribute more to it than to endeavor to civilize the Algonquins, the Hurons and other Indians who have embraced Christianity, and to induce them to come and settle in common with the French, to live with them and raise their children according to our manners and customs.

*   *   *

Recommendation to mould the Indians, settled near us, after our manners and language.

I confess that I agreed with you that very little regard has been paid, up to the present time, in New France, to the police and civilization of the Algonquins and Hurons (who were a long time ago subjected to the King's domination,) through our neglect to de-

* Quoted in *ibid.,* p. 548.

tach them from their savage customs and to oblige them to adopt ours, especially to become acquainted with our language. On the contrary, to carry on some traffic with them, our French have been necessitated to attract those people, especially such as have embraced Christianity, to the vicinity of our settlements, if possible to mingle there with them, in order that through course of time, having only but one law and one master, they might likewise constitute only one people and one race.

* * *

Amidst all the plans presented to me to attract the Indians among us and to accustom them to our manners, that from which most success may be anticipated, without fearing the inconveniences common to all the others, is to establish Villages of those people in our midst.

British Proclamation of 1763*

Following Britain's triumph over France in the "French and Indian War," the Proclamation of 1763 was issued. In it may be seen two major elements of general British policy, namely, the attempted separation of colonists and Indians spatially and the treatment of each Indian tribe as a distinct political entity with which it was necessary to make a treaty.

And whereas, it is just and reasonable, and essential to our interest and the security of our colonies, that the several nations or tribes of Indians with whom we are connected, and who live under our protection, should not be molested or disturbed in the possession of such parts of our dominions and territories as, not having been ceded to, or purchased by us, are reserved to them, or any of them, as their hunting grounds; we do, therefore, with the advice of our privy council, declare it to be our royal will and pleasure, that no Governor or commander-in-chief, in any of our colonies of Quebec, East Florida, or West Florida, do presume, upon any pretence whatever, to grant warrants of survey, or pass any patents for lands beyond the bounds of their respective governments, as described in their commissions; as, also, that no Governor or commander in chief of our other colonies or plantations in America, do presume for the present, and until our further pleasure be known, to grant warrants of survey, or pass patents for any lands beyond the heads or sources of any of the rivers which fall into the Atlantic ocean from the West or Northwest; or upon any lands whatever, which, not having been ceded to, or purchased by, us, as aforesaid, are reserved to the said Indians or any of them.

And we do further declare it to be our royal will and pleasure, for the present, as aforesaid, to reserve under our sovereignty, protection, and dominion, for the use of the said Indians, all the land and territories not included within the limits of our said three new Governments, or within the limits of the territory granted to the Hudson's Bay Company; as also all the lands and territories lying to the Westward of the sources of the rivers which fall into the sea from the West and Northwest as aforesaid; and we do hereby strictly forbid, on pain of our displeasure, all our loving subjects from making any purchases or settlements whatever, or taking possession of any of the lands above reserved, without our special leave and license for that purpose first obtained.

* Quoted in *ibid.,* p. 558.

And we do further strictly enjoin and require all persons whatever, who have either wilfully or inadvertently seated themselves upon any lands within the countries above described, or upon any other lands, which, not having been ceded to, or purchased by, us, are still reserved to the said Indians as aforesaid, forthwith to remove themselves from such settlements.

And whereas great frauds and abuses have been committed in the purchasing lands of the Indians, to the great prejudice of our interests, and to the great dissatisfaction of the said Indians; in order, therefore, to prevent such irregularities for the future, and to the end that the Indians may be convinced of our justice and determined resolution to remove all reasonable cause of discontent, we do, with the advice of our privy council, strictly enjoin and require that no private person do presume to make any purchase from the said Indians, of any lands reserved to the said Indians, within those parts of our colonies where we have thought proper to allow settlement; but that, if, at any time, any of the said Indians should be inclined to dispose of the said lands, the same shall be purchased only for us, in our name, at some public meeting or assembly of the said Indians, to be held for that purpose, by the Governor or commander-in-chief of our colony, respectively, within which they shall lie: and in case they shall lie within the limits of any proprietaries, conformable to such directions and instructions as we or they shall think proper to give for that purpose.

The Pickering Treaty between the U.S. and the Six Nations*

One of the earliest treaties made between the United States and any Indian nation was one negotiated by Timothy Pickering with the Six Nations in 1794.

A TREATY

Between the United States of America, and the Tribes of Indians called the Six Nations.

The President of the United States having determined to hold a conference with the Six Nations of Indians, for the purpose of removing from their minds all causes of complaint, and establishing a firm and permanent friendship with them; and Timothy Pickering being appointed sole agent for that purpose; and the agent having met and conferred with the Sachems, Chiefs and Warriors of the Six Nations, in a general council: Now, in order to accomplish the good design of this conference, the parties have agreed on the following articles; which, when ratified by the President, with the advice and consent of the Senate of the United States, shall be binding on them and the Six Nations.

ARTICLE I

Peace and friendship are hereby firmly established, and shall be perpetual, between the United States and the Six Nations.

ARTICLE II

The United States acknowledge the lands reserved to the Oneida, Onondaga and Cayuga Nations, in their respective treaties with the state of New-York, and called their reservations, to be their property; and the United States will never claim the same, nor disturb them or either of the Six Nations, nor their Indian friends residing thereon and united with them, in the free use and enjoyment thereof: but the said reservations shall remain theirs, until they choose to sell the same to the people of the United States, who have the right to purchase.

* *Public Statutes at Large of the United States of America,* Vol. VII, Chas. Little and J. Brown, Boston, 1848, pp. 44–47.

ARTICLE III

The land of the Seneka nation is bounded as follows: Beginning on Lake Ontario, at the north-west corner of the land they sold to Oliver Phelps, the line runs westerly along the lake, as far as O-yōng-wong-yeh Creek, at Johnson's Landing-place, about four miles eastward from the fort of Niagara; then southerly up that creek to its main fork, then straight to the main fork of Stedman's creek, which empties into the river Niagara, above fort Schlosser, and then onward, from that fork, continuing the same straight course, to that river; (this line, from the mouth of O-yōng-wong-yeh Creek to the river Niagara, above fort Schlosser, being the eastern boundary of a strip of land, extending from the same line to Niagara river, which the Seneka nation ceded to the King of Great-Britain, at a treaty held about thirty years ago, with Sir William Johnson;) then the line runs along the river Niagara to Lake Erie; then along Lake Erie to the north-east corner of a triangular piece of land which the United States conveyed to the state of Pennsylvania, as by the President's patent, dated the third day of March, 1792; then due south to the northern boundary of that state; then due east to the south-west corner of the land sold by the Seneka nation to Oliver Phelps; and then north and northerly, along Phelps's line, to the place of beginning on Lake Ontario. Now, the United States acknowledge all the land within the aforementioned boundaries, to be the property of the Seneka nation; and the United States will never claim the same, nor disturb the Seneka nation, nor any of the Six Nations, or of their Indian friends residing thereon and united with them, in the free use and enjoyment thereof: but it shall remain theirs, until they choose to sell the same to the people of the United States, who have the right to purchase.

ARTICLE IV

The United States having thus described and acknowledged what lands belong to the Oneidas, Onondagas, Cayugas and Senekas, and engaged never to claim the same, nor to disturb them, or any of the Six Nations, or their Indian friends residing thereon and united with them, in the free use and enjoyment thereof: Now, the Six Nations, and each of them, hereby engage that they will never claim any other lands within the boundaries of the United States; nor ever disturb the people of the United States in the free use and enjoyment thereof.

ARTICLE V

The Seneka nation, all others of the Six Nations concurring, cede to the United States the right of making a waggon road from Fort Schlosser to Lake Erie, as far south as Buffaloe Creek; and the people of the United States shall have the free and undisturbed use of this road, for the purposes of travelling and transportation. And the Six Nations, and each of them, will forever allow to the people of the United States, a free passage through their lands, and the free use of the harbours and rivers adjoining and within their respective tracts of land, for the passing and securing of vessels and boats, and liberty to land their cargoes where necessary for their safety.

ARTICLE VI

In consideration of the peace and friendship hereby established, and of the engagements entered into by the Six Nations; and because the United States desire, with humanity and kindness, to contribute to their comfortable support; and to render the peace and friendship hereby established, strong and perpetual; the United States now deliver to the Six Nations, and the Indians of the other nations residing among and united with them, a quantity of goods of the value of ten thousand dollars. And for the same considerations, and with a view to promote the future welfare of the Six Nations, and of their Indian friends aforesaid, the United States will add the sum of three thousand dollars to the one thousand five hundred dollars, heretofore allowed them by an article ratified by the President, on the twenty-third day of April, 1792; making in the whole, four thousand five hundred dollars; which shall be expended yearly forever, in purchasing clothing, domestic animals, implements of husbandry, and other utensils suited to their circumstances, and in compensating useful artificers, who shall reside with or near them, and be employed for their benefit. The immediate application of the whole annual allowance now stipulated, to be made by the superintendant appointed by the President for the affairs of the Six Nations, and their Indian friends aforesaid.

ARTICLE VII

Lest the firm peace and friendship now established should be interrupted by the misconduct of individuals, the United States and Six Nations agree, that for injuries done by individuals on either side, no private revenge or retaliation shall take place; but, instead thereof, complaint shall be made by the party injured, to the other: By the Six Nations or any of them, to the President of the United States, or the Superintendant by him appointed: and by the Superintendant, or other person appointed by the President, to the principal chiefs of the Six Nations, or of the nation to which the offender belongs: and such prudent measures shall then be pursued as shall be necessary to preserve our peace and friendship unbroken; until the legislature (or great council) of the United States shall make other equitable provision for the purpose.

NOTE. It is clearly understood by the parties to this treaty, that the annuity stipulated in the sixth article, is to be applied to the benefit of such of the Six Nations and of their Indian friends united with them as aforesaid, as do or shall reside within the boundaries of the United States: For the United States do not interfere with nations, tribes or families, of Indians elsewhere resident.

In Witness whereof, the said Timothy Pickering, and the Sachems and War-chiefs of the said Six Nations, have hereto set their hands and seals.

Done at Kon-on-daigua, in the state of New York, the eleventh day of November, in the Year one thousand seven hundred and ninety-four.　Timothy Pickering

O-no-ye-ah-nee,
Kon-ne-at-or-lee-ooh, or Hand-
  some Lake.
Te-kenh-you-hau, alias Capt. Key.
O-nes-hau-ee,
Ko-nooh-qung,
Tos-song-gau-lo-lus,
John Sken-en-do-a,
O-ne-at-or-lee-ooh,
Kus-sau-wa-tau,
E-yoo-ten-yoo-tau-ook,
Kohn-ye-au-gong, alias Jake
  Stroud.
Sha-gui-e-sa,
Teer-oos, alias Capt. Prantup.
Soos-ha-oo-wau,
Henry Young Brant,
Sonh-yoo-wau-na, or Big Sky.
O-na-ah-hah,
Hot-osh-a-henh,
Kau-kon-da-nai-ya,
Non-di-yau-ka,
Kos-sish-to-wau,
Oo-jau-geht-a, or Fish Carrier.
To-he-ong-go,
Oot-a-guas-so,
Joo-non-dau-wa-onh,
Ki-yau-ha-onh,
Oo-tau-je-au-genh, or Broken Axe.
Tau-ho-on-dos, or Open the Way.
Twau-ke-wash-a,
Se-qui-dong-quee, alias Little
  Beard.
Kod-je-ote, or Half Town.

Hendrick Aupaumut,
David Neesoonhuk,
Kanatsoyh, alias Nicholas Kusik,
Soh-hon-te-o-quent,
Oo-duht-sa-it,
Ken-jau-au-gus, or Stinking Fish.
Soo-noh-quau-kau,
Twen-ni-ya-na,
Jish-kaa-ga, or Green Grass-hop-
  per, alias Little Billy.
Tug-geh-shot-ta,
Teh-ong-ya-gau-na,
Teh-ong-yoo-wush,
Kon-ne-yoo-we-sot,
Ti-ooh-quot-ta-kau-na, or Woods
  on Fire.
Ta-oun-dau-deesh,
Ho-na-ya-wus, alias Farmer's
  Brother.
Sog-goo-ya-waut-hau, alias Red
  Jacket.
Kon-yoo-ti-a-yoo,
Sauh-ta-ka-ong-yees, (or Two
  Skies of a length.)
Oun-na-shatta-kau,
Ka-ung-ya-neh-quee,
Soo-a-yoo-wau,
Kau-je-a-ga-onh, or Heap of
  Dogs.
Soo-nooh-shoo-wau,
T-ha-oo-wau-ni-as,
Soo-nong-joo-wau,
Kiant-whau-ka, alias Cornplanter.
Kau-neh-shong-goo.

Witnesses:—Israel Chapin, James Smedley, Augustus Porter, Wm. Ewing, Wm. Shepard, jun. John Wickham, James K. Garnsey, Israel Chapin, jun. Interpreters, Horatia Jones, Joseph Smith, Jasper Parish. Henry Abeele.

To the Indian names are subjoined a mark and seal.

DOCUMENT NO. 11

Cherokee Nation v. the State of Georgia*

In 1831 the U.S. Supreme Court rendered the decision in which the concept of "domestic dependent nation" was defined.

Mr. Chief Justice Marshall delivered the opinion of the Court:
This bill is brought by the Cherokee nation, praying an injunction to restrain the state of Georgia from the execution of certain laws of that state, which, as is alleged, go directly to annihilate the Cherokees as a political society, and to seize, for the use of Georgia, the lands of the nation which have been assured to them by the United States in solemn treaties repeatedly made and still in force.

If courts were permitted to indulge their sympathies, a case better calculated to excite them can scarcely be imagined. A people once numerous, powerful, and truly independent, found by our ancestors in the quiet and uncontrolled possession of an ample domain, gradually sinking beneath our superior policy, our arts and our arms, have yielded their lands by successive treaties, each of which contains a solemn guarantee of the residue, until they retain no more of their formerly extensive territory than is deemed necessary to their comfortable subsistence. To preserve this remnant, the present application is made.

Before we can look into the merits of the case, a preliminary inquiry presents itself. Has this court jurisdiction of the cause?

The third article of the constitution describes the extent of the judicial power. The second section closes an enumeration of the cases to which it is extended, with "controversies" "between a state or the citizens thereof, and foreign states, citizens, or subjects." A subsequent clause of the same section gives the supreme court original jurisdiction in all cases in which a state shall be a party. The party defendant may then unquestionably be sued in this court. May the plaintiff sue in it? Is the Cherokee nation a foreign state in the sense in which that term is used in the constitution?

The counsel for the plaintiffs have maintained the affirmative of this proposition with great earnestness and ability. So much of the argument as was intended to prove the character of the Cherokees as a state, as a distinct political society, separated from others, capable of managing its own affairs and governing itself, has, in the opinion of a majority of the judges, been completely successful. They have been uniformly treated as a state from the settlement of our country. The numerous treaties made with them by the United

* U.S. Supreme Court *Reports,* 5 Peters 15–18.

States recognize them as a people capable of maintaining the relations of peace and war, of being responsible in their political character for any violation of their engagements, or for any aggression committed on the citizens of the United States by any individual of their community. Laws have been enacted in the spirit of these treaties. The acts of our government plainly recognize the Cherokee nation as a state, and the courts are bound by those acts.

A question of much more difficulty remains. Do the Cherokees constitute a foreign state in the sense of the constitution?

The counsel have shown conclusively that they are not a state of the union, and have insisted that individually they are aliens, not owing allegiance to the United States. An aggregate of aliens composing a state must, they say, be a foreign state. Each individual being foreign, the whole must be foreign.

This argument is imposing, but we must examine it more closely before we yield to it. The condition of the Indians in relation to the United States is perhaps unlike that of any other two people in existence. In the general, nations not owing a common allegiance are foreign to each other. The term foreign nation is, with strict propriety, applicable by either to the other. But the relation of the Indians to the United States is marked by peculiar and cardinal distinctions which exist no where else.

The Indian territory is admitted to compose a part of the United States. In all our maps, geographical treaties, histories, and laws, it is so considered. In all our intercourse with foreign nations, in our commercial regulations, in any attempt at intercourse between Indians and foreign nations, they are considered as within the jurisdictional limits of the United States, subject to many of those restraints which are imposed upon our own citizens. They acknowledge themselves in their treaties to be under the protection of the United States; they admit that the United States shall have the sole and exclusive right of regulating the trade with them, and managing all their affairs as they think proper; and the Cherokees in particular were allowed by the treaty of Hopewell, which preceded the constitution, "to send a deputy of their choice, whenever they think fit, to congress." Treaties were made with some tribes by the state of New York, under a then unsettled construction of the confederation, by which they ceded all their lands to that state, taking back a limited grant to themselves, in which they admit their dependence.

Though the Indians are acknowledged to have an unquestionable, and, heretofore, unquestioned right to the lands they occupy, until that right shall be extinguished by a voluntary cession to our government; yet it may well be doubted whether those tribes which reside within the acknowledged boundaries of the United States can, with strict accuracy, be denominated foreign nations. They may, more correctly be denominated domestic dependent nations. They occupy a territory to which we assert a title independent of their will, which must take effect in point of possession when their right of possession ceases. Meanwhile, they are in a state of pupilage. Their relation to the United States resembles that of a ward to his guardian.

They look to our government for protection; rely upon its kindness and its power; appeal to it for relief to their wants; and address the president as their great father. They and their country are considered by foreign nations, as well as by ourselves, as being so completely under the sovereignty and dominion of the United States, that any attempt to acquire their lands, or to form a political connexion with them, would be considered by all as an invasion of our territory, and an act of hostility.

These considerations go far to support the opinion, that the framers of our constitution had not the Indian tribes in view, when they opened the courts of the union to controversies between a state or the citizens thereof, and foreign states.

In considering this subject, the habits and usages of the Indians, in their intercourse with their white neighbours, ought not to be entirely disregarded. At the time the constitution was framed, the idea of appealing to an American court of justice for an assertion of right or a redress of wrong, had perhaps never entered the mind of an Indian or of his tribe. Their appeal was to the toma-hawk, or to the government. This was well understood by the statesmen who framed the constitution of the United States, and might furnish some reason for omitting to enumerate them among the parties who might sue in the courts of the union. Be this as it may, the peculiar relations between the United States and the Indians occupying our territory are such, that we should feel much difficulty in considering them as designated by the term foreign state, were there no other part of the constitution which might shed light on the meaning of these words. But we think that in construing them, considerable aid is furnished by that clause in the eighth section of the third article; which empowers congress to "regulate commerce with foreign nations, and among the several states, and with the Indian tribes."

In this clause they are as clearly contradistinguished by a name appropriate to themselves, from foreign nations, as from the several states composing the union. They are designated by a distinct appellation; and as this appellation can be applied to neither of the others, neither can the appellation distinguishing either of the others be in fair construction applied to them. The objects, to which the power of regulating commerce might be directed, are divided into three distinct classes—foreign nations, the several states, and Indian tribes. When forming this article, the convention considered them as entirely distinct. We cannot assume that the distinction was lost in framing a subsequent article, unless there be something in its language to authorize the assumption.

The counsel for the plaintiffs contend that the words "Indian tribes" were introduced into the article, empowering congress to regulate commerce, for the purpose of removing those doubts in which the management of Indian affairs was involved by the language of the ninth article of the confederation. Intending to give the whole power of managing those affairs to the government about to be instituted, the convention conferred it explicitly; and omitted those qualifications which embarrassed the exercise of it as granted in the confederation. This may be admitted without weakening the construction which has been intimated. Had the Indian tribes been foreign nations, in the view of the convention; this exclusive power of regulating intercourse with them might have been, and most probably would have been, specifically given, in language indicating that idea, not in language contradistinguishing them from foreign nations. Congress might have been empowered "to regulate commerce with foreign nations, including the Indian tribes, and among the several states." This language would have suggested itself to statesmen who considered the Indian tribes as foreign nations, and were yet desirous of mentioning them particularly.

It has been also said, that the same words have not necessarily the same meaning attached to them when found in different parts of the same instrument: their meaning is controlled by the context. This is undoubtedly true. In common language the same word has various meanings, and the peculiar sense in which it is used in any sentence is to be determined by the context. This may not be equally true with respect to proper names. Foreign nations is a general term, the application of which to Indian tribes, when used in the American constitution, is at best extremely questionable. In one article in which a power is given to be exercised in regard to foreign nations generally, and to the Indian tribes particularly, they are mentioned as separate in terms clearly contradistinguishing from each other. We perceive plainly that the constitution in this article does not comprehend Indian tribes in the general term "foreign nations," not we presume because a tribe may not be a nation, but because it is not foreign to the United States. When, afterwards, the term "foreign state" is introduced, we cannot impute to the convention the intention to desert its former meaning, and to comprehend Indian tribes within it, unless the context force that construction on us. We find nothing in the context, and nothing in the subject of the article, which leads to it.

The court has bestowed its best attention on this question, and, after mature deliberation, the majority is of opinion that an Indian tribe or nation within the United States is not a foreign state in the sense of the constitution, and cannot maintain an action in the courts of the United States.

A serious additional objection exists to the jurisdiction of the court. Is the matter of the bill the proper subject for judicial inquiry and decision? It seeks to restrain a state from the forcible exercise of legislative power over a neighbouring people asserting their independence; their right to which the state denies. On several of the matters alleged in the bill, for example on the laws making it criminal to exercise the usual powers of self-government in their own country by the Cherokee nation, this court cannot interpose; at least in the form in which those matters are presented.

That part of the bill which respects the land occupied by the Indians, and prays the aid of the court to protect their possession, may be more doubtful. The mere question of right might perhaps be decided by this court in a proper case with proper parties. But the court is asked to do more than decide on the title. The bill requires us to control the legislature of Georgia, and to restrain the exertion of its physical force. The propriety of such an inter-position by the court may be well questioned. It savours too much of the exercise of political power to be within the proper province of the judicial department. But the opinion on the point respecting parties makes it unnecessary to decide this question.

If it be true that the Cherokee nation have rights, this is not the tribunal in which those rights are to be asserted. If it be true that wrongs have been inflicted, and that still greater are to be apprehended, this is not the tribunal which can redress the past or prevent the future.

The motion for an injunction is denied.

Samuel A. Worcester v. the
State of Georgia*

In a second decision of 1832 Chief Justice Marshall amplified the court's ideas concerning Indian self-government, which were still further developed by Associate Justice McLean.

The Indian nations had always been considered as distinct, independent political communities, retaining ˜their original natural rights, as the undisputed possessors of the soil, from time immemorial, with the single exception of that imposed irresistible power, which excluded them from intercourse with any other European potentate than the first discoverer of the coast of the particular region claimed: and this was a restriction which those European potentates imposed on themselves, as well as on the Indians. The very term, "nation," so generally applied to them, means "a People distinct from other." The constitution by declaring treaties already made, as well as those to be made, to be the supreme law of the land, had adopted and sanctioned the previous treaties with the Indian nations, and, consequently, admits their rank among those Powers who are capable of making treaties. The words "treaty" and "nation" are words of our own language, selected in our diplomatic and legislative proceedings, by ourselves, having each a definite and well understood meaning. We have applied them to Indians, as we have applied them to the other nations of the earth. They are applied to all in the same sense.

Georgia, herself, has furnished conclusive evidence that her former opinions on this subject concurred with those entertained by her sister States, and by the Government of the United States. Various acts of her Legislature have been cited in the argument, including the contract of cession made in the year 1802, all tending to prove her acquiescence in the universal conviction that the Indian nations possessed a full right to the lands they occupied, until that right should be extinguished by the United States, with their consent; that their territory was separated from that of any State within whose chartered limits they might reside, by a boundary line, established by treaties; that, within their boundary, they possessed rights with which no State could interfere; and that the whole power of regulating the intercourse with them, was vested in the United States. A review of these acts, on the part of Georgia, would occupy

* U.S. Supreme Court *Reports,* 6 Peters 559–561.

too much time, and is the less necessary, because they have been accurately detailed in the argument at the bar. Her new series of laws, manifesting her abandonment of these opinions, appears to have commenced in December, 1828.

In opposition to this original right, possessed by the undisputed occupants of every country, to this recognition of that right, which is evidenced by our history, in every change through which we have passed, is placed the charters granted by the monarch of a distant and distinct region, parcelling out a territory in possession of others, whom he could not remove, and did not attempt to remove, and the cession made of his claims, by the treaty of peace.

The actual state of things at the time, and all history since, explain these charters; and the King of Great Britain, at the treaty of peace, could cede only what belonged to his crown. These newly asserted titles can derive no aid from the articles so often repeated in Indian treaties, extending to them, first, the protection of Great Britain, and afterwards that of the United States. These articles are associated with others, recognizing their title to self government. The very fact of repeated treaties with them recognized it; and the settled doctrine of the law of nations is, that a weaker power does not surrender its independence—its right to self government— by associating with a stronger, and taking its protection. A weak state, in order to provide for its safety, may place itself under the protection of one more powerful, without stripping itself of the right of government, and ceasing to be a State. Examples of this kind are not wanting in Europe. "Tributary and feudatory States," says Vattel, "do not thereby cease to be sovereign and independent States, so long as self-government and sovereign and independent authority is left in the administration of the State." At the present day, more than one State may be considered as holding its right of self government under the guarantee and protection of one or more allies.

The Cherokee nation, then, is a distinct community, occupying its own territory, with boundaries accurately described, in which the laws of Georgia can have no force, and which the citizens of Georgia have no right to enter, but with the assent of the Cherokees themselves, or in conformity with treaties, and with the acts of Congress. The whole intercourse between the United States and this nation, is by our constitution and laws, vested in the Government of the United States.

The act of the State of Georgia, under which the plaintiff in error was prosecuted is consequently void, and the judgment a nullity. Can this court revise and reverse it?

If the objection to the system of legislation, lately adopted by the Legislature of Georgia, in relation to the Cherokee nation, was confined to its extra-territorial operation, the objection, though complete, so far as respected mere right, would give this Court no power over the subject. But it goes much further. If the view which has been taken be correct, and we think it is, the acts of Georgia are repugnant to the constitution, laws, and treaties, of the United States.

They interfere forcibly with the relations established between the United States and the Cherokee nation, the regulation of which, according to the settled principles of our constitution, are committed exclusively to the Government of the Union.

They are in direct hostility with treaties, repeated in a succession of years, which mark out the boundary that separates the Cherokee country from Georgia; guaranty to them all the land within their boundary; solemnly pledge the faith of the United States to restrain their citizens from trespassing on it; and recognize the pre-existing power of the nation to govern itself.

They are in equal hostility with the acts of Congress for regulating this intercourse and giving effect to the treaties.

The forcible seizure and abduction of the plaintiff in error, who was residing in the nation, with its permission, and by authority of the President of the United States, is also a violation of the acts which authorize the Chief Magistrate to exercise this authority.

Will these powerful considerations avail the plaintiff in error? We think they will. He was seized, and forcibly carried away, while under guardianship of treaties guarantying the country in which he resided, and taking it under the protection of the United States. He was seized while performing under the sanction of the Chief Magistrate of the Union, those duties which the humane policy adopted by Congress had recommended. He was apprehended, tried, and condemned, under color of a law which has been shown to be repugnant to the constitution, laws, and treaties, of the United States. Had a judgement liable to the same objections, been rendered for property, none would question the jurisdiction of this Court. It cannot be less clear when the judgement affects personal liberty, and inflicts disgraceful punishment, if punishment could disgrace when inflicted on innocence. The plaintiff in error is not less interested in the operation of this unconstitutional law than if it affected his property. He is not less entitled to the protection of the constitution, laws, and treaties, of his country.

It is the opinion of the Court that the judgement of the Superior Court for the county of Gwinnett, in the State of Georgia, condemning Samual A. Worcester to hard labor, in the penitentiary of the State of Georgia, for four years, was pronounced by that Court under color of a law which is void, as being repugnant to the constitution, treaties, and laws of the United States, and ought, therefore, to be reversed and annulled.

Justice McLean concurred with the opinion of the Court but added some further remarks to clarify the position of the United States relative to Indian tribes.

The exercise of the power of self-government by the Indians, within a State is undoubtedly contemplated to be temporary. This is shown by the unsettled policy of the Government, in the extinguishment of their title, and especially, by the compact with the State of Georgia. It is a question, not of abstract right, but of public policy. I do not mean to say, that the same moral rule which should regulate the affairs of private life, should not be regarded by communities or nations. But, a sound national policy does require that the Indian tribes within our States should exchange their territories, upon equitable principles, or eventually, consent to become amalgamated in our political communities.

At best, they can enjoy a very limited independence within the boundaries of a State and such a residence must always subject them to encroachments from the settlements around them; and their existence within a State, as a separate and independent community, may seriously embarrass or obstruct the political welfare of the States, and the social advance of their citizens, that an independent and permanent power should exist within their limits, this power must give way to the greater power which surrounds it, or seek its exercise beyond the sphere of State authority.

This state of things can only be produced by a co-operation of the State and Federal Governments. The latter has the exclusive regulation of intercourse with the Indians; and, so long as this power shall be exercised, it cannot be obstructed by the State. It is a power given by the constitution, and sanctioned by the most solemn acts of both the Federal and State Government. Consequently, it cannot be abrogated at the will of a State. It is one of the powers parted with by the States, and vested in the Federal Government. But, if a contingency shall occur, which shall render the Indians who reside in a State, incapable of self-government, either by moral degradation or a reduction of their numbers, it would undoubtedly be in the power of a State Government to extend to them the aegis of its laws. Under such circumstances, the agency of the General Government, of necessity, must cease.

But, if it shall be the policy of the Government to withdraw its protection from the Indians who reside within the limits of the respective States, and who not only claim the right of self-government, but have uniformly exercised it; the laws and treaties which impose duties and obligations on the General Government should be abrogated by the powers competent to do so. So long as those laws and treaties exist, having been formed within the sphere of the Federal powers, they must be respected and enforced by the appropriate organs of the Federal Government.

Treaty with the Navajos*

One of the last treaties made by the U.S. government with an Indian tribe was the Navajo Treaty of 1868.

Articles of a treaty and agreement made and entered into at Fort Sumner, New Mexico, on the first day of June, one thousand eight hundred and sixty eight, by and between the United States, represented by it commissioners, Lieutenant-General W. T. Sherman and Colonel Samuel F. Tappan, of the one part, and the Navajo Nation or tribe of Indians, represented by their chiefs and head-men, duly authorized and empowered to act for the whole people of said nation or tribe, (the names of said chiefs and head-men being hereto subscribed,) of the other part witness:

ARTICLE 1. From this day forward all war between the parties to this agreement shall forever cease. The Government of the United States desires peace, and its honor is hereby pledged to keep it. The Indians desire peace, and they now pledge their honor to keep it.

If bad men among the whites, or among other people subject to the authority of the United States, shall commit any wrong upon the person or property of the Indians, the United States will, upon proof made to the agent and forwarded to the Commissioner of Indian Affairs at Washington City, proceed at once to cause the offender to be arrested and punished according to the laws of the United States, and also to reimburse the injured persons for the loss sustained.

If the bad men among the Indians shall commit a wrong or depredation upon the person or property of any one, white, black, or Indian, subject to the authority of the United States and at peace therewith, the Navajo tribe agree that they will, on proof made to their agent, and on notice by him, deliver up the wrongdoer to the United States, to be tried and punished according to its laws; and in case they wilfully refuse so to do, the person injured shall be reimbursed for his loss from the annuities or other moneys due or to become due to them under this treaty, or any others that may be made with the United States. And the President may proscribe such rules and regulations for ascertaining damages under this article as in his judgment may be proper; but no such damage shall

* Ruth Underhill, *Here Come the Navajo!* United States Indian Service, Haskell Institute Print Shop, Lawrence, Kansas, 1953.

be adjusted and paid until examined and passed upon by the Commissioner of Indian Affairs, and no one sustaining loss whilst violating, or because of his violating the provisions of this treaty or the laws of the United States, shall be reimbursed therefor.

ARTICLE 2. The United States agrees that the following district of country, to wit: bounded on the north by the 37th degree of north latitude, south by an east and west line crossing through the site of old Fort Defiance, in Canon Bonito, east by parallel of longitude which, if prolonged south, would pass through old Fort Lyon, or the Ojo-de-oso, Bear Spring, and west by a parallel of longitude about 109° 30′ west of Greenwich, provided it embraces the outlet of the Canon de Chelly, which canon is to be all included in this reservation, shall be, and the same is hereby, set apart for the use and occupation of the Navajo tribe of Indians, and for such other friendly tribes or individual Indians as from time to time they may be willing, with the consent of the United States, to admit among them; and the United States agrees that no persons except those herein authorized to do so, and except such officers, soldiers, agents, and employees of the Government, or of the Indians, as may be authorized to enter upon Indian reservations in discharge of duties imposed by law, or the orders of the President, shall ever be permitted to pass over, settle upon, or reside in, the territory described in this article.

ARTICLE 3. The United States agrees to cause to be built, at some point within the said reservation, where timber and water may be convenient, the following buildings: a warehouse, to cost not exceeding twenty-five hundred dollars; an agency building for the residence of the agent, not to cost exceeding three thousand dollars; a carpenter shop and blacksmith shop, not to cost exceeding one thousand dollars each; and a schoolhouse and chapel, so soon as a sufficient number of children can be induced to attend school, which shall not cost to exceed five thousand dollars.

ARTICLE 4. The United States agrees that the agent for the Navajos shall make his home at the agency building; that he shall reside among them, and shall keep an office open at all times for the purpose of prompt and diligent inquiry into such matters of complaint by or against the Indians as may be presented for investigation, as also for the faithful discharge of other duties enjoined by law. In all cases of depredation on person or property he shall cause the evidence to be taken in writing and forwarded together with his finding, to the Commissioner of Indian Affairs, whose decision shall be binding on the parties to this treaty.

ARTICLE 5. If any individual belonging to said tribe, or legally incorporated with it, being the head of a family, shall desire to commence farming, he shall have the privilege to select, in the presence and with the assistance of the agent then in charge, a tract of land within said reservation, not exceeding one hundred and sixty acres in extent, which tract, when so selected, certified, and recorded in the "land book" as herein described, shall cease to be held in common, but the same may be occupied and held in the exclusive possession of the person selecting it, and of his family, so long as he or they may continue to cultivate it.

Any person over eighteen years of age, not being the head of a family, may in like manner select, and cause to be certified to him or her for purposes of cultivation, a quantity of land, not exceeding eighty acres in extent, and thereupon be entitled to the exclusive possession of the same as above directed.

For each tract of land so selected a certificate containing a description thereof, and the name of the person selecting it, with a certificate endorsed thereon, that the same has been recorded, shall be delivered to the party entitled to it by the agent, after the same shall have been recorded by him in a book to be kept in his office, subject to inspection, which said books shall be known as the "Navajo land-book."

The President may at any time order a survey of the reservation, and when so surveyed, Congress shall provide for protecting the rights of said settlers in their improvements, and may fix the character of the title held by each.

The United States may pass such laws on the subject of alienation and descent of property between the Indians and their descendants as may be thought proper.

ARTICLE 6. In order to insure the civilization of the Indians entering into this treaty, the necessity of education is admitted, especially of such of them as may be settled on said agricultural parts of this reservation, and they therefore pledge themselves to compel their children male and female, between the ages of six and sixteen years, to attend school; and it is hereby made the duty of the agent for said Indians to see that this stipulation is strictly complied with; and the United States agrees that, for every thirty children between said ages who can be induced or compelled to attend school, a house shall be provided, and a teacher competent to teach the elementary branches of an English education shall be furnished, who will reside among said Indians, and faithfully discharge his or her duties as a teacher.

The provisions of this article to continue for not less than ten years.

ARTICLE 7. When the head of a family shall have selected lands and received his certificate as above directed, and the agent shall be satisfied that he intends in good faith to commence cultivating the soil for a living, he shall be entitled to receive seeds and agricultural implements for the first year, not exceeding in value one hundred dollars, and for each succeeding year he shall continue to farm, for a period of two years, he shall be entitled to receive seeds and implements to the value of twenty-five dollars.

ARTICLE 8. In lieu of all sums of money or other annuities provided to be paid to the Indians herein named under any treaty or treaties heretofore made, the United States agrees to delivery at the agency-house on the reservation herein named, on the first day of September of each year for ten years, the following articles, to wit:

Such articles of clothing, goods, or raw materials in lieu thereof, as the agent may make his estimate for, not exceeding in value five dollars per Indian—each Indian being encouraged to manufacture their own clothing, blankets, &c.; to be furnished with no article which they can manufacture themselves. And, in order that the Commissioner of Indian Affairs may be able to estimate properly for the articles herein named, it shall be the duty of the agent each year to forward to him a full and exact census of the Indians, on which the estimate from year to year can be based.

And in addition to the articles herein named, the sum of ten dollars for each person entitled to the beneficial effects of this treaty shall be annually appropriated for a period of ten years, for each person who engages in farming or mechanical pursuits, to be used by the Commissioner of Indian Affairs in the purchase of such articles as from time to time the condition and necessities of the Indians may indicate to be proper; and if within the ten years at any time it shall appear that the amount of money needed for clothing under the article, can be appropriated to better uses for the Indians named herein, the Commissioner of Indian Affairs may change the appropriation to other purposes, but in no event shall the amount of this appropriation be withdrawn or discontinued for the period named, provided they remain at peace. And the President shall annually detail an officer of the Army to be present and attest the delivery of all the goods herein named to the Indians, and he shall inspect and report on the quantity and quality of the goods and the manner of their delivery.

ARTICLE 9. In consideration of the advantages and benefits conferred by this treaty, and the many pledges of friendship by the United States, the tribes who are parties to this agreement hereby stipulate that they will relinquish all right to occupy any territory outside their reservation, as herein defined, but retain the right to hunt on any unoccupied lands contiguous to their reservation, so long as the large game may range thereon in such numbers as to justify the chase; and they, the said Indians, further expressly agree:

1st. That they will make no opposition to the construction of railroads now being built or hereafter to be built across the continent.

2nd. That they will not interfere with the peaceful construction of any railroad not passing over their reservation as herein defined.

3rd. That they will not attack any persons at home or travelling, nor molest or disturb any wagon-trains, coaches, mules, or cattle belonging to the people of the United States, or to persons friendly therewith.

4th. That they will never capture or carry off from the settlements women or children.

5th. They will never kill or scalp white men, nor attempt to do them harm.

6th. They will not in future oppose the construction of railroads, wagon-roads, mail stations, or other works of utility or necessity which may be ordered or permitted by the laws of the United States; but should such roads or other works be constructed on the lands of their reservation, the Government will pay the tribe whatever amount of damage may be assessed by three disinterested commissioners to be appointed by the President for that purpose, one of said commissioners to be a chief or head-man of the tribe.

7th. They will make no opposition to the military posts or roads now established, or that may be established, not in violation of treaties heretofore made or hereafter to be made with any of the Indian tribes.

ARTICLE 10. No future treaty for the cession of any portion or part of the reservation herein described, which may be held in common, shall be of any validity or force against said Indians unless agreed to and executed by at least three-fourths of all the adult male Indians occupying or interested in the same; and no cession by the tribe shall be understood or construed in such manner as to deprive, without his consent, any individual member of the tribe of his rights to any tract of land selected by him as provided in article (5) of this treaty.

ARTICLE 11. The Navajos also agree that at any time after the signing of these presents they will proceed in such a manner as may be required of them by the agent, or by the officer charged with their removal to the reservation herein provided for, the United States paying for their subsistence enroute, and providing a reasonable amount of transportation for the sick and feeble.

ARTICLE 12. It is further agreed by and between the parties to this agreement that the sum of one hundred and fifty thousand dollars appropriated or to be appropriated shall be disbursed as follows, subject to any condition provided in the law, to wit:

1st. The actual cost of the removal of the tribe from the Bosque Redondo reservation to the reservation, say fifty thousand dollars.

2nd. The purchase of fifteen thousand sheep and goats at a cost not to exceed thirty thousand dollars.

3rd. The purchase of five hundred beef cattle and a million pounds of corn, to be collected and sold at the military post nearest the reservation, subject to the orders of the agent, for the relief of the needy during the coming winter.

4th. The balance, if any, of the appropriation to be invested for the maintenance of the Indians pending their removal, in such manner as the agent who is with them may determine.

5th. The removal of this tribe to be made under the supreme control and direction of the military commander of the Territory of New Mexico, and when completed, the management of the tribe to revert to the proper agent.

ARTICLE 13. The tribe herein named, by their representatives, parties to this treaty, agree to make the reservation herein described their permanent home, and they will not as a tribe make any permanent settlement elsewhere, reserving the right to hunt on the lands adjoining the said reservation formerly called theirs, subject to the modifications named in this treaty and the orders of the commander of the department in which said reservation may be for the time being; and it is further agreed and understood by the parties to this treaty, that if any Navajo Indian or Indians shall leave the reservation herein described to settle elsewhere, he or they shall forfeit all the rights, privileges, and annuities conferred by the terms of this treaty; and it is further agreed by the parties to this treaty, that they will do all they can to induce Indians now away from the reservations set apart for the exclusive use and occupation of the Indians, leading a nomadic life, or engaged in war against the people of the United States, to abandon such a life and settle permanently in one of the territorial reservations set apart for the exclusive use and occupation of the Indians.

The General Allotment Act of 1887

This legislation is sometimes called the Dawes Act.

ACT OF FEBRUARY 8, 1887 (24 Stat. L., 338).

AN ACT To provide for the allotment of lands in severalty to Indians on the various reservations, and to extend the protection of the laws of the United States and the Territories over the Indians, and for other purposes.

Be it enacted by the Senate and House of Representatives of the United States of America in Congress assembled, That in all cases where any tribe or band of Indians has been, or shall hereafter be, located upon any reservation created for their use, either by treaty stipulation or by virtue of an act of Congress or Executive order setting apart the same for their use, the President of the United States be, and he hereby is, authorized, whenever in his opinion any reservation or any part thereof of such Indians is advantageous for agricultural and grazing purposes, to cause said reservation, or any part thereof, to be surveyed, or resurveyed if necessary, and to allot the lands in said reservation in severalty to any Indian located thereon in quantities as follows:

To each head of a family, one-quarter of a section;

To each single person over eighteen years of age, one-eighth of a section;

To each orphan child under eighteen years of age, one-eighth of a section; and

To each other single person under eighteen years now living, or who may be born prior to the date of the order of the President directing an allotment of the lands embraced in any reservation, one-sixteenth of a section: *Provided,* That in case there is not sufficient land in any of said reservations to allot lands to each individual of the classes above named in quantities as above provided, the lands embraced in such reservation or reservations shall be allotted to each individual of each of said classes pro rata in accordance with the provisions of this act: *And provided further,* That where the treaty or act of Congress setting apart such reservation provides for the allotment of lands in severalty in quantities in excess of those herein provided, the President, in making allotments upon such reservation, shall allot the lands to each individual Indian belonging thereon in quantity as specified in such treaty or act: *And provided further,* That when the lands allotted are only valuable for grazing purposes, an additional allotment of such grazing lands, in quantities as above provided, shall be made to each individual.

SEC. 2. That all allotments set apart under the provisions of this act shall be selected by the Indians, heads of families selecting for their minor children, and the agents shall select for each orphan child, and in such manner as to embrace the improvements of the Indians making the selection. Where the improvements of two or more Indians have been made on the same legal subdivision of land, unless they shall otherwise agree, a provisional line may be run dividing said lands between them, and the amount to which each is entitled shall be equalized in the assignment of the remainder of the land to which they are entitled under this act: *Provided,* That if any one entitled to an allotment shall fail to make a selection within four years after the President shall direct that allotments may be made on a particular reservation, the Secretary of the Interior may direct the agent of such tribe or band, if such there be, and if there be no agent, then a special agent appointed for that purpose, to make a selection for such Indian, which selection shall be allotted as in cases where selections are made by the Indians, and patents shall issue in like manner.

SEC. 3. That the allotments provided for in this act shall be made by special agents appointed by the President for such purpose, and the agents in charge of the respective reservations on which the allotments are directed to be made, under such rules and regulations as the Secretary of the Interior may from time to time prescribe, and shall be certified by such agents to the Commissioner of Indian Affairs, in duplicate, one copy to be retained in the Indian Office and the other to be transmitted to the Secretary of the Interior for his action, and to be deposited in the General Land Office.

SEC. 4. That where any Indian not residing upon a reservation, or for whose tribe no reservation has been provided by treaty, act of Congress, or Executive order, shall make settlement upon any surveyed or unsurveyed lands of the United States not otherwise appropriated, he or she shall be entitled, upon application to the local land office for the district in which the lands are located, to have the same allotted to him or her, and to his or her children, in quantities and manner as provided in this act for Indians residing upon reservations; and when such settlement is made upon unsurveyed lands, the grant to such Indians shall be adjusted upon the survey of the lands so as to conform thereto; and patents shall be issued to them for such lands in the manner and with the restrictions as herein provided. And the fees to which the officers of such local land office would have been entitled had such lands been entered under the general laws for the disposition of the public lands shall be paid to them, from any moneys in the Treasury of the United States not otherwise appropriated, upon a statement of an account in their behalf for such fees by the Commissioner of the General Land Office, and a certification of such account to the Secretary of the Treasury by the Secretary of the Interior.

SEC. 5. That upon the approval of the allotments provided for in this act by the Secretary of the Interior, he shall cause patents to issue therefore in the name of the allottees, which patents shall be of the legal effect, and declare that the United States does and will hold the land thus allotted, for the period of twenty-five years, in trust for the sole use and benefit of the Indian to whom such allotment shall have been made, or, in case of his decease, of his heirs according to the laws of the State or Territory where such land is located, and that at the expiration of said period the United States will convey the same by patent to said Indian, or his heirs as aforesaid, in fee, discharged of said trust and free of all charge or incumbrance whatsoever: *Provided,* That the President of the United States may in any case in his discretion extend the period. And if any conveyance shall be made of the lands set apart and allotted as herein provided, or any contract made touching the same, before the expiration of the time above mentioned, such conveyance or contract shall be absolutely null and void: *Provided,* That the law of descent and partition in force in the State or Territory where such lands are situate shall apply thereto after patents therefor have been executed and delivered, except as herein otherwise provided; and the laws of the State of Kansas regulating the descent and partition of real estate shall, so far as practicable, apply to all lands in the Indian Territory which may be allotted in severalty under the provisions of this act: *And provided further,* That at any time after lands have been allotted to all the Indians of any tribe as herein provided, or sooner if in the opinion of the President it shall be for the best interests of said tribe, it shall be lawful for the Secretary of the Interior to negotiate with such Indian tribe for the purchase and release by said tribe, in conformity with the treaty or statute under which such reservation is held, of such portions of its reservation not allotted as such tribe shall, from time to time, consent to sell, on such terms and conditions as shall be considered just and equitable between the United States and said tribe of Indians, which purchase shall not be complete until ratified by Congress, and the form and manner of executing such release shall also be prescribed by Congress: *Provided, however,* That all lands adapted to agriculture, with or without irrigation so sold or released to the United States by any Indian tribe shall be held by the United States for the sole purpose of securing homes to actual settlers and shall be disposed of by the United States to actual and bona fide settlers only in tracts not exceeding one hundred and sixty acres to any one person, on such terms as Congress shall prescribe, subject to grants which Congress may make in aid of education: *And provided further,* That no patents shall issue therefor except to the person so taking the same as and for a homestead, or his heirs, and after the expiration of five years occupancy thereof as such homestead; and any conveyance of said lands so taken as a homestead, or any contract touching the same, or lien thereon, created prior to the date of such patent, shall be null and void. And the sums agreed to be paid by the United

THE GENERAL ALLOTMENT ACT OF 1887 203

States as purchase money for any portion of any such reservation shall be held in the Treasury of the United States for the sole use of the tribe or tribes of Indians; to whom such reservations belonged; and the same, with interest thereon at three per cent per annum, shall be at all times subject to appropriation by Congress for the education and civilization of such tribe or tribes of Indians or the members thereof. The patents aforesaid shall be recorded in the General Land Office, and afterward delivered, free of charge to the allottee entitled thereto. And if any religious society or other organization is now occupying any of the public lands to which this act is applicable, for religious or educational work among the Indians, the Secretary of the Interior is hereby authorized to confirm such occupation to such society or organization, in quantity not exceeding one hundred and sixty acres in any one tract, so long as the same shall be so occupied, on such terms as he shall deem just; but nothing herein contained shall change or alter any claim of such society for religious or educational purposes heretofore granted by law. And hereafter in the employment of Indian police, or any other employees in the public service among any of the Indian tribes or bands affected by this act, and where Indians can perform the duties required, those Indians who have availed themselves of the provisions of this act and become citizens of the United States shall be preferred.

SEC. 6. That upon the completion of said allotments and the patenting of the lands to said allottees, each and every member of the respective bands or tribes of Indians to whom allotments have been made shall have the benefit of and be subject to the laws, both civil and criminal, of the State or Territory in which they may reside; and no Territory shall pass or enforce any law denying any such Indian within its jurisdiction the equal protection of the law. And every Indian born within the territorial limits of the United States to whom allotments shall have been made under the provisions of this act, or under any law or treaty, and every Indian born within the territorial limits of the United States who has voluntarily taken up, within said limits, his residence separate and apart from any tribe of Indians therein, and has adopted the habits of civilized life, is hereby declared to be a citizen of the United States, and is entitled to all the rights, privileges, and immunities of such citizens, whether said Indian has been or not, by birth or otherwise a member of any tribe of Indians within the territorial limits of the United States without in any manner impairing or otherwise affecting the right of any such Indian to tribal or other property.

SEC. 7. That in cases where the use of water for irrigation is necessary to render the lands within any Indian reservation available for agricultural purposes, the Secretary of the Interior be, and he is hereby, authorized to prescribe such rules and regulations as he may deem necessary to secure a just and equal distribution thereof among the Indians residing upon any such reservations; and no other appropriation or grant of water by any riparian proprietor shall be authorized or permitted to the damage of any other riparian proprietor.

SEC. 8. That the provisions of this act shall not extend to the territory occupied by the Cherokees, Creeks, Choctaws, Chickasaws, Seminoles, and Osage, Miamies and Peorias, and Sacs and Foxes, in the Indian Territory, nor to any of the reservations of the Seneca Nation of New York Indians in the State of New York, nor to that strip of territory in the State of Nebraska adjoining the Sioux Nation on the south added by Executive order.

SEC. 9. That for the purpose of making the surveys and resurveys mentioned in section two of this act, there be, and hereby is, appropriated, out of any moneys in the Treasury not otherwise appropriated, the sum of one hundred thousand dollars, to be repaid proportionately out of the proceeds of the sales of such land as may be acquired from the Indians under the provisions of this act.

SEC. 10. That nothing in this act contained shall be so construed as to affect the right and power of Congress to grant the right of way through any lands granted to an Indian, or a tribe of Indians, for railroads or other highways, or telegraph lines, for the public use, or to condemn such lands to public uses, upon making just compensation.

SEC. 11. That nothing in this act shall be so construed as to prevent the removal of the Southern Ute Indians from their present reservation in Southwestern Colorado to a new reservation by and with the consent of a majority of the adult male members of said tribe.

Approved, February 8, 1887.

Stephens v. the Cherokee Nation*

The rejection of treaty-making by the U.S. government in 1871 and the enactment of the General Allotment Act led to revisions of John Marshall's decisions on Indian status. The Cherokee effort to test the constitutionality of the Curtis Act resulted in Chief Justice Fuller's decision in 1898.

It is true that the Indian tribes were for many years allowed by the United States to make all laws and regulations for the government and protection of their persons and property, not inconsistent with the Constitution and laws of the United States; and numerous treaties were made by the United States with those tribes as distinct political societies. The policy of the government, however, in dealing with the Indian nations was definitively expressed in a proviso inserted in the Indian appropriation act of March 3, 1871 (16 Stat. at L. 544, 566, chap. 120), to the effect:

"That hereafter no Indian nation or tribe within the territory of the United States shall be acknowledged or recognized as an independent nation, tribe, or power with whom the United States may contract by treaty: Provided, further, That nothing herein contained shall be construed to invalidate or impair the obligation of any treaty heretofore lawfully made and ratified with any such Indian nation or tribe," which was carried forward into section 2079 of the Revised Statutes, which reads:

"Sec. 2079. No Indian nation or tribe within the territory of the United States shall be acknowledged or recognized as an independent nation, tribe or power with whom the United States may contract by treaty; but no obligation of any treaty lawfully made and ratified with any such Indian nation or tribe prior to March third, eighteen hundred and seventy-one, shall be hereby invalidated or impaired."

The treaties referred to in argument were all made and ratified prior to March 3, 1871, but it is "well settled that an act of Congress may supersede a prior treaty and that any questions that may arise are beyond the sphere of judicial cognizance, and must be met by the political department of the government." Thomas v. Gay, 169 U.S. 264, 271 (42:740, 743), and cases cited.

As to the general power of Congress we need not review the decisions on the subject, as they are sufficiently referred to by Mr. Justice Harlan in Cherokee Nation v. Southern Kansas Railway Company, 135 U.S. 641, 653 (34: 295, 301), from whose opinion we quote as follows:

* U.S. Supreme Court *Reports,* 171–174, Book 43, pp. 1055–1056 (483, 486).

"The proposition that the Cherokee Nation is sovereign in the sense that the United States is sovereign, or in the sense that the nation alone can exercise the power of eminent domain within its limits, finds no support in the numerous treaties with the Cherokee Indians, or in the decisions of this court, or in the acts of Congress defining the relations of that people with the United States. From the beginning of the government to the present time, they have been treated as 'wards of the nation,' in a state of pupilage, 'dependent political communities,' holding such relations to the general government that they and their country, as declared by Chief Justice Marshall in Cherokee Nation v. Georgia, 5 Pet. 1, 17 (8:25, 31), 'are considered by foreign nations, as well as by ourselves, as being so completely under the sovereignty and dominion of the United States that any attempt to acquire their lands, or to form a political connection with them, would be considered by all as an invasion of our territory and an act of hostility.' It is true, as declared in Worcester v. Georgia, 6 Pet. 515, 557, 569 (8:483, 499, 504), that the treaties and laws of the United States contemplate the Indian territory as completely separated from the states and the Cherokee Nation as a distinct community, and (in the language of Mr. Justice McLean in the same case, p. 583 (8:509), that 'in the executive, legislative, and judicial branches of our government, we have admitted, by the most solemn sanction, the existence of the Indians as a separate and distinct people, and as being vested with rights which constitute them a state, or separate community.' But that falls far short of saying that they are a sovereign state, with no superior within the limits of its territory. By the treaty of New Echota, 1835, the United States covenanted and agreed that the lands ceded to the Cherokee Nation should at no future time, without their consent, be included within the territoral limits or jurisdiction of any state or territory, and that the government would secure to that nation 'the right by their national councils to make and carry into effect all such laws as they may deem necessary for the government of the persons and property within their own country, belonging to their people or such persons as have connected themselves with them'; and, by the treaties of Washington, 1846 and 1866, the United States guaranteed to the Cherokees the title and possession of their lands, and jurisdiction over their country. Revision of Indian Treaties, pp. 65, 79, 85. But neither these nor any previous treaties evinced any intention, upon the part of the government, to discharge them from their condition of pupilage or dependency, and constitute them a separate, independent, sovereign people, with no superior within its limits. This is made clear by the decisions of this court, rendered since the cases already cited. In United States v. Rogers, 4 How. 567, 572 (11:1105, 1107), in court, referring to the locality in which a particular crime had been committed, said: 'It is true that it is occupied by the tribe of Cherokee Indians. But it has been assigned to them by the United States as a place of domicil for the tribe, and they hold and occupy it with the consent of the United

States, and under their authority. . . . We think it too firmly and clearly established to admit of dispute that the Indian tribes residing within the territorial limits of the United States are subject to their authority.' In United States v. Kagama, 118 U.S. 375, 379 (30: 228, 230), the court, after observing that the Indians were within the geographical limits of the United States, said: 'The soil and the people within these limits are under the political control of the government of the United States, or the states of the Union. There exist within the broad domain of sovereignty but these two. . . . They were, and always have been, regarded as having a semi-independent position when they preserved their tribal relations; not as states, not as nations, not as possessed of the full attributes of sovereignty, but as a separate people, with the power of regulating their internal and social relations, and thus far not brought under the laws of the Union or of the state within whose limits they resided. . . . The power of the general government over these remnants of a race once powerful, now weak and diminished in numbers, is necessary to their protection, as well as to the safety of those among whom they dwell. It must exist in that government, because it has never existed anywhere else, because the theater of its exercise is within the geographical limits of the United States, because it has never been denied, and because it alone can enforce its laws on all the tribes.' The latest utterance upon this general subject is in Choctaw Nation v. United States, 119 U.S. 1, 27 (30: 396, 315), where the court, after stating that the United States is a sovereign nation limited only by its own Constitution, said: 'On the other hand, the Choctaw Nation falls within the description in the terms of our Constitution, not of an independent state or sovereign nation, but of an Indian tribe. As such, it stands in a peculiar relation to the United States. It was capable under the terms of the Constitution of entering into treaty relations with the government of the United States, although, from the nature of the case, subject to power and authority of the laws of the United States when Congress should choose, as it did determine in the act of March 3, 1871, embodied in section 2079 of the Revised Statutes, to exert its legislative power.' "

Such being the position occupied by these tribes (and it has often been availed of to their advantage), and the power of Congress in the premises having the plenitude thus indicated, we are unable to perceive that the legislation in question is in contravention of the Constitution.

Lone Wolf v. Hitchcock*

The concept of Indians as "wards of the government," first suggested by John Marshall was taken up later by the Supreme Court as in Lone Wolf v. Hitchcock in 1902.

By the sixth article of the first of the two treaties referred to in the preceding statement, proclaimed on August 25, 1868 (15 Stat. at L. 581), it was provided that heads of families of the tribes affected by the treaty might select, within the reservation, a tract of land of not exceeding 320 acres in extent, which should thereafter cease to be held in common, and should be for the exclusive possession of the Indian making the selection so long as he or his family might continue to cultivate the land. The twelfth article reads as follows:

> Article 12. No treaty for the cession of any portion or part of the reservation herein described, which may be held in common, shall be of any validity or force, as against the said Indians, unless executed and signed by at least three fourths of all the adult male Indians occupying the same, and no cession by the tribe shall be understood or construed in such manner as to deprive, without his consent, any individual member of the tribe of his rights to any tract of land selected by him as provided in article 3 (6) of this treaty.

The appellants base their right to relief on the proposition that by the effect of the article just quoted the confederated tribes of Kiowas, Comanches, and Apaches were vested with an interest in the lands held in common within the reservation, which interest could not be devested by Congress in any other mode than that specified in the said twelfth article, and that as a result of the said stipulation the interest of the Indians in the common lands fell within the protection of the 5th Amendment to the Constitution of the United States, and such interest—indirectly at least—came under the control of the judicial branch of the government. We are unable to yield our assent to this view.

The contention in effect ignores the status of the contracting Indians and the relation of dependency they bore and continue to bear towards the government of the United States. To uphold the claim would be to adjudge that the indirect operation of the treaty was to materially limit and qualify the controlling authority of Congress in respect to the care and protection of the Indians, and to deprive Congress, in a possible emergency, when the necessity might be urgent for a partition and disposal of the tribal lands, of all power to act, if the assent of the Indians could not be obtained.

* U.S. Supreme Court *Reports,* 187–190, Book 47, pp. 305, 307 (564, 568).

Now, it is true that in decisions of this court, the Indian right of occupancy of tribal lands, whether declared in a treaty or otherwise created, has been stated to be sacred, or, as sometimes expressed, as sacred as the fee of the United States in the same lands. Johnson v. M'Intosh (1823) 8 Wheat. 543, 574, 5 L. ed. 681, 688; Cherokee Nation v. Georgia (1831) 5 Pet. 515, 581, 8 L. ed. 483, 508; United States v. Cook (1873) 19 Wall. 591, 592, 22 L. ed. 210, 211; Leavenworth, L. & G. R. Co. v. United States (1875) 92 U.S. 733, 755, 23 L. ed. 634, 643; Beecher v. Wetherby (1877) 95 U.S. 525, 24 L. ed. 441. But in none of these cases was there involved a controversy between Indians and the government respecting the power of Congress to administer the property of the Indians. The questions considered in the cases referred to, which either directly or indirectly had relation to the nature of the property rights of the Indians, concerned the character and extent of such rights as respected states or individuals. In one of the cited cases it was clearly pointed out that Congress possessed a paramount power over the property of the Indians, by reason of its exercise of guardianship over their interests, and that such authority might be implied, even though opposed to the strict letter of a treaty with the Indians. Thus, in Beecher v. Wetherby, 95 U.S. 525, 24 L. ed. 441, discussing the claim that there had been a prior reservation of land by treaty to the use of a certain tribe of Indians, the court said (p. 525, L. ed. p. 441):

> But the right which the Indians held was only that of occupancy. The fee was in the United States, subject to that right, and could be transferred by them whenever they chose. The grantee, it is true, would take only the naked fee, and could not disturb the occupancy of the Indians; that occupancy could only be interfered with or determined by the United States. It is to be presumed that in this matter the United States would be governed by such considerations of justice as would control a Christian people in their treatment of an ignorant and dependent race. Be that as it may, the propriety or justice of their action towards the Indians with respect to their lands is a question of governmental policy, and is not a matter open to discussion in a controversy between third parties, neither of whom derives title from the Indians.

Plenary authority over the tribal relations of the Indians has been exercised by Congress from the beginning, and the power has always been deemed a political one, not subject to be controlled by the judicial department of the government. Until the year 1871, the policy was pursued of dealing with the Indian tribes by means of treaties, and, of course, a moral obligation rested upon Congress to act in good faith in its behalf. But, as with treaties made with foreign nations (Chinese Exclusion Case, 130 U.S. 581, 600, 32 L. ed. 1068, 1073, 9 Sup. Ct. Rep. 623), the legislative power might pass laws in conflict with treaties made with the Indians, Thomas v. Gay, 169 U.S. 264, 270, 42 L. ed. 740, 743, 18 Sup. Ct. Rep. 340; Ward v. Race Horse, 163 U.S. 504, 511, 41 L. ed. 244, 246, 16 Sup. Ct. Rep. 1076;

Spalding v. Chandler, 160 U.S. 394, 405, 40 L. ed. 469, 473, 16 Sup. Ct. Rep. 360; Missouri K. & T. R. Co. v. Roberts, 152 U.S. 114, 117, 38 L. ed. 377, 379, 14 Sup. Ct. Rep. 496; Cherokee Tobacco, 11 Wall. 616, sub nom. 207 Half Pound Papers of Smoking Tobacco v. United States, 20 L. ed. 227.

The power exists to abrogate the provisions of an Indian treaty, though presumably such power will be exercised only when circumstances arise which will not only justify the government in disregarding the stipulations of the treaty, but may demand, in the interest of the country and the Indians themselves, that it should do so. When, therefore, treaties were entered into between the United States and a tribe of Indians, it was never doubted that the power to abrogate existed in Congress, and that in a contingency such power might be availed of from considerations of governmental policy, particularly if consistent with perfect good faith towards the Indians. In United States v. Kagama (1885) 118 U.S. 375, 30 L. ed. 228, 6 Sup. Ct. Rep. 1109, speaking of the Indians, the court said (p. 382, L. ed. p. 230, Sup. Ct. Rep. p. 1113):

> After an experience of a hundred years of the treaty-making system of government Congress has determined upon a new departure, to govern them by acts of Congress. This is seen in the act of March 3, 1871, embodied in 2079 of the Revised Statutes: "No Indian nation or tribe, within the territory of the United States, shall be acknowledged or recognized as an independent nation, tribe, or power with whom the United States may contract by treaty; but no obligation of any treaty lawfully made and ratified with any such Indian nation or tribe prior to March 3rd, 1871, shall be hereby invalidated or impaired."

In upholding the validity of an act of Congress which conferred jurisdiction upon the court of the United States for certain crimes committed on an Indian reservation within a state, the court said (p. 383, L. ed. p. 231, Sup. Ct. Rep. p. 1114):

> It seems to us that this is within the competency of Congress. These Indian tribes are the wards of the nation. They are communities dependent on the United States. Dependent largely for their daily food. Dependent for their political rights. They owe no allegiance to the states, and receive from them no protection. Because of the local ill feeling, the people of the states where they are found are often their deadliest enemies. From their very weakness, and helplessness, so largely due to the course of dealing of the Federal government with them and the treaties in which it has been promised, there arises the duty of protection, and with it the power. This has always been recognized by the executive and by Congress, and by this court, whenever the question has arisen.
>
> The power of the general government over these remnants of a race once powerful, now weak and diminished in numbers, is necessary to their protection, as well as to the safety of those among whom they dwell. It must exist in that government, because it never has existed anywhere else, because the theater of its exercise is within the geographical limits of the United States, because it has never been denied, and because it alone can enforce its laws on all the tribes.

That Indians who had not been fully emancipated from the control and protection of the United States are subject, at least so far as the tribal lands were concerned, to be controlled by direct legislation of Congress, is also declared in Choctaw Nation v. United States, 119 U.S. 1, 27, 30 L. ed. 306, 314, 7 Sup. Ct. Rep. 75, and Stephens v. Choctaw Nation, 174 U.S. 445, 483, 43 L. ed. 1041, 1054, 19 Sup. Ct. Rep. 722.

In view of the legislative power possessed by Congress over treaties with the Indians and Indian tribal property, we may not specially consider the contentions pressed upon our notice, that the signing by the Indians of the agreement of October 6, 1892, was obtained by fraudulent misrepresentations, and concealment, that the requisite three fourths of adult male Indians had not signed, as required by the twelfth article of the treaty of 1867, and that the treaty as signed had been amended by Congress without submitting such amendments to the action of the Indians, since all these matters, in any event, were solely within the domain of the legislative authority, and its action is conclusive upon the courts.

The act of June 6, 1900, which is complained of in the bill, was enacted at a time when the tribal relations between the confederated tribes of Kiowas, Comanches, and Apaches still existed, and that statute and the statutes supplementary thereto dealt with the disposition of tribal property, and purported to give an adequate consideration for the surplus lands not allotted among the Indians or reserved for their benefit. Indeed, the controversy which this case presents is concluded by the decision in Cherokee Nation v. Hitchcock, 187 U.S. 294, ante, 183, 23 Sup. Ct. Rep. 115, decided at this term, where it was held that full administrative power was possessed by Congress over Indian tribal property. In effect, the action of Congress now complained of was but an exercise of such power, a mere change in the form of investment of Indian tribal property, the property of those who, as we have held, were in substantial effect the wards of the government. We must presume that Congress acted in perfect good faith in the dealings with the Indians of which complaint is made, and that the legislative branch of the government exercised its best judgment in the premises. In any event, as Congress possessed full power in the matter, the judiciary cannot question or inquire into the motives which prompted the enactment of this legislation. If injury was occasioned, which we do not wish to be understood as implying, by the use made by Congress of its power, relief must be sought by an appeal to that body for redress, and not to the courts. The legislation in question was constitutional, and the demurrer to the bill was therefore rightly sustained.

Indian Reorganization Act of 1934*

AN ACT

To conserve and develop Indian lands and resources; to extend to Indians the right to form business and other organizations; to establish a credit system for Indians; to grant certain rights of home rule to Indians; to provide for vocational education for Indians; and for other purposes.

Be it enacted by the Senate and House of Representatives of the United States of America in Congress assembled, That hereafter no land of any Indian reservation, created or set apart by treaty or agreement with the Indians, Act of Congress, Executive order, purchase, or otherwise, shall be allotted in severalty to any Indian.

Section 2. The existing periods of trust placed upon any Indian lands and any restriction on alienation thereof are hereby extended and continued until otherwise directed by Congress.

Section 3. The Secretary of the Interior, if he shall find it to be in the public interest, is hereby authorized to restore to tribal ownership the remaining surplus lands of any Indian reservation heretofore opened, or authorized to be opened, to sale, or any other form of disposal by Presidential proclamation, or by any of the public-land laws of the United States: Provided, however, That valid rights or claims of any persons to any lands so withdrawn existing on the date of the withdrawal shall not be affected by this Act: Provided further, That this section shall not apply to lands within any reclamation project heretofore authorized in any Indian reservation: Provided further, That the order of the Department of the Interior signed, dated, and approved by Honorable Ray Lyman Wilbur, as Secretary of the Interior, on October 28, 1932, temporarily withdrawing lands of the Papago Indian Reservation in Arizona from all forms of mineral entry or claim under the public land mining laws, is hereby revoked and rescinded, and the lands of the said Papago Indian Reservation are hereby restored to exploration and location, under the existing mining laws of the United States, in accordance with the express terms and provisions declared and set forth in the Executive orders establishing said Papago Indian Reservation: Provided further, That damages shall be paid to the Papago Tribe for loss of any improvements on any land located for mining in such a sum as may be determined by the Secretary of the Interior but not to exceed the cost of said improvements: Provided further, That a yearly rental not to exceed five cents per acre shall be paid to the Papago Tribe for loss of the use or occupancy of any land with-

* Public Law No. 383–73D CONGRESS.

drawn by the requirements of mining operations, and payments derived from damages or rentals shall be deposited in the Treasury of the United States to the credit of the Papago Tribe: Provided further, That in the event any person or persons, partnership, corporation, or association, desires a mineral patent, according to the mining laws of the United States, he or they shall first deposit in the Treasury of the United States to the credit of the Papago Tribe the sum of $1.00 per acre in lieu of annual rental, as hereinbefore provided, to compensate for the loss or occupancy of the lands withdrawn by the requirements of mining operations: Provided further, That patentee shall also pay into the Treasury of the United States to the credit of the Papago Tribe damages for the loss of improvements not heretofore paid in such a sum as may be determined by the Secretary of the Interior, but not to exceed the cost thereof; the payment of $1.00 per acre for surface use to be refunded to patentee in the event that patent is not acquired.

Nothing herein contained shall restrict the granting or use of permits for easements or rights-of-way; or ingress or egress over the lands for all proper and lawful purposes; and nothing contained herein, except as expressly provided, shall be construed as authority for the Secretary of the Interior, or any other person, to issue or promulgate a rule or regulation in conflict with the Executive order of February 1, 1917, creating the Papago Indian Reservation in Arizona or the Act of February 21, 1931 (46 Stat. 1202).

Section 4. Except as herein provided, no sale, devise, gift, exchange or other transfer of restricted Indian lands or of shares in the assets of any Indian tribe or corporation organized hereunder, shall be made or approved: Provided, however, That such lands or interests may, with the approval of the Secretary of the Interior, be sold, devised, or otherwise transferred to the Indian tribe in which the lands or shares are located or from which the shares were derived or to a successor corporation; and in all instances such lands or interests shall descend or be devised, in accordance with the then existing laws of the State, or Federal laws where applicable; in which said lands are located or in which the subject matter of the corporation is located, to any member of such tribe or of such corporation or any heirs of such member: Provided further, That the Secretary of the Interior may authorize voluntary exchanges of lands of equal value and the voluntary exchange of shares of equal value whenever such exchange, in his judgment, is expedient and beneficial for or compatible with the proper consolidation of Indian lands and for the benefit of cooperative organizations.

Section 5. The Secretary of the Interior is hereby authorized, in his discretion, to acquire through purchase, relinquishment, gift, exchange, or assignment, any interest in lands, water rights or surface rights to lands, within or without existing reservations, including trust or otherwise restricted allotments whether the allottee be living or deceased, for the purpose of providing land for Indians.

For the acquisition of such lands, interests in land, water rights, and surface rights, and for expenses incident to such acquisition, there is hereby authorized to be appropriated, out of any funds in the Treasury not otherwise appropriated, a sum not to exceed $2,000,000 in any one fiscal year: Provided, That no part of such funds shall be used to acquire additional land outside of the exterior boundaries of Navajo Indian Reservation for the Navajo Indians in Arizona and New Mexico, in the event that the proposed Navajo boundary extension measures now pending in Congress and embodied in the bills (S. 2499 and H.R. 8927) to define the exterior boundaries of the Navajo Indian Reservation in Arizona, and for other purposes, and the bills (S. 2531 and H.R. 8982) to define the exterior boundaries of the Navajo Indian Reservation in New Mexico and for other purposes, or similar legislation, become law.

The unexpended balances of any appropriations made pursuant to this section shall remain available until expended.

Title to any lands or rights acquired pursuant to this Act shall be taken in the name of the United States in trust for the Indian tribe or individual Indian for which the land is acquired, and such lands or rights shall be exempt from State and local taxation.

Section 6. The Secretary of the Interior is directed to make rules and regulations for the operation and management of Indian forestry units on the principle of sustained-yield management, to restrict the number of livestock grazed on Indian range units to the estimated carrying capacity of such ranges, and to promulgate such other rules and regulations as may be necessary to protect the range from deterioration, to prevent soil erosion, to assure full utilization of the range, and like purposes.

Section 7. The Secretary of the Interior is hereby authorized to proclaim new Indian reservations on lands acquired pursuant to any authority conferred by this Act, or to add such lands to existing reservations: Provided, That lands added to existing reservations shall be designated for the exclusive use of Indians entitled by enrollment or by tribal membership to residence at such reservations.

Section 8. Nothing contained in this Act shall be construed to relate to Indian holdings of allotments or homesteads upon the public domain outside of the geographic boundaries of any Indian reservation now existing or established hereafter.

Section 9. There is hereby authorized to be appropriated, out of any funds in the Treasury not otherwise appropriated, such sums as may be necessary, but not to exceed $250,000 in any fiscal year, to be expended at the order of the Secretary of the Interior, in defraying the expenses of organizing Indian chartered corporations or other organizations created under this Act.

Section 10. There is hereby authorized to be appropriated, out of any funds in the Treasury not otherwise appropriated, the sum of $10,000,000 to be established as a revolving fund from which the Secretary of the Interior, under such rules and regulations as he may prescribe, may make loans to Indian chartered corporations for the purpose of promoting the economic development of such tribes and of their members, and may defray the expenses of administering such loans. Repayment of amounts loaned under this authorization shall be credited to the revolving fund and shall be available for the purposes for which the fund is established. A report shall be made annually to Congress of transactions under this authorization.

Section 11. There is hereby authorized to be appropriated, out of any funds in the United States Treasury not otherwise appropriated, a sum not to exceed $25,000 annually, together with any unexpended balances of previous appropriations made pursuant to this section, for loans to Indians for the payment of tuition and other expenses in recognized vocational and trade schools: Provided, That not more than $50,000 of such sum shall be available for loans to Indian students in high schools and colleges. Such loans shall be reimbursable under rules established by the Commissioner of Indian Affairs.

Section 12. The Secretary of the Interior is directed to establish standards of health, age, character, experience, knowledge, and ability for Indians who may be appointed, without regard to civil-service laws, to the various positions maintained, now or hereafter, by the Indian Office, in the administration of functions or services affecting any Indian tribe. Such qualified Indians shall hereafter have the preference to appointment to vacancies in any such positions.

Section 13. The provisions of this Act shall not apply to any of the Territories, colonies, or insular possessions of the United States, except that sections 9, 10, 11, 12, and 16, shall apply to the Territory of Alaska: Provided, That Sections 2, 4, 7, 16, 17, and 18 of this Act shall not apply to the following-named Indian tribes, the members of such Indian tribes, together with members of other tribes affiliated with such named tribes located in the state of Oklahoma, as follows: Cheyenne, Arapaho, Apache, Comanche, Kiowa, Caddo, Delaware, Wichita, Osage, Kaw, Otoe, Tonkawa, Pawnee, Ponca, Shawnee, Ottawa, Quapaw, Seneca, Wyandotte, Iowa, Sac and Fox, Kickapoo, Pottawatomi, Cherokee, Chickasaw, Choctaw, Creek, and Seminole. Section 4 of this Act shall not apply to the Indians of the Klamath Reservation in Oregon.

Section 14. The Secretary of the Interior is hereby directed to continue the allowance of the articles enumerated in section 17 of the Act of March 2, 1889 (23 Stat. L. 894), or their commuted cash value under the Act of June 10, 1896 (29 Stat. L. 334), to all Sioux Indians who would be eligible, but for the provisions of this Act, to receive allotments of lands in severalty under section 19 of the Act of May 29, 1908 (25 Stat. L. 451), or under any prior Act, and who have the prescribed status of the head of a family or single person over the age of eighteen years, and his approval shall be final and conclusive, claims therefor to be paid as formerly from the permanent appropriation made by said section 17 and carried on the books of the Treasury for this purpose. No person shall receive in his own right more than one allowance of the benefits, and application must be made and approved during the lifetime of the allottee or the right shall lapse. Such benefits shall continue to be paid upon such reservation until such time as the lands available therein for allotment at the time of the passage of this Act would have been exhausted by the award to each person receiving such benefits of an allotment of eighty acres of such land.

Section 15. Nothing in this Act shall be construed to impair or prejudice any claim or suit of any Indian tribe against the United States. It is hereby declared to be the intent of Congress that no expenditures for the benefit of Indians made out of appropriations authorized by this Act shall be considered as offsets in any suit brought to recover upon any claim of such Indians against the United States.

Section 16. Any Indian tribe or tribes, residing on the same reservation, shall have the right to organize for its common welfare, and may adopt an appropriate constitution and bylaws, which shall become effective when ratified by a majority vote of the adult members of the tribe, or of the adult Indians residing on such reservation, as the case may be, at a special election authorized and called by the Secretary of the Interior under such rules and regulations as he may prescribe. Such constitution and bylaws when ratified as aforesaid and approved by the Secretary of the Interior shall be revocable by an election open to the same voters and conducted in the same manner as hereinabove provided. Amendments to the constitution and bylaws may be ratified and approved by the Secretary in the same manner as the original constitution and bylaws.

In addition to all powers vested in any Indian tribe or tribal council by existing law, the constitution adopted by said tribe shall also vest in such tribe or its tribal council the following rights and powers: To employ legal counsel, the choice of counsel and fixing of fees to be subject to the approval of the Secretary of the Interior; to prevent the sale, disposition, lease, or encumbrance of tribal lands, interests in lands, or other tribal assets without the consent of the tribe; and to negotiate with the Federal, State, and local Governments. The Secretary of the Interior shall advise such tribe or its tribal council of all appropriation estimates or Federal projects for the benefit of the tribe prior to the submission of such estimates to the Bureau of the Budget and the Congress.

Section 17. The Secretary of the Interior may, upon petition by at least one-third of the adult Indians, issue a charter of incorporation to such tribe: Provided, That such charter shall not become operative until ratified at a special election by a majority vote of the adult Indians living on the reservation. Such charter may convey to the incorporated tribe the power to purchase, take by gift, or bequest, or otherwise, own, hold, manage, operate and dispose of property of every description, real and personal, including the power to purchase restricted Indian lands and to issue in exchange therefor interests in corporate property, and such further powers as may be incidental to the conduct of corporate business, not inconsistent with law, but no authority shall be granted to sell, mortgage, or lease for a period exceeding ten years any of the land included in the limits of the reservation. Any charter so issued shall not be revoked or surrendered except by Act of Congress.

Section 18. This Act shall not apply to any reservation wherein a majority of the adult Indians, voting at a special election duly called by the Secretary of the Interior, shall vote against its application. It shall be the duty of the Secretary of the Interior, within one year after the passage and approval of this Act, to call such an election, which election shall be held by secret ballot upon thirty days' notice.

Section 19. The term "Indian" as used in this Act shall include all persons of Indian descent who are members of any recognized Indian tribe now under Federal jurisdiction, and all persons who are descendants of such members who were, on June 1, 1934, residing within the present boundaries of any Indian reservation, and shall further include all other persons of one-half or more Indian blood. For the purposes of this Act, Eskimos and other aboriginal peoples of Alaska shall be considered Indians. The term "tribe" wherever used in this Act shall be construed to refer to any Indian tribe, organized band, pueblo, or the Indians residing on one reservation. The words "adult Indians" wherever used in this Act shall be construed to refer to Indians who have attained the age of twenty one years.

Approved, June 18, 1934.

House Concurrent Resolution 108*

This resolution provided the impetus for the legislation which led in 1954 to the "termination" of the Klamath, the Menominee, and other tribes.

Whereas it is the policy of Congress, as rapidly as possible, to make the Indians within the territorial limits of the United States subject to the same laws and entitled to the same privileges and responsibilities as are applicable to other citizens of the United States, to end their status as wards of the United States, and to grant them all of the rights and prerogatives pertaining to American citizenship; and

Whereas the Indians within the territorial limits of the United States should assume their full responsibilities as American citizens: Now, therefore, be it

Resolved by the House of Representatives (the Senate concurring), That it is declared to be the sense of Congress that, at the earliest possible time, all of the Indian tribes and the individual members thereof located within the States of California, Florida, New York, and Texas, and all of the following named Indian tribes and individual members thereof, should be freed from Federal supervision and control and from all disabilities and limitations specially applicable to Indians: The Flathead Tribe of Montana, the Klamath Tribe of Oregon, the Menominee Tribe of Wisconsin, the Potowatamie Tribe of Kansas and Nebraska, and those members of the Chippewa Tribe who are on the Turtle Mountain Reservation, North Dakota. It is further declared to be the sense of Congress that, upon the release of such tribes and individual members thereof from such disabilities and limitations, all offices of the Bureau of Indian Affairs in the State of California, Florida, New York, and Texas and all other offices of the Bureau of Indian Affairs whose primary purpose was to serve any Indian tribe or individual freed from Federal supervision should be abolished. It is further declared to be the sense of Congress that the Secretary of the Interior should examine all existing legislation dealing with such Indians, and treaties between the Government of the United States and each such tribe, and report to Congress at the earliest practicable date, but not later than January 1, 1954, his recommendations for such legislation as, in his judgment, may be necessary to accomplish the purposes of this resolution.

Attest: LYLE O. SNADER,
Clerk of the House of Representatives.
Attest: J. MARK TRICE,
Secretary of the Senate.

* 83d CONGRESS, 1ST SESSION, Passed August 1, 1953.

Warren Trading Post v. Arizona State Tax Commission*

The question of federal, state, and tribal jurisdiction on Indian reservations was a live issue still in the 1960s.

No. 115   October Term, 1964

Warren Trading Post Company, Appellant,

v

Arizona State Tax Commission et al.

On Appeal From the Supreme Court of Arizona.

(April 29, 1965.)

Mr. Justice Black delivered the opinion of the Court.

Arizona has levied a tax of 2% on the "gross proceeds of sales, or gross income" of appellant Warren Trading Post Company, which does a retail trading business with Indians on the Arizona part of the Navajo Indian Reservation under a license granted by the United States Indian Commissioner pursuant to 25 U. S. C. 261 (1958 ed.). Appellant claimed that as applied to its income from trading with reservation Indians on the reservation the state tax was invalid as (1) in violation of Art. 1, & 8, cl. 3, of the United States Constitution, which provides that "Congress shall have Power . . . To regulate Commerce . . . with the Indian Tribes"; (2) inconsistent with the comprehensive congressional plan, enacted under authority of Arts. 1, & 8, to regulate Indian trade and traders and to have Indian tribes on reservations govern themselves. The Supreme Court rejected these contentions and upheld the tax, one Justice dissenting. 95 Ariz. 110, 387 P. 2d 809. The case is properly here on appeal under 28 U. S. C. & 1257 (2) (1958 ed.). Since we held that this State tax cannot be imposed consistently with federal statutes applicable to the Indians on the Navajo Reservation, we find it unnecessary to consider whether the tax is also barred by that part of the Commerce Clause giving Congress power to regulate commerce with the Indian tribes.

The Navajo Reservation was set apart as a "permanent home for" the Navajos in a treaty made with the "Navajo nation or tribe of Indians" on June 1, 1868. Long before that, in fact from the very

* Supreme Court Reporter, Vol. 85A, West Publishing Company, St. Paul, Minn., 1966, pp. 1243–1246.

first days of our Government, the Federal Government had been permitting the Indians largely to govern themselves, free from state interference, and had exercised through statutes and treaties a sweeping and dominant control over persons who wished to trade with Indians and Indian tribes. As Chief Justice John Marshall recognized in Worcester v. Georgia, 6 Pet. 515, 556–557:

> From the commencement of our government, congress has passed acts to regulate trade and intercourse with the Indians; which treat them as nations, respect their rights, and manifest a firm purpose to afford that protection which treaties stipulate.

He went on to say that:

> The treaties and laws of the United States contemplate the Indian territory as completely separated from that of the states; and provide that all intercourse with them shall be carried on exclusively by the government of the union. (*Id., at 557.*)

See also, e.g., United States v. Forty-three Gallons of Whiskey, 93 U.S. 188. In the very first volume of the federal statutes is found an Act, passed in 1790 by the first Congress, "to regulate trade and intercourse with the Indian tribes," requiring that Indian traders obtain a license from a federal official, and specifying in detail the conditions on which such licenses would be granted.

Such comprehensive federal regulation of Indian traders has continued from that day to this. Existing statutes make specific restrictions on trade with the Indians, and one of them, passed in 1876 and tracing back to comprehensive enactments of 1802 and 1834, provides that the Commissioner of Indian Affairs shall have "the sole power and authority to appoint traders to the Indian tribes" and to specify "the kind and quantity of goods and the prices at which such goods shall be sold to the Indians." Acting under authority of this statute and one added in 1901, the Commissioner has promulgated detailed regulations prescribing in the most minute fashion who may qualify to be a trader and how he shall be licensed; penalties for acting as a trader without a license; conditions under which government employees may trade with Indians; articles that cannot be sold to Indians; and conduct forbidden on licensed records to be kept and that government officials be allowed to inspect these records to make sure that prices charged are fair and reasonable; that traders pay Indians in money; that bonds be executed by proposed licensees; and that the governing body of an Indian reservation may assess from a trader "such fees, etc. as it may deem appropriate." It was under these comprehensive statutes and regulations that the Commissioner of Indian Affairs licensed appellant to trade with the Indians on the Navajo Reservation. These apparently all-inclusive regulations and the statutes authorizing them would seem in themselves sufficient to show that Congress has taken the business of Indian trading on reservations so fully in hand that no room remains for state laws imposing additional burdens upon traders. In fact, the Solicitor's Office of the Department of the Interior in 1940 and again in 1943 interpreted these statutes to bar States from taxing federally licensed Indian traders on their sales to reservation Indians on a reservation. We think those rulings were correct.

Congress has, since the creation of the Navajo Reservation nearly a century ago, left the Indians on it largely free to run the reservation and its affairs without state control, a policy which has automatically relieved Arizona of all burdens for carrying on those same responsibilities. And in compliance with its treaty obligations the Federal Government has provided for roads, education and other services needed by the Indians. We think the assessment and collection of this tax would to a substantial extent frustrate the evident congressional purpose of ensuring that no burden shall be imposed upon Indian traders for trading with Indians on reservations except as authorized by Acts of Congress or by valid regulations promulgated under those Acts. This state tax on gross income would put financial burdens on appellant or the Indians with whom it deals in addition to those Congress or the tribes have prescribed, and could thereby disturb and disarrange the statutory plan Congress set up in order to protect Indians against prices deemed unfair or unreasonable by the Indian Commissioner. And since federal legislation has left the State with no duties or responsibilities respecting the reservation Indians, we cannot believe that Congress intended to leave to the State the privilege of levying this tax. Insofar as they are applied to this federally licensed Indian trader with respect to sales made to reservation Indians on the reservation, these state laws imposing taxes cannot stand. Cf. Rice v. Santa Fe Elevator Corp., 331 U.S. 218. The judgment of the Supreme Court of Arizona is reversed and the cause remanded for further proceedings not inconsistent with this opinion.

Reversed and remanded.

Bureau of Indian Affairs
Task Force Report*

In 1960 the Bureau of Indian Affairs set up a task force to hold hearings for developing federal Indian policy on a broader base than that from which "termination" legislation had proceeded. The following is the introduction to the Task Force Report.

I. INTRODUCTION

OPENING STATEMENT

During the 90 years which have elapsed since the United States Government ceased to make treaties with Indian tribes, Congress has appropriated millions of dollars[1] to finance its programs for the protection, subsistence and acculturation of this relatively small group of Americans. Both with and without Federal assistance, many Indians have left the reservations and taken up new lives for themselves among their non-Indian neighbors. However, significant numbers have remained in Indian country and preserved their tribal identities.[2]

From time to time during these 90 years, critics of the Federal Indian program have raised the question of how long the Government must continue its special relationship with Indians. Underlying their concern has been an awareness of the accelerating cost of the program, a belief that to provide special services for Indians places them in a privileged category, and a contention that, because of excessive paternalism, the Federal program prevents Indians from achieving their maximum degree of self-sufficiency.

An examination of the history and present status of Indian affairs reveals a certain justification for the reservations which these critics

---

* *Report to the Secretary of the Interior by the Task Force on Indian Affairs,* July 10, 1961. Mimeographed.

[1] Since 1789, the U.S. Government has appropriated nearly $3 billion for Indian affairs. The bulk of this amount has been spent since 1871, when the policy of negotiating treaties with Indian tribes was discontinued. (Committee on Interior and Insular Affairs, House Committee Print No. 38, 85th Congress, 2d Session, 1959, pp. 20 and 21.)

[2] In its most recent request for appropriations, the Bureau of Indian Affairs estimates that there are 360,000 Indians still living on reservations and 160,000 living in other areas (Department of the Interior Justifications for Appropriations, Fiscal Year Ending June 30, 1962, Bureau of Indian Affairs, p. 30).

have expressed. Annual direct expenditures by the Federal Government for its services to Indians have risen from slightly over $7 million in 1871 to more than $160 million in 1961. Many treaties and hundreds of Federal statutes qualify Indians for services in the fields of health, education, welfare, banking and land management which are not available from governmental sources to any other group of Americans. Furthermore, the administration of these services has often been characterized by a paternalistic emphasis which has fostered continuing Indian dependence.

Beset by criticisms based on pragmatic and philosophical considerations such as those listed above, Federal administrators and Congressmen have at various times offered proposals for terminating the special relationship between Indians and the Federal Government. A paramount feature of many of these proposals has been the abolition of the Bureau of Indian Affairs. Such demands were strongly made in the last decade of the 19th century, during the years 1917–1918 and 1922–1924, and have dominated much of the Federal Indian policy in recent years.

Yet, even those who are most eager to end this special relationship are troubled by the fact that the bulk of the reservation Indian population is less well educated than other Americans, has a shorter life span, and has a much lower standard of living. Furthermore, critics of the present program know that States in which many of these Indians reside have limited financial resources and, unless they are subsidized from the Federal Treasury, cannot undertake the rehabilitation programs which are necessary if Indians within their jurisdictions are to advance economically, socially and politically.

The distinct legal status of Indians is a further hindrance to the abolishment of the Bureau of Indian Affairs and the withdrawal of the Federal Government from this field. In many decisions, the United States Supreme Court has upheld Washington's responsibility for helping Indians find solutions to their problems. Treaties and statutes still in effect recognize Indians as partial wards of the Federal Government and as representatives of "domestic, dependent nations," while also recognizing them as citizens of the United States.

Through the years, the Indians themselves have come to have an ambivalent regard for the Federal Government. They look to it for aid, but also resent and resist its attempts to undermine their social and cultural identity. Seldom do they perceive any connection between what they want and the demands upon them which securing it imposes. Similarly, many well-intentioned non-Indians who recognize and respect the underlying philosophies of the Indian way of life ignore or fail to see this connection. Thus, while urging Indians on the one hand to retain the old ways, they exhort the Federal Government to improve Indian health and the Indian standard of living, changes which cannot be provided without affecting the old ways they wish to preserve.

Confronted by conflicting opinions as to what the Indian's place in American society is and should be, we have had Indian policies enunciated by Congress and the Executive which, over the past 75 years, have run the gamut from extreme harshness to extreme paternalism. Inevitably, the results have disappointed both the Indians and those who were sincerely and deeply concerned about their welfare.

The Task Force will not concede that, even with all its complexities, the job of developing and administering an effective program for American Indians is impossible of execution. However, it must be a joint effort. Responsibility for the solution of the many problems confronting each tribe and reservation lies not only with the Bureau of Indian Affairs, but also with the Congress, with the Indians, with local agencies of Government and, very importantly, with the American people. Furthermore, this solution cannot be found through a return to the extremes of the past.

The programs which the Task Force suggests in the pages which follow are programs of development—development of people and development of resources. What we are attempting to do for those in the underdeveloped areas of the world, we can and must also do for the Indians here at home. Furthermore, to insure the success of our endeavor, we must solicit the collaboration of those whom we hope to benefit—the Indians themselves. To do otherwise is contrary to the American concept of democracy. Basically, we must not forget that ours is a program which deals with human beings. We must have faith in their abilities to help themselves and be willing to take some risks with them.

STATEMENT OF OBJECTIVES

In preparing their report, the members of the Task Force attempted to define what they feel the objectives of the Federal Indian program should be and to offer proposals aimed at fulfilling these objectives. At the present time, the Bureau of Indian Affairs defines its aims as follows:[3]

1. To create conditions under which the Indians will advance their social, economic and political adjustment to achieve a status comparable to that of their non-Indian neighbors.
2. To encourage Indians and Indian tribes to assume an increasing measure of self-sufficiency.
3. To terminate, at appropriate times, Federal supervision and services special to Indians.

The Task Force feels that recent Bureau policy has placed more emphasis on the last of these three objectives than on the first two. As a result, Indians, fearful that termination will take place before they are ready for it, have become deeply concerned. Their preoccupation was reflected in vigorous denunciation of the so-called "termination policy" during the many hearings which the Task Force con-

[3] *Indian Affairs Manual*, Volume 1.

ducted with Indian leaders. No other topic was accorded similar attention. It is apparent that Indian morale generally has been lowered and resistance to transition programs heightened as a result of the fear of premature Federal withdrawal. Now, many Indians see termination written into every new bill and administrative decision and sometimes are reluctant to accept help which they need and want for fear that it will carry with it a termination requirement. During the Task Force hearings in Oklahoma City, Acting Commissioner Crow pointed out to those present that a few years ago it was possible for Bureau employees to sit down with Indians and talk constructively about the time when special Federal services for Indians would no longer be provided. "Now," said the Commissioner, "we have reached a point where we can't talk about it to each other; we don't want to talk about it, and if we do talk about it, we have rather harsh words on the subject."

The experience of the past few years demonstrates that placing greater emphasis on termination than on development impairs Indian morale and produces a hostile or apathetic response which greatly limits the effectiveness of the Federal Indian program. The Task Force believes it is wiser to assist the Indians to advance socially, economically and politically to the point where special services to this group of Americans are no longer justified. Then, termination can be achieved with maximum benefit for all concerned. Furthermore, if development, rather than termination, is emphasized during the transitional period, Indian cooperation—an essential ingredient of a successful program—can be expected.

It is for the above reasons that the Task Force prefers not to list termination *per se* as a major objective of the Federal Indian program.

On the other hand, members of the Task Force believe that wherever the availability of special Federal services for Indians occasions resentment among their neighbors and results in discrimination, and wherever State and local governments use the Federal relationship with Indians as an excuse for denying Indians equal treatment with other citizens, a sympathetic effort should be made to develop programs which will meet their needs without placing Indians in a special category. In this respect such legislation as the Social Security Act, the Area Redevelopment Bill, and Public Laws 815 and 874 (81st Congress)—all of which treat Indian and non-Indian needs on the same basis—is highly desirable.

Finally, the Task Force believes that eligibility for special Federal services should be withdrawn from Indians with substantial incomes and superior educational experience, who are as competent as most non-Indians to look after their own affairs. Furthermore, Indians should not receive federally administered services which duplicate State and local benefits to which they are entitled as citizens of the States, counties and communities in which they reside.

In concluding its remarks concerning objectives, the Task Force acknowledges the wisdom of basing future policies and programs of the Bureau of Indian Affairs on the first two aims listed above.[4] However, it wishes to restate the first of these, in order to emphasize the importance of helping Indians achieve an adjustment which will be contributory, rather than passive. Membership in a society imposes obligations as well as bestows privileges. Assisting Indians to recognize and fulfill their obligations is as important as helping them to take advantage of their privileges and must be an essential part of the Federal program if it is to benefit both the Indians and the United States.

In the opinion of the Task Force, the Bureau of Indian Affairs should seek attainment of the following related objectives:

1. Maximum Indian economic self-sufficiency.
2. Full participation of Indians in American life.
3. Equal citizenship privileges and responsibilities for Indians.

The Task Force strongly emphasizes that the aid of the tribe—or, more properly, the Indian community—is crucial to the achievement of these objectives and this support should be secured before projects are commenced. The Indians can retain their tribal identities and much of their culture while working toward a greater adjustment and, for the further enrichment of our society, it is in our best interests to encourage them to do so.

[4] As set forth in the *Indian Affairs Manual,* these "aims" are actually statements of programs, as well as objectives.

White Viewpoints

The policy of the U.S. government has grown out of the conceptions and misconceptions about Indians held by White men. The nature of some of the recurring ideas of Whites is suggested in the following brief selections.

DOCUMENT NO. 21

An Opinion of Thomas Jefferson*

Writing to Benjamin Hawkins, United States agent to the Creeks, in 1803, Thomas Jefferson expressed a current White viewpoint.

I consider the business of hunting as already become insufficient to furnish clothing and subsistence to the Indians. The promotion of agriculture, therefore, and household manufacture, are essential in their preservation, and I am disposed to aid and encourage it. This will enable them to live on much smaller portions of land . . . while they are learning to do better on less land, our increasing numbers will be calling for more land, and thus a coincidence of interests between those who have such necessaries to spare, and want lands. . . . Surely it will be better for them to be identified with us, and preserve the occupation of their lands, than be exposed to the many casualties that may endanger them while a separate people.

* P. L. Ford, editor, *The Writings of Thomas Jefferson*, New York, 1892–99, Vol. III, p. 214.

Andrew Jackson's Opinions*

General Andrew Jackson wrote to President Monroe in 1817 presenting the frontiersman's view of Indian rights to land and self-determination, a position which was not translated fully into federal policy for another 70 years.

. . . The policy of government in open violation of the Constitution, which secures property from being taken for public use without just compensation being made, has by law, prevented the individuals from taking possession of their lands, and reserved them for hunting grounds for the Indians. The game being destroyed as acknowledged by all, the right of possession, granted to the Indians for the purpose of hunting ceases, and justice, sound policy, and the constitutional rights of the citizen, would require its being resigned to him.

It may be asked how this land is to be obtained from the Indians, they having refused to relinquish their claim to the commissioners lately appointed and authorized to make this purchase from them, one of whom, I was. . . . I have long viewed treaties with the Indians an absurdity not to be reconciled to the principles of our government. The Indians are the subjects of the United States, inhabiting its territory and acknowledging its sovereignty, then is it not absurd for the sovereign to negotiate by treaty with the subject? I have always thought, that congress had as much right to regulate by acts of legislation, all Indian concerns, as they had of territories; there is only this difference, that the inhabitants of territories, are citizens of the United States and entitled to all the rights thereof; the Indians are subjects and entitled to their protection and fostering care, the proper guardian of this protection and fostering care is the legislature of the Union.

To this might be opposed the policy and practice of government so long pursued towards them, to which I would answer, that this policy grew out of the weakness of the arm of government . . . and not from rights acknowledged to be possessed by them.

* John S. Bassett, editor, *Correspondence of Andrew Jackson,* Washington, 1926–35, Vol. II, pp. 277–82.

James Monroe and Indian Removal*

President James Monroe in a message to Congress in 1825 presented the case for Indian removal.

Being deeply impressed with the opinion, that the removal of the Indian tribes from the lands which they now occupy within the limits of the several States and Territories, to the country lying westward and northward thereof, within our own acknowledged boundaries, is of very high importance to our Union, and may be accomplished on conditions, and in a manner, to promote the interest and happiness of those tribes, the attention has long been drawn, with great solicitude, to the object. For the removal of the tribes within the State of Georgia, the motive has been peculiarly strong, arising from the compact with that State, whereby the United States are bound to extinguish the Indian title to the lands within it, whenever it may be done peaceably and on reasonable conditions. In the fulfilment of this compact I have thought that the United States should act with a generous spirit, that they should omit nothing which should comport with a liberal construction of the instrument, and likewise be in accordance with the just rights of these tribes. From the view which I have taken of the subject, I am satisfied that, in the discharge of those important duties, in regard to both the parties alluded to, the United States will have to encounter no conflicting interests with either; on the contrary, that the removal of the tribes, from the territory which they now inhabit, to that which was designated in the message at the commencement of the session, which would accomplish the object for Georgia, under a well digested plan for their government and civilization, which should be agreeable to themselves, would not only shield them from impending ruin, but promote their welfare and happiness. Experience has clearly demonstrated, that in their present state, it is impossible to incorporate them, in such masses, in any form whatever, into our system. It has also demonstrated, with equal certainty, that, without a timely anticipation of, and provision against, the dangers to which they are exposed, under causes which it will be difficult, if not impossible, to control, their degradation and extermination will be inevitable. . . .

To the United States, the proposed arrangement offers many advantages in addition to those which have been already enumerated.

* Henry R. Schoolcraft, *Historical and Statistical Information Respecting the History, Conditions and Prospects of the Indian Tribes of the United States,* Philadelphia, Lippincott, 1851–57, 6 Vols., Vol. VI, p. 407.

By the establishment of such a government over these tribes, with their consent, we become, in reality their benefactors. The relation of conflicting interests, which has heretofore existed between them and our frontier settlements, will cease. There will be no more wars between them and the United States. Adopting such a government, their movement will be in harmony with us, and its good effect be felt throughout the whole extent of our territory, to the Pacific. It may fairly be presumed, that, through the agency of such a government, the condition of all the tribes inhabiting that vast region may be essentially improved; that permanent peace may be preserved with them and our commerce be much extended.

A Century of Dishonor*

In the introduction to her indictment of the U.S. government for failure to keep faith and treaties with the Indians, Helen Hunt Jackson invoked the conscience of the American people, voicing what has continued ever since to be an important element in the spectrum of White sentiment.

The history of the United States Government's repeated violations of faith with the Indians thus convicts us, as a nation, not only of having outraged the principles of justice, which are the basis of international law; and of having laid ourselves open to the accusation of both cruelty and perfidy; but of having made ourselves liable to all punishments which follow upon such sins—to arbitrary punishment at the hands of any civilized nation who might see fit to call us to account, and to that more certain natural punishment which, sooner or later, as surely comes from evil-doing as harvests come from sown seed.

To prove all this it is only necessary to study the history of any one of the Indian tribes. I propose to give in the following chapters merely outline sketches of the history of a few of them, not entering more into details than is necessary to show the repeated broken faith of the United States Government toward them. A full history of the wrongs they have suffered at the hands of the authorities, military and civil, and also of the citizens of this country, it would take years to write and volumes to hold.

There is but one hope of righting this wrong. It lies in appeal to the heart and the conscience of the American people. What the people demand, Congress will do. It has been—to our shame be it spoken—at the demand of part of the people that all these wrongs have been committed, these treaties broken, these robberies done, by the Government.

So long as there remains on our frontier one square mile of land occupied by a weak and helpless owner, there will be a strong and unscrupulous frontiersman ready to seize it, and a weak and unscrupulous politician, who can be hired for a vote or for money, to back him.

The only thing that can stay this is a mighty outspoken sentiment and purpose of the great body of the people. Right sentiment and right purpose in a Senator here and there, and a Representative here and there, are little more than straws which make momentary

* Helen Hunt Jackson, *A Century of Dishonor*, Roberts Bros., Boston, 1886, pp. 29–31.

eddies, but do not obstruct the tide. The precedents of a century's unhindered and profitable robbery have mounted up into a very Gibraltar of defence and shelter to those who care for nothing but safety and gain. That such precedents should be held, and openly avowed as standards, is only one more infamy added to the list. Were such logic employed in the case of an individual man, how quick would all men see its enormity. Suppose that a man had had the misfortune to be born into a family whose name had been blackened by generations of criminals; that his father, his grandfather, and his great-grandfather before them had lived in prisons, and died on scaffolds, should that man say in his soul, "Go to! What is the use? I also will commit robbery and murder, and get the same gain by it which my family must have done?" Or shall he say in his soul, "God help me! I will do what may be within the power of one man, and the compass of one generation, to atone for the wickedness, and to make clean the name of my dishonored house!"

What an opportunity for the Congress of 1880 to cover itself with a lustre of glory, as the first to cut short our nation's record of cruelties and perjuries! the first to attempt to redeem the name of the United States from the stain of a century of dishonor!

An Opposing View of the General Allotment Act*

In 1881 Senator Teller of Colorado spoke on the Senate floor against an early version of the General Allotment Act, demonstrating that there were other viewpoints besides that which prevailed in the passage of the act.

The civilized Indians in the Indian territory hold all their land by a common tenure, and yet they do not work an acre of it in common any more than white men would do under the same circumstances. Each Indian goes upon the reservation and takes for himself such land as is unoccupied and works it, and he works it just as long as he sees fit . . . When he abandons it and goes away from it then any other Indian may step in and take his place. Knowing that fact, and knowing that the Indians protect these possessions with as much scrupulous honesty as we protect the fee simple title, I say that when it is asserted that they will not work because the title is not secure, it is nonsense.

They know what a paper title from the Government means, and they want the title not to themselves, but to their tribe; they want it where it will be understood that they cannot be disturbed; they want it so that an act of Congress cannot move them without their consent.

You propose to divide all this land and to give each Indian his quarter section, or whatever he may have, and for twenty-five years he is not to sell it, mortgage it, or dispose of it in any shape, and at the end of that time he may sell it. It is safe to predict that when that shall have been done, in thirty years there after there will not be an Indian on the continent, or there will be very few at least, that will have any land . . .

It is in the interest of speculators; it is in the interest of the men who are clutching up this land, but not in the interest of the Indians at all; and there is the baneful feature of it that when you have allotted the Indians land on which they cannot make a living the Secretary of the Interior may then proceed to purchase their land, and Congress will, as a matter of course, ratify the purchase, and the Indians will become the owners in a few years in fee and away goes their title.

* Congressional Record, 46th Congress, 3rd Session, Vol. XI, June 10, 1881.

If I stand alone in the Senate, I want to put upon the record my prophecy in this matter, that when thirty or forty years shall have passed and these Indians shall have parted with their title, they will curse the hand that was raised professedly in their defense to secure this kind of legislation, and if the people who are clamoring for it understood Indian character, and Indian laws, and Indian morals, and Indian religion, they would not be here clamoring for this at all.

Forced Assimilation*

The view that forcible assimilation of the Indians was fully justified received expression in statements of many government officials and others from the 1870s into the 1900s. Some of the major emphases are set forth in the following excerpts from various documents.

DOCUMENT NO. 26A

In our intercourse with the Indians it must always be borne in mind that we are the most powerful party . . . We . . . claim the right to control the soil which they occupy, and we assume that it is our duty to coerce them, if necessary, into the adoption and practice of our habits and customs. (Columbus Delano, *Report of the Secretary of the Interior, 1872*, pp. 3–4.)

DOCUMENT NO. 26B

The education of small numbers is overborne and lost in the mass of corrupting and demoralizing surroundings. Children at [the non-reservation boarding] school are hostages for good behavior of parents. (R. H. Pratt in *U.S. Bureau of Indian Affairs Annual Report*, 1878, pp. 173–75.)

DOCUMENT NO. 26C

Agents are expected to keep the [boarding] schools filled with Indian pupils, first by persuasion; if this fails, then by withholding rations or annuities or by such other means as may reach the desired end. (U.S. Bureau of Indian Affairs, *Regulations*, 1884, p. 94.)

DOCUMENT NO. 26D

The multiplicity of tribes represented, enabled a mixing of tribes in dormitory rooms. The rooms held three to four each and it was arranged that no two of the same tribe were placed in the same room. This not only helped in the acquirement of English but broke up tribal and race clannishness, a most important victory in getting the Indian toward real citizenship. (R. H. Pratt, *The Indian Industrial School: Carlisle, Penna.* Carlisle, Penna., 1908, p. 21.)

* The first four are quoted in J. S. Slotkin, *The Peyote Religion*, Glencoe, Ill., 1956, p. 85; the last three in Loring B. Priest, *Uncle Sam's Stepchildren*, New Brunswick, N.J., 1942, pp. 242–43.

DOCUMENT NO. 26E

We have a full right, by our own best wisdom, and then even by compulsion, to dictate terms and conditions to them; to use constraint and force; to say what we intend to do, and what they must and shall do. . . . This rightful power of ours will relieve us from conforming to, or even consulting to any troublesome extent, the views and inclinations of the Indians whom we are to manage. A vast deal of folly and mischief has come of our attempts to accommodate ourselves to them, to humor their whims and caprices, to indulge them in their barbarous ways and their inveterate obstinacy. Henceforward they must conform to our best views of what is for their good. The Indian must be made to feel he is in the grasp of a superior. (George E. Ellis, *The Red Man and the White Man in North America,* Boston, 1882, p. 572.)

DOCUMENT NO. 26F

I believe the Government should adopt a more vigorous policy with the Indian people. I can see no reason why a strong Government like ours should not govern and control them and compel each one to settle down and stay in one place, his own homestead, wear the white man's clothing, labor for his own support, and send his children to school. I can see no reason why . . . good and true men and women should come to an Indian agency and labor honestly and earnestly for three or four or a dozen years trying to coax or persuade the Indians to forsake their heathenish life and adopt the white man's manner of living, and then go away feeling they have thrown away, almost, the best years of their lives. The truth is the Indians hate the white man's life in their hearts, and will not adopt it until driven by necessity. (United States Indian Office, *Annual Report of the Commissioner of Indian Affairs,* 1884 [Statement by Agent Armstrong of the Crows], p. 111.)

DOCUMENT NO. 26G

Some races are plastic and can be molded: some races are elastic and can be bent; but the Indian is neither; he is formed out of rock, and when you change his form you annihilate his substance. . . . Civilization destroys the Indian . . . and the sooner the country understands that all these efforts are valueless unless they are based upon force supplemented by force and continued by force, the less money we shall waste and the less difficulty we shall have. (United States Congress, *Congressional Record,* IV, p. 3953 [Senator Ingalls of Kansas].)

The Views of Theodore Roosevelt*

Squarely in opposition to Helen Hunt Jackson, Theodore Roosevelt was a vigorous apologist for prevailing federal policy of the end of the 19th century. The combination of sound information and extensive misinformation regarding Indian history was probably characteristic of all American political leaders of the period whether in high or low positions.

It is greatly to be wished that some competent person would write a full and true history of our national dealings with the Indians. Undoubtedly the latter have often suffered terrible injustice at our hands. A number of instances, such as the conduct of the Georgians to the Cherokees in the early part of the present century, or the whole treatment of Chief Joseph and his Nez Percés, might be mentioned, which are indelible blots on our fair fame; and yet, in describing our dealings with the red men as a whole, historians do us much less than justice.

It was wholly impossible to avoid conflicts with the weaker race, unless we were willing to see the American continent fall into the hands of some other strong power; and even had we adopted such a ludicrous policy, the Indians themselves would have made war upon us. It cannot be too often insisted that they did not own the land; or, at least, that their ownership was merely such as that claimed often by our own white hunters. If the Indians really owned Kentucky in 1775, then in 1776 it was the property of Boon and his associates; and to dispossess one party was as great a wrong as to dispossess the other. To recognize the Indian ownership of the limitless prairies and forests of this continent—that is, to consider the dozen squalid savages who hunted at long intervals over a territory of a thousand square miles as owning it outright—necessarily implies a similar recognition of the claims of every white hunter, squatter, horse-thief, or wandering cattle-man. Take as an example the country round the Little Missouri. When the cattle-men, the first actual settlers, came into this land in 1882, it was already scantily peopled by a few white hunters and trappers. The latter were extremely jealous of intrusion; they had held their own in spite of the Indians, and, like the Indians, the inrush of settlers and the consequent destruction of the game meant their own undoing; also, again like the Indians, they felt that their having hunted over the

* Theodore Roosevelt, *The Winning of the West,* New York, 1889–96, 4 vols., Vol. I, pp. 331–35.

soil gave them a vague prescriptive right to its sole occupation, and they did their best to keep actual settlers out. In some cases, to avoid difficulty, their nominal claims were bought up; generally, and rightly, they were disregarded. Yet they certainly had as good a right to the Little Missouri country as the Sioux have to most of the land on their present reservations. In fact, the mere statement of the case is sufficient to show the absurdity of asserting that the land really belonged to the Indians. The different tribes have always been utterly unable to define their own boundaries. Thus the Delawares and Wyandots, in 1785, though entirely separate nations, claimed and, in a certain sense, occupied almost exactly the same territory.

Moreover, it was wholly impossible for our policy to be always consistent. Nowadays we undoubtedly ought to break up the great Indian reservations, disregard the tribal governments, allot the land in severalty (with, however, only a limited power of alienation), and treat the Indians as we do other citizens, with certain exceptions, for their sakes as well as ours. But this policy, which it would be wise to follow now, would have been wholly impracticable a century since. Our central government was then too weak either effectively to control its own members or adequately to punish aggressions made upon them; and even if it had been strong, it would probably have proved impossible to keep entire order over such a vast, sparsely-peopled frontier, with such turbulent elements on both sides. The Indians could not be treated as individuals at that time. There was no possible alternative, therefore, to treating their tribes as nations, exactly as the French and English had done before us. Our difficulties were partly inherited from these, our predecessors, were partly caused by our own misdeeds, but were mainly the inevitable result of the conditions under which the problem had to be solved; no human wisdom or virtue could have worked out a peaceable solution. As a nation, our Indian policy is to be blamed, because of the weakness it displayed, because of its shortsightedness, and its occasional leaning to the policy of the sentimental humanitarians; and we have often promised what was impossible to perform; but there has been little wilful wrong-doing. Our government almost always tried to act fairly by the tribes; the governmental agents (some of whom have been dishonest, and others foolish, but who, as a class, have been greatly traduced), in their reports, are far more apt to be unjust to the whites than to the reds; and the Federal authorities, though unable to prevent much of the injustice, still did check and control the white borderers very much more effectually than the Indian sachems and war-chiefs controlled their young braves. The tribes were warlike and bloodthirsty, jealous of each other and of the whites; they claimed the land for their hunting grounds, but their claims all conflicted with one another; their knowledge of their own boundaries was so indefinite that they were always willing, for inadequate compensation, to sell land to which they had merely the vaguest title; and yet, when once they had received the goods, were generally reluctant to make over even what they could; they coveted the goods and scalps of the whites, and the young warriors were always on the alert to commit outrages when they could do it with impunity. On the other hand, the evil-disposed whites regarded the Indians as fair game for robbery and violence of any kind; and the far larger number of well-disposed men, who would not willingly wrong any Indian, were themselves maddened by the memories of hideous injuries received. They bitterly resented the action of the government, which, in their eyes, failed to properly protect them, and yet sought to keep them out of waste, uncultivated lands which they did not regard as being any more the property of the Indians than of their own hunters. With the best intentions, it was wholly impossible for any government to evolve order out of such a chaos without resort to the ultimate arbitrator—the sword.

The purely sentimental historians take no account of the difficulties under which we labored, nor of the countless wrongs and provocations we endured, while grossly magnifying the already lamentably large number of injuries for which we really deserve to be held responsible. To get a fair idea of the Indians of the present day, and of our dealings with them, we have fortunately one or two excellent books, notably "Hunting Grounds of the Great West," and "Our Wild Indians," by Col. Richard I. Dodge (Hartford, 1882), and "Massacres of the Mountains," by J. P. Dunn (New York, 1886). As types of the opposite class, which are worse than valueless, and which nevertheless might cause some hasty future historian, unacquainted with the facts, to fall into grievous error, I may mention, "A Century of Dishonor," by H. H. (Mrs. Helen Hunt Jackson), and "Our Indian Wards," (Geo. W. Manypenny). The latter is a mere spiteful diatribe against various army officers, and neither its manner nor its matter warrants more than an allusion. Mrs. Jackson's book is capable of doing more harm because it is written in good English, and because the author, who had lived a pure and noble life, was intensely in earnest in what she wrote, and had the most praiseworthy purpose—to prevent our committing any more injustice to the Indians. This was all most proper; every good man or woman should do whatever is possible to make the government treat the Indians of the present time in the fairest and most generous spirit, and to provide against any repetition of such outrages as were inflicted upon the Nez Percés and upon part of the Cheyennes, or the wrongs with which the civilized nations of the Indian territory are sometimes threatened. The purpose of the book is excellent, but the spirit in which it is written cannot be called even technically honest. As a polemic, it is possible that it did not do harm (though the effect of even a polemic is marred by hysterical indifference to facts.) As a history it would be beneath criticism, were it not that the high character of the author and her excellent literary work in other directions have given it a fictitious value and made it much quoted by the large class of amiable but maudlin fanatics concerning whom it may be said that the excellence of their intentions but indifferently atones for the invariable folly and ill effect of their actions. It is not too much to say that the book is thoroughly untrustworthy from cover to cover, and that not a single statement it contains should be accepted without independent proof; for even those that are not absolutely false, are often as bad on account of so much of the truth having been suppressed. One effect of this is of course that the author's recitals of the many real wrongs of Indian tribes utterly fail to impress us, because she lays quite as much stress on those that are non-existent, and on the equally numerous cases where the wrong-doing was wholly the other way. To get an idea of the value of the work, it is only necessary to compare her statements about almost any tribe with the real facts, choosing at random; for instance, compare her accounts of the Sioux and the plains tribes generally, with those given by Col. Dodge in his two books; or her recital of the Sandy Creek massacre with the facts as stated by Mr. Dunn—who is apt, if any thing, to lean to the Indian's side.

These foolish sentimentalists not only write foul slanders about their own countrymen, but are themselves the worst possible advisers on any point touching Indian management. They would do well to heed General Sheridan's bitter words, written when many Easterners were clamoring against the army authorities because they took partial vengeance for a series of brutal outrages: "I do not know how far these humanitarians should be excused on account of their ignorance; but surely it is the only excuse that can give a shadow of justification for aiding and abetting such horrid crimes."

DOCUMENT NO. 28

Bureau of Indian Affairs Paternalism

The dominance of the paternalistic approach to Indian affairs was voiced by various officials of the Bureau during the first quarter of the 20th century, but nowhere so succinctly as in the following statements by Commissioners of Indian affairs. (The first was written by Commissioner Francis E. Leupp in 1910 and occurs in the Preface of his book The Indian and His Problem, *Charles Scribner's Sons, New York, 1910. The second was written as a letter "To All Indians" in 1923 by Commissioner Burke, U.S. National Archives, File: 10429-22-063, Part 1. But this Commissioner's special concern was the Pueblo Indians' religion.)*

DOCUMENT NO. 28A

The Indian problem has now reached a stage where its solution is almost wholly a matter of administration. Mere sentiment has spent its day; the moral questions involved have pretty well settled themselves. What is most needed from this time forth is the guidance of affairs by an independent mind, active sympathies free from mawkishness, an elastic patience and a steady hand.

DOCUMENT NO. 28B

To All Indians:

Not long ago I held a meeting of Superintendents, Missionaries and Indians, at which the feeling of those present was strong against Indian dances, as they are usually given, and against so much time as is often spent by the Indians in a display of their old customs at public gatherings held by the whites. From the views of this meeting and from other information I feel that something must be done to stop the neglect of stock, crops, gardens, and home interests caused by these dances or by celebrations, pow-wows, and gatherings of any kind that take the time of the Indians for many days.

Now, what I want you to think about very seriously is that you must first of all try to make your own living, which you cannot do unless you work faithfully and take care of what comes from your labor, and go to dances or other meetings only when your home work will not suffer by it. I do not want to deprive you of decent amusements or occasional feast days, but you should not do evil or foolish things or take so much time for these occasions. No good comes from your "giveaway" custom at dances and it should be stopped. It is not right to torture your bodies or to handle poisonous snakes in your ceremonies. All such extreme things are wrong and should be put aside and forgotten. You do yourselves and your families great injustice when at dances you give away money or other property, perhaps clothing, a cow, a horse or a team and wagon, and then after an absence of several days go home to find everything going to waste and yourselves with less to work with than you had before.

I could issue an order against these useless and harmful performances, but I would much rather have you give them up of your own free will and, therefore, I ask you now in this letter to do so. I urge you to come to an understanding and an agreement with your Superintendent to hold no gatherings in the months when the seedtime, cultivation and the harvest need your attention, and at other times to meet for only a short period and to have no drugs, intoxicants, or gambling, and no dancing that the Superintendent does not approve.

If at the end of one year the reports which I receive show that you are doing as requested, I shall be very glad for I will know that you are making progress in other and more important ways, but if the reports show that you reject this plea, then some other course will have to be taken.

With best wishes for your happiness and success, I am,

Sincerely yours,
CHARLES H. BURKE,
Commissioner.

The Meriam Report*

In the Meriam Report, published in 1928, is to be found the fullest realization of the effects of U.S. Indian policy in the period following 1871. The excerpts below suggest the nature of the views engendered by this extensive non-government sponsored study.

RECOMMENDATIONS. The fundamental requirement is that the task of the Indian Service be recognized as primarily educational, in the broadest sense of that word, and that it be made an efficient educational agency, devoting its main energies to the social and economic advancement of the Indians, so that they may be absorbed into the prevailing civilization or be fitted to live in the presence of that civilization at least in accordance with a minimum standard of health and decency.

To achieve this end the Service must have a comprehensive, well-rounded educational program, adequately supported, which will place it at the forefront of organizations devoted to the advancement of a people. This program must provide for the promotion of health, the advancement of productive efficiency, the acquisition of reasonable ability in the utilization of income and property, guarding against exploitation and the maintenance of reasonably high standards of family and community life. It must extend to adults as well as children and must place special emphasis on the family and the community. Since the great majority of the Indians are ultimately to merge into the general population, it should cover the transitional period and should endeavor to instruct Indians in the utilization of the services provided by public and quasi public agencies for the people at large in exercising the privileges of citizenship and in making their contribution in service and in taxes for the maintenance of the government. It should also be directed toward preparing the white communities to receive the Indian. By improving the health of the Indian, increasing his productive efficiency, raising his standard of living, and teaching him the necessity for paying taxes, it will remove the main objections now advanced against permitting Indians to receive the full benefit of services rendered by progressive states and local governments for their populations. By actively seeking coöperation with state and local governments and by making a fair contribution in payment for services rendered by them to untaxed Indians, the national government can expedite the transition and hasten the day when there will no longer

* Lewis Meriam and Associates, *The Problem of Indian Administration*, The Brookings Institution, Baltimore, 1928, pp. 21–23, 32–33, 51.

be a distinctive Indian problem and when the necessary governmental services are rendered alike to whites and Indians by the same organization without discrimination.

In the execution of this program scrupulous care must be exercised to respect the rights of the Indian. This phrase "rights of the Indian" is often used solely to apply to his property rights. Here it is used in a much broader sense to cover his rights as a human being living in a free country. Indians are entitled to unfailing courtesy and consideration from all government employees. They should not be subjected to arbitrary action. Recognition of the educational nature of the whole task of dealing with them will result in taking the time to discuss with them in detail their own affairs and to lead rather than force them to sound conclusions. The effort to substitute educational leadership for the more dictatorial methods now used in some places will necessitate more understanding of and sympathy for the Indian point of view. Leadership will recognize the good in the economic and social life of the Indians in their religion and ethics, and will seek to develop it and build on it rather than to crush out all that is Indian. The Indians have much to contribute to the dominant civilization, and the effort should be made to secure this contribution, in part because of the good it will do the Indians in stimulating a proper race pride and self respect.

Planning and Development Program. To plan and develop such a broad educational program obviously requires the services of a considerable number of persons expert in the special fields of activity which are involved in it. They must not be burdened with the details of routine administration, but must have their time almost entirely free to devote to research, planning, and the establishing of contacts and coöperative arrangements essential to the preparation of such a program. The Indian Service as it is at present organized does not possess such a staff of specialists in the several fields. Without any reflection whatsoever on its central staff, it may fairly be said to consist mainly of persons with administrative experience rather than technical and scientific training for planning and developing a program in specialized fields. Those specialists that it does have are primarily engaged in administration and cannot devote their energies to planning and development unless arrangements can be made to free them from their present heavy administrative responsibilities.

The survey staff, therefore, recommends that the Secretary of the Interior ask Congress for an appropriation of at least $250,000 a year to establish, in connection with the central office but with many duties in the field, a scientific and technical Division of Planning and Development.

School System. The first and foremost need in Indian education is a change in point of view. Whatever may have been the official governmental attitude, education for the Indian in the past has proceeded largely on the theory that it is necessary to remove the Indian child as far as possible from his home environment; whereas the modern point of view in education and social work lays stress on upbringing in the natural setting of home and family life. The Indian educational enterprise is peculiarly in need of the kind of approach that recognizes this principle; that is less concerned with a conventional school system and more with the understanding of human beings.

The methods must be adapted to individual abilities, interests, and needs. Indian tribes and individual Indians within the tribes vary so greatly that a standard content and method of education, no matter how carefully they might be prepared, would be worse than futile.

Routinization must be eliminated. The whole machinery of routinized boarding school and agency life works against that development of initiative and independence which should be the chief concern of Indian education in and out of school. The routinization characteristic of the boarding schools, with everything scheduled, no time left to be used at the child's own initiative, every moment determined by a signal or an order, leads just the other way.

For the effort to bring Indian schools up to standard by prescribing from Washington a uniform course of study for all Indian schools and by sending out from Washington uniform examination questions, must be substituted the only method of fixing standards that has been found effective in other school systems, namely, that of establishing reasonably high minimum standards for entrance into positions in the Indian school system. Only thus can the Service get first class teachers and supervisors who are competent to adapt the educational system to the needs of the pupils they are to teach, with due consideration of the economic and social conditions of the Indians in their jurisdiction and of the nature and abilities of the individual child.

The curriculum must not be uniform and standardized. The text books must not be prescribed. The teacher must be free to gather material from the life of the Indians about her, so that the little children may proceed from the known to the unknown and not be plunged at once into a world where all is unknown and unfamiliar. The little desert Indian in an early grade who is required to read in English from a standard school reader about the ship that sails the sea has no mental background to understand what it is all about and the task of the teacher is rendered almost impossible. The material, particularly the early material, must come from local Indian life, or at least be within the scope of the child's experience.

* * *

The belief is that it is a sound policy of national economy to make generous expenditures in the next few decades with the object of winding up the national administration of Indian affairs. The people of the United States have the opportunity, if they will, to write the closing chapters of the history of the relationship of the national government and the Indians. The early chapters contain little of which the country may be proud. It would be something of a national atonement to the Indians if the closing chapters should disclose the national government supplying the Indians with an Indian Service which would be a model for all governments concerned with the development and advancement of a retarded race.

Commissioner Collier's Views*

The viewpoint underlying the Indian Reorganization Act of 1934 was most fully and clearly expressed by John Collier, as in this memorandum written while he was Commissioner of Indian Affairs in 1943.

I see the broad function of Indian policy and Indian administration to be the development of Indian democracy and equality within the framework of American and world democracy. . . .

The most significant clue to achieving full Indian democracy within and as a part of American democracy, is the continued survival, through all historical change and disaster, of the Indian tribal group, both as a real entity and a legal entity. I suspect the reason we do not always give this fact the recognition it deserves is that we do not want to recognize it. Indian "tribalism" seems to be foreign to our American way of life. It seems to block individual development. We do not know how to deal with it. Consciously or unconsciously, we ignore it or try to eliminate it. Remove the tribe, rehabilitate the individual, and our problem is solved—so runs our instinctive thinking. . . .

We can discard everything else if we wish, and think of the tribe merely as a fact of law. At the minimum, the tribe is a legally recognized holding corporation—a holder of property and a holder of tangible rights granted by treaty or statute, by virtue of which a member enjoys valuable privileges which as a non-member he could not have. Through court decisions—many of them Supreme Court decisions—an important body of legal doctrine has grown up about the concept of the tribal entity. This fact of law is an enormously important, persistent, stubborn, living reality. . . .

Now this fact of law was greatly clarified and strengthened by the Indian Reorganization Act, which converted the tribe from a static to a dynamic concept. Congress, through the Indian Reorganization Act, invoked the tribe as a democratic operational mechanism. It reaffirmed the powers inherent in Indian tribes and set those powers to work for modern community development. In doing so, Congress recognized that most Indians were excluded from local civic government and that no human beings can prosper, or even survive, in a vacuum. If we strip the word tribe of its primitive and atavistic connotations, and consider tribes merely as primary or somewhat localized human groups, we can see that Indian tribal government, for

* Quoted in Harold E. Fey and D'Arcy McNickle, *Indians and Other Americans,* Harper and Bros., New York, 1959, pp. 131–33.

most Indians, is the only presently feasible type of local civic self-government they can share in and use for their advancement. We can divest ourselves of the lingering fear that tribalism is a regression, and we can look upon it as a most important single step in assimilating Indians to modern democratic life. . . .

I cannot predict how long tribal government will endure. I imagine it will be variable in duration. I can imagine some tribes will remain cohesive social units for a very long time; others will more or less rapidly diffuse themselves among the rest of the population. It is not our policy to force this issue. Indians have the right of self-determination. And cultural diversity is by no means inimical to national unity, as the magnificent war effort of the Indians proves. . . .

During this transitional period (however short or long it may prove to be) the federal government is forced both by the fact of law and the fact of self-interest to continue to give a friendly guiding and protective hand to Indian advancement. As to law: there is a large body of treaties and statutes to be interpreted and enforced; Indian property must continue to be protected against unfair practices by the dominant group; Indians must be assisted in attaining self-subsistence and full citizenship. As to government self-interest: the complete withdrawal of this protection would merely substitute a more difficult problem in place of the one that is on the way to solution. It would create a permanently dispossessed and impoverished group that will either have to live on the dole or become one more sore spot in the body politic. . . .

The government's relationship to Indians is itself in a transition period. The Indian Reorganization Act made that inevitable. The Indian office is moving from guardian to advisor, from administrator to friend in court. In this transition, many powers hitherto exercised by the Indian service have been transferred to the organized tribes; many more such powers will be transferred. As Indians advance in self-government, they will begin to provide many of their own technical and social services or will depend more and more on the services ordinarily provided to American communities. I think we can agree, however, that federal advisory supervision ought not to be withdrawn until Indians have attained a fair political, economic, and cultural equality.

Views of Social Scientists*

In 1954 a conference of social scientists, mainly anthropologists, met under the chairmanship of former Assistant Commissioner of Indian Affairs John H. Provinse for the purpose of pooling their knowledge and bringing it to bear on federal Indian policy. A portion of the statement they produced follows.

An assumption which seems to underlie the basic philosophy of much of the United States approach centers about the idea that assimilation of the American Indian into the normal stream of American life is inevitable, that Indian tribes and communities will disappear.

There was complete agreement on the part of the discussants that this prediction is unwarranted. Most Indian groups in the United States, after more than 100 years of Euro-American contact and in spite of strong external pressures, both direct and fortuitous, have not yet become assimilated in the sense of a loss of community identity and the full acceptance of American habits of thought and conduct. Nor can one expect such group assimilation within any short, predictable time period, say, one to four generations. The urge to retain tribal identity is strong, and operates powerfully for many Indian groups. It finds support in some of the attitudes and behavior of the general American public, and has been encouraged by federal policy for the past twenty years. Group feeling and group integrity among the American Indians are as likely to gain strength in the decades ahead as they are to lose it.

On the other hand we may expect continuing adaptation of the Indian groups to the non-Indian society surrounding them. Modification will occur in Indian material culture, in Indian thought and value systems, and in tribal organizational arrangements. But the process of change will be so varied in degree or amount, so selective in type or aspect of cultual feature, and so dependent on social factors of racial prejudice, local attitudes, administrative practices in the larger American society, plus Indian group resistances, that it cannot be taken for granted for any particular group of Indians, much less for all.

Further, the group was unanimously of the opinion that forced, or coercive, assimilation is self-defeating in practice, tending to antagonize and drive underground in the Indian groups those

* John Provinse and Others, "The American Indian in Transition," Wenner-Gren Supper Conference, *American Anthropologist*, 1954, Vol. 56, No. 3, pp. 388–89.

leaders who might otherwise develop constructive and cooperative attitudes toward greater acceptance of non-Indian society. Also, the extent of coercion that would have to be applied in order to force assimilation—coercion sufficient to disperse the Indian communities—would not be permitted by the American public. Meanwhile, the current practice of telling Indians that their assimilation is inevitable is probably more deterrent than contributory to adjustive changes, since it gives rise to feelings of anxiety and resistance that lead to rejection of new ideas and institutions.

While tribal groups may be expected to survive indefinitely, individuals will continue to leave them, either to join already existing Indian communities in towns and cities, or to enter the larger American society as acculturated, relatively well accepted and adjusted individuals. Despite such individual out-migration the population of the Indian groups will probably maintain itself or increase due to high birth rates and falling death rates.

The general prediction, therefore, is that Indian communities will maintain themselves as cultural islands, more or less well adjusted to or integrated into the American system, at the same time that a growing number of individual Indians will make personal adjustments in the general society. With respect to the communities, therefore, the conference agreed that *despite external pressures, and internal change, most of the present identifiable Indian groups residing on reservations (areas long known to them as homelands) will continue indefinitely as distinct social units, preserving their basic values, personality, and Indian way of life, while making continual adjustments, often superficial in nature, to the economic and political demands of the larger society.*

It was noted that cultural islands of many kinds presently exist in America, retaining their cultural identity in thought, value system, and custom, as they make adjustment to the political and economic pressures of the powerful culture surrounding them. The existence of such cultural islands is generally accepted as proper by the American public, if they do not violate the public sense of basic decency and are not considered an economic burden. There is also a contradictory feeling that differences should disappear in time, and in public and governmental thinking about Indian policy the feeling that differences should disappear seems generally to take precedence over the feeling that groups have a right to self-determination. It is likely that this choice is made, not too consciously, because assimilation is thought to solve a problem—the present economic burden of nonproductive Indian groups—which problem is not seen as solvable in any other way.

SECTION 4

Indian Prophets and Spokesmen

Through three and a half centuries Indian religious leaders, states-men, and observers have looked into the future, urged action on their people, and interpreted history. Their differing points of view have shaped Indian lives and molded the course of events. The following samples give some suggestion of the nature of the human situation as experienced by Indians.

DOCUMENT NO. 32

The Delaware Prophet*

Through the eyes of a contemporary Moravian missionary, John Heckewelder, a glimpse of the teachings of the first influential Algonkian prophet comes down to us.

In the year 1762 there was a ramous preacher of the Delaware nation, who resided at Cayahaga, near Lake Erie, and travelled about the country, among the Indians, endeavouring to persuade them that he had been appointed by the Great Spirit to instruct them in those things that were agreeable to him, and point out to them the offences by which they had drawn his displeasure on themselves, and the means by which they might recover his favour for the future. He had drawn, as he pretended, by the direction of the Great Spirit, a kind of map on a piece of deerskin, somewhat dressed like parchment, which he called "the great Book or Writing." This, he said, he had been ordered to shew to the Indians, that they might see the situation in which the Mannitto had originally placed them, the misery which they had brought upon themselves by neglecting their duty, and the only way

* James Mooney, The Ghost Dance Religion and the Sioux Outbreak of 1890. *14th Annual Report, Bureau of American Ethnology,* Gov't. Printing Office, Washington, D.C. 1896, pp. 666–67.

251

that was now left them to regain what they had lost. This map he held before him while preaching, frequently pointing to particular marks and spots upon it, and giving explanations as he went along.

The size of this map was about fifteen inches square, or, perhaps, something more. An inside square was formed by lines drawn within it, of about eight inches each way; two of these lines, however, were not closed by about half an inch at the corners. Across these inside lines, others of about an inch in length were drawn with sundry other lines and marks, all which was intended to represent a strong inaccessible barrier, to prevent those without from entering the space within, otherwise than at the place appointed for that purpose. When the map was held as he directed, the corners which were not closed lay at the left-hand side, directly opposite to each other, the one being at the southeast by south, and the nearest at the northeast by north. In explaining or describing the particular points on this map, with his fingers always pointing to the place he was describing, he called the space within the inside lines "the heavenly regions," or the place destined by the Great Spirit for the habitation of the Indians in future life. The space left open at the southeast corner he called the "avenue," which had been intended for the Indians to enter into this heaven, but which was now in the possession of the white people; wherefore the Great Spirit had since caused another "avenue" to be made on the opposite side, at which, however, it was both difficult and dangerous for them to enter, there being many impediments in their way, besides a large ditch leading to a gulf below, over which they had to leap; but the evil spirit kept at this very spot a continual watch for Indians, and whoever he laid hold of never could get away from him again, but was carried to his regions, where there was nothing but extreme poverty; where the ground was parched up by the heat for want of rain, no fruit came to perfection, the game was almost starved for want of pasture, and where the evil spirit, at his pleasure, transformed men into horses and dogs, to be ridden by him and follow him in his hunts and wherever he went.

The space on the outside of this interior square was intended to represent the country given to the Indians to hunt, fish, and dwell in while in this world; the east side of it was called the ocean or "great salt-water lake." Then the preacher, drawing the attention of his hearers particularly to the southeast avenue, would say to them, "Look here! See what we have lost by neglect and disobedience; by being remiss in the expression of our gratitude to the Great Spirit for what he has bestowed upon us; by neglecting to make to him sufficient sacrifices; by looking upon a people of a different colour from our own, who had come across a great lake, as if they were a part of ourselves; by suffering them to sit down by our side, and looking at them with indifference, while they were not only taking our country from us, but this (pointing to the spot), this, our own avenue, leading into those beautiful regions which were destined for us. Such is the sad condition to which we are reduced. What is now to be done, and what remedy is to be applied? I will tell you, my friends. Hear what the Great Spirit has ordered me to tell you! You are to make sacrifices, in the manner that I shall direct; to put off entirely from yourselves the customs which you have adopted since the white people came among us. You are to return to that former happy state, in which we lived in peace and plenty, before these strangers came to disturb us; and, above all, you must abstain from drinking their deadly *beson,* which they have forced upon us, for the sake of increasing their gains and diminishing our numbers. Then will the Great Spirit give success to our arms; then he will give us strength to conquer our enemies, to drive them from hence, and recover the passage to the heavenly regions which they have taken from us."

Such was in general the substance of his discourses. After having dilated more or less on the various topics which I have mentioned, he commonly concluded in this manner: "And now, my friends, in order that what I have told you may remain firmly impressed on your minds, and to refresh your memories from time to time, I advise you to preserve, in every family at least, such a book or writing as this, which I will finish off for you, provided you bring me the price, which is only one buckskin or two doeskins apiece." The price was of course bought (*sic*), and the book purchased. In some of those maps, the figure of a deer or turkey, or both, was placed in the heavenly regions, and also in the dreary region of the evil spirit. The former, however, appeared fat and plump, while the latter seemed to have nothing but skin and bones.

A Cherokee Treaty-Making Speech*

A leading "beloved man" of the Cherokees—called Old Tassel by the Whites—spoke as follows at treaty negotiations with the Americans in the 1780s.

It is surprising that when we enter into treaties with our fathers the white people, their whole cry is more land. Indeed it has seemed a formality with them to demand what they know we dare not refuse. But on the principles of fairness of which we have received assurance during the conduct of this treaty I must refuse your demand.

What did you do? You marched into our towns with a superior force. Your numbers far exceeded us, and we fled to the strongholds of our woods, there to secure our women and children. Our towns left to your mercy. You killed a few scattered and defenseless individuals, spread fire and desolation wherever you pleased, and returned to your own habitations.

If you term this a conquest, you have overlooked the most essential point. You should have fortified the junction of Holston and Tennessee Rivers, and thereby conquered all the waters above. It is now too late for us to suffer from your mishap of generalship. Will you claim our lands by right of conquest? No! If you do, I will tell you that WE marched over them, even up to this very place; and some of our young warriors whom we have not had opportunity to recall are still in the woods and continue to keep your people in fear.

Much has been said of the want of what you term "civilization" among the Indians. Many proposals have been made to us to adopt your laws, your religions, your manners, and your customs, We do not see the propriety of such a reformation. We should be better pleased with beholding the good effect of these doctrines in your own practices than with hearing you talk about them, or of reading your papers to us on such subjects. You say, "Why do not the Indians till the ground and live as we do?" May we not ask with equal propriety, "Why do not the white people hunt and live as we do?"

We wish, however, to be at peace with you, and to do as we would be done by. We do not quarrel with you for the killing of an occasional buffalo or deer on our lands, but your people go much farther. They hunt to gain a livelihood. They kill all our game; but it is very criminal in our young men if they chance to kill a cow or a hog for their sustenance when they happen to be in your lands.

* John P. Brown, *Old Frontiers*, Kingsport, Tennessee, 1938.

The Great Spirit has placed us in different situations. He has given you many advantages, but he has not created us to be your slaves. We are a separate people! He has stocked your lands with cows, ours with buffalo; yours with hogs, ours with bears; yours with sheep, ours with deer. He has given you the advantage that your animals are tame, while ours are wild an demand not only a larger space for range, but art to hunt and kill them. They are, nevertheless, as much our property as other animals are yours, and ought not to be taken from us without our consent, or for something of equal value.

The Code of Handsome Lake*

The "Great Message," or Code of Handsome Lake, the Seneca religious leader, is preserved in several forms. The following excerpts are translated from the Seneca version written down about 1903 by So-son-dowa (Edward Cornplanter), a leading preacher of the Longhouse Religion.

THE GREAT MESSAGE

SECTION 1

"Now the beings spoke saying, 'We must now relate our message. We will uncover the evil upon the earth and show how men spoil the laws the Great Ruler has made and thereby made him angry.'

" 'The Creator made man a living creature.'

" 'Four words tell a great story of wrong and the Creator is sad because of the trouble they bring, so go and tell your people.'

" 'The first word is One'ga'.[1] It seems that you never have known that this word stands for a great and monstrous evil and has reared a high mound of bones. Ga''nigoĕntdo'" tha, you lose your minds and one'ga' causes it all. Alas, many are fond of it and are too fond of it. So now all must now say, "I will use it nevermore. As long as I live, as long as the number of my days is I will never use it again. I now stop." So must all say when they hear this message.' Now the beings, the servants of the Great Ruler, the messengers of him who created us, said this. Furthermore they said that the Creator made one'ga' and gave it to our younger brethren, the white man, as a medicine but they use it for evil for they drink it for other purposes than medicine and drink instead of work and idlers drink one'ga'. No, the Creator did not make it for you."

So they said and he said. Eniä'iehŭk! [2]

* * *

SECTION 25

" 'Now another message.

" 'Three things that our younger brethren (the white people) do are right to follow.

* Arthur C. Parker, The Code of Handsome Lake, the Seneca Prophet, *New York State Museum Bulletin 163*, Albany, 1912, pp. 27, 38, 39, 40, 41, 47, 48.
[1] Whiskey or Rum.
[2] Eniä'iehŭk meaning, *It was that way.*

" 'Now, the first. The white man works on a tract of cultivated ground and harvests food for his family. So if he should die they still have the ground for help. If any of your people have cultivated ground let them not be proud on that account. If one is proud there is sin within him but if there be no pride there is no sin.

" 'Now, the second thing. It is the way a white man builds a house. He builds one warm and fine appearing so if he dies the family has the house for help. Whoso among you does this does right, always providing there is no pride. If there is pride it is evil but if there is none, it is well.

" 'Now the third. The white man keeps horses and cattle. Now there is no evil in this for they are a help to his family. So if he dies his family has the stock for help. Now all this is right if there is no pride. No evil will follow this practice if the animals are well fed, treated kindly and not overworked. Tell this to your people.' "

So they said and he said. Eniaiehuk.

SECTION 26

" 'Now another message to tell your relatives.

" 'This concerns education. It is concerning studying in English schools.

" 'Now let the Council appoint twelve people to study, two from each nation of the six. So many white people are about you that you must study to know their ways.' "

So they said and he said. Eniaiehuk.

SECTION 27

" 'Now another message to tell your people.

" 'Now some men have much work and invite all their friends to come and aid them and they do so. Now this is a good plan and the Creator designed it. He ordained that men should help one another[3] (ādanidä'oshä').' "

So they said and he said. Eniaiehuk.

SECTION 28

" 'Now another message of things not right.

" 'People do wrong in the world and the Creator looks at all things.

" 'A woman sees some green vegetables and they are not hers. She takes them wrongly. Now she is yeno$^{n'}$skwaswa'do^n, a thieving woman. Tell your people that petty thieving must cease.' So they said.

" 'Now the Creator gave Diohe$^{n'}$ko^n [4] for a living. When a woman sees a new crop and wishes to eat of it in her own house, she must

[3] The bee is a very popular institution among the Iroquois. See Museum Bulletin 144, p. 31.

[4] Meaning, "our life givers," the corn, beans and squashes. See Iroquois Uses of Maize, p. 36.

ask the owner for a portion and offer payment. Then may the owner use her judgment and accept recompense or give the request freely.' " [5]

So they said and he said. Eniaiehuk.

SECTION 29

" 'Now another message for you to tell your people.

" 'It is not right for you to have so many dances[6] and dance songs.

" 'A man calls a dance in honor of some totem animal from which he desires favor or power. This is very wrong, for you do not know what injury it may work upon other people.

" 'Tell your people that these things must cease. Tell them to repent and cease.' "

So they said and he said. Eniaiehuk.

" 'Now this shall be the way: They who belong to these totem animal societies[7] must throw tobacco and disband.' So they said.

[5] One of the old methods of gardening was to clear a small patch in the woods by girdling the trees and planting in the mellow forest mold. The name and totem of the owner of the garden was painted on a post, signifying that the ground was private property. The clan totem gave permission to any hard-pressed clansman to take what he wished in emergency but only in such a case. These isolated gardens in the forests were objects of temptation sometimes, as the prophet intimates.

[6] The Seneca had thirty-three dances, ten of which were acquired from other tribes. See p. 81.

[7] Animal Societies and Totems. The Seneca firmly believe that by using the proper formula the favor of various animals can be purchased. The animal petitioned it is believed will make the person successful in any pursuit in which itself is proficient. The charm-animal was sometimes revealed in a dream, sometimes by a diviner of mysteries and was often sought directly. A warrior wishing to become a successful fisherman, for instance, might do any one of three things. He might seek for a dream that would show him what animal would make him an expert fisher, he might consult a "clairvoyant" or he might go directly to a stream of water and selecting some animal petition its favor.

The patron of the fisheries was the otter and there is a special society of those who have the otter for a "friend." The Society of Otters preserves the rites of invocation and the method of propitiation and also the method of healing afflicted members.

Other animals which are thought to be "great medicine" are the eagle, the bear, the buffalo and the mythical nia'gwahē or mammoth bear that was alternately a man and a beast. To be ungrateful to these givers of luck is a sin that arouses the ire of the animal who will punish the offender by inflicting him with some strange sickness. The offense may be one of neglect or altogether unintentional and unknown. It is then the duty of the society to appease the offended animal by performing the rites on a grand scale that the individual has failed to do in the ordinary way. The ordinary individual ceremony consisted simply of going to the bank of some clear stream, in the case of the Otters for instance, and after smoking sacred tobacco, casting the pulverized tobacco into the water at intervals during a thanksgiving and praise chant. Then will

"Now in those days when the head men heard this message they said at once, in anger, 'We disband,' and they said this without holding a ceremony as the messenger had directed." [8]

Eniaiehuk.

SECTION 30

" 'Now another message to tell your people.

" 'Four words the Creator has given for bringing happiness. They are amusements devised in the heaven world, the Osto'wägo'wa,[9] Gonē'owo", Ado"wē" and Ganäwe"'gowa.' "

So they said and he said. Eniaiehuk.

SECTION 31

" 'Now another message to tell your people.

" 'The Creator has sanctioned four dances for producing a joyful spirit and he has placed them in the keeping of Honon'diont[10] who have authority over them. The Creator has ordered that on certain times and occasions there should be thanksgiving ceremonies. At such times all must thank the Creator that they live. After that, let the chiefs thank him for the ground and the things on the ground and then upward to the sky and the heaven-world where he is. Let the children and old folk come and give thanks. Let the old women who can scarcely walk come. They may lean against the middle benches and after listening to three or four songs must say, "I thank the Great Ruler that I have seen this day." Then will the Creator call them right before him.

" 'It seems that you have never known that when Osto'wägo'wa was being celebrated that one of the four beings was in the midst of it, but it is so. Now when the time for dancing comes you must wash your faces and comb your hair, paint your face with red spots on either cheek, and with a thankful heart go to the ceremony. This preparation will be sufficient, therefore, do not let your style of dress hold you back.

" 'You have not previously been aware that when a Godi'ont is appointed that you have not appointed her. No, for the Great Ruler

the otters know that their human brothers are not ungrateful for the fortune they are receiving.

There were four societies, having as their genii the spirits of the bear, the birds (eagle), the buffalo and the otter, respectively, and taking their names from their guardian animal (Secret Medicine Societies of the Seneca p. 113).

[8] This was done at the suggestion of Cornplanter who is accused of endeavoring to upset the plans and prophecies of Handsome Lake in many sly ways.

[9] The Great Feather dance, the Harvest dance, the Sacred Song and the Peach Stone game.

[10] *Honon'diont, overseers* or *keepers of ceremonies,* more often women than men. The word means *They are mountains.* (Hodi'ont is masc. sing.; Godi'ont, fem. sing.).

has chosen her. A road leads from the feet of every godi'ont and hodi'ont toward heaven. Truly this is so only of they who do right before the Creator.' "

So they said and he said. Eniaiehuk.

*   *   *

SECTION 48

"Now another story.

1 "Now it was that when the people reviled me, the proclaimer of the prophecy, the impression came to me that it would be well to depart and go to Tonawanda. In that place I had relatives and friends and thought that my bones might find a resting place there. Thus I thought through the day.

"Then the messengers came to me and said 'We understand your thoughts. We will visit you more frequently and converse with you. Wherever you go take care not to be alone. Be cautious and move secretly.'

"Then the messengers told me that my life journey would be in three stages and when I entered the third I would enter into the eternity of the New World,[11] the land of our Creator. So they said." Eniaiehuk.

2 "The day was bright when I went into the planted field and alone I wandered in the planted field and it was the time of the second hoeing. Suddenly a damsel[12] appeared and threw her arms about my neck and as she clasped me she spoke saying, 'When you leave this earth for the new world above, it is our wish to follow you.' I looked for the damsel but saw only the long leaves of corn twining round my shoulders. And then I understood that it was the spirit of the corn who had spoken, she the sustainer of life. So I replied, 'O spirit of the corn, follow not me but abide still upon the earth and be strong and be faithful to your purpose. Ever endure and do not fail the children of women. It is not time for you to follow for Gai'wiio' is only in its beginning.' " Eniaiehuk.

SECTION 49

" 'Now another message to tell your people.

" 'There is a dispute in the heaven-world between two parties. It is a controversy about you, the children of earth. Two great beings are disputing—one is the Great Ruler, the Creator, and the other is the evil-minded spirit.

" 'You who are on earth do not know the things of heaven.

" 'Now the evil one said, "I am the ruler of the earth because when I command I speak but once and man obeys." '

[11] The heaven described by Ganioda'io' was called the New World because it had not been previously known. The generations before had not gone there, not having known the will of the Creator as revealed by the prophet.

[12] The Spirit of the Corn.

" 'Then answered the Great Ruler, "The earth is mine for I have created it and you have helped me in no part."

" 'Now the evil one answered, "I do not acknowledge that you have created the earth and that I helped in no part, but I say that when I say to men, 'Obey me,' they straightway obey, but they do not hear your voice."

" 'Then the Great Ruler replied, "Truly the children are my own for they have never done evil."

" 'And the evil one answering said, "Nay, the children are mine for when I bid one saying, 'Pick up that stick and strike your fellow,' they obey me quickly. Aye, the children are mine."

" 'Then was the Great Ruler very sad and he said, "Once more will I send my messengers and tell them my heart and they will tell my people and thus I will redeem my own."

" 'Then the evil one replied, "Even so it will not be long before men transgress your commands. I can destroy it with a word for they will do my bidding. Verily I delight in the name Hanïssë'ono. It is very true that they who love my name, though they be on the other side of the earth, will find me at their backs the moment they pronounce my name."

" 'Now at that time the Great Ruler spoke to the four messengers saying, "Go tell mankind that at present they must not call me Hawi'n'io', the Great Ruler, until a later time, for the Evil One calls himself the Ruler of Mankind. So now whosoever is turned into my way must say when he calls upon my name, Hodiänok'doo^n Hëd'iohe', our Creator. So also whosoever speaks the name of the evil one must say, Segoewa'tha, The Tormentor. Then will the evil one know that you have discovered who he is, for it is he who will punish the wicked when they depart from this world." [13]

So they said and he said. Eniaiehuk.

[13] A typical example of Iroquois philosophy. The Iroquois were fond of devising stories of this character and many of them reveal the subtle reasoning powers of the Indian in a striking manner.

Red Jacket's Reply to a Missionary*

The following exchange between a missionary and a Seneca leading man took place at Buffalo Creek, New York, in 1805.

In the summer of 1805, a number of the principal Chiefs and Warriors of the Six Nations, principally Senecas, assembled at Buffalo Creek, in the state of New York, at the particular request of Rev. Mr. Cram, a Missionary from the state of Massachusetts. The Missionary being furnished with an Interpreter, and accompanied by the Agent of the United States for Indian affairs, met the Indians in Council, when the following talk took place:

First, By the Agent:

"*Brothers of the Six Nations;* I rejoice to meet you at this time, and thank the Great Spirit, that he has preserved you in health, and given me another opportunity of taking you by the hand.

"*Brothers;* The person who sits by me, is a friend who has come a great distance to hold a talk with you. He will inform you what his business is, and it is my request that you would listen with attention to his words."

Missionary:

"*My Friends;* I am thankful for the opportunity afforded us of uniting together at this time. I had a great desire to see you, and inquire into your state and welfare; for this purpose I have travelled a great distance, being sent by your old friends, the Boston Missionary Society. You will recollect they formerly sent missionaries among you, to instruct you in religion, and labor for your good. Although they have not heard from you for a long time, yet they have not forgotten their brothers the Six Nations, and are still anxious to do you good.

"*Brothers;* I have not come to get your lands or your money, but to enlighten your minds, and to instruct you how to worship the Great Spirit agreeably to his mind and will, and to preach to you the gospel of his son Jesus Christ. There is but one religion, and but one way to serve God, and if you do not embrace the right way, you cannot be happy hereafter. You have never worshipped the Great Spirit in a manner acceptable to him; but have, all your lives, been in great errors and darkness. To endeavor to remove these errors, and open your eyes, so that you might see clearly, is my business with you.

"*Brothers;* I wish to talk with you as one friend talks with another; and, if you have any objections to receive the religion which I preach,

* Quoted in Wilcomb E. Washburn, *The Indian and the White Man,* Doubleday and Co., Garden City, N.Y., 1964, pp. 209–14.

I wish you to state them; and I will endeavor to satisfy your minds, and remove the objections.

"*Brothers;* I want you to speak your minds freely; for I wish to reason with you on the subject, and, if possible, remove all doubts, if there be any on your minds. The subject is an important one, and it is of consequence that you give it an early attention while the offer is made you. Your friends, the Boston Missionary Society, will continue to send you good and faithful ministers, to instruct and strengthen you in religion, if, on your part, you are willing to receive them.

"*Brothers;* Since I have been in this part of the country, I have visited some of your small villages, and talked with your people. They appear willing to receive instructions, but, as they look up to you as their older brothers in council, they want first to know your opinion on the subject.

"You have now heard what I have to propose at present. I hope you will take it into consideration, and give me an answer before we part."

After about two hours consultation among themselves, the Chief, commonly called by the white people, Red Jacket, (whose Indian name is Sagu-yu-what-hah, which interpreted is *Keeper awake*) rose and spoke as follows:

"*Friend and Brother;* It was the will of the Great Spirit that we should meet together this day. He orders all things, and has given us a fine day for our Council. He has taken his garment from before the sun, and caused it to shine with brightness upon us. Our eyes are opened, that we see clearly; our ears are unstopped, that we have been able to hear distinctly the words you have spoken. For all these favors we thank the Great Spirit; and Him *only.*

"*Brother;* This council fire was kindled by you. It was at your request that we came together at this time. We have listened with attention to what you have said. You requested us to speak our minds freely. This gives us great joy; for we now consider that we stand upright before you, and can speak what we think. All have heard your voice, and all speak to you now as one man. Our minds are agreed.

"*Brother;* You say you want an answer to your talk before you leave this place. It is right you should have one, as you are a great distance from home, and we do not wish to detain you. But we will first look back a little, and tell you what our fathers have told us, and what we have heard from the white people.

"*Brother;* Listen to what we say.

"There was a time when our forefathers owned this great island. There seats extended from the rising to the setting sun. The Great Spirit had made it for the use of Indians. He had created the buffalo, the deer, and other animals for food. He had made the bear and the beaver. Their skins served us for clothing. He had scattered them over the country, and taught us how to take them. He had caused the earth to produce corn for bread. All this He had done for his red children, because He loved them. If we had some disputes about our hunting ground, they were generally settled without the shedding of much blood. But an evil day came upon us. Your forefathers crossed the great water, and landed on this island. Their numbers were small. They found friends and not enemies. They told us they had fled from their own country for fear of wicked men, and had come here to enjoy their religion. They asked for a small seat. We took pity on them, granted their request; and they sat down amongst us. We gave them corn and meat, they gave us poison (alluding, it is supposed, to ardent spirits) in return.

"The white people had now found our country. Tidings were carried back, and more came amongst us. Yet we did not fear them. We took them to be friends. They called us brothers. We believed them, and gave them a larger seat. At length their numbers had greatly increased. They wanted more land; they wanted our country. Our eyes were opened, and our minds became uneasy. Wars took place. Indians were hired to fight against Indians, and many of our people were destroyed. They also brought strong liquor amongst us. It was strong and powerful, and has slain thousands.

"*Brother;* Our seats were once large and yours were small. You have now become a great people, and we have scarcely a place left to spread our blankets. You have got our country, but are not satisfied; you want to force your religion upon us.

"*Brother;* Continue to listen.

"You say that you are sent to instruct us how to worship the Great Spirit agreeably to his mind, and, if we do not take hold of the religion which you white people teach, we shall be unhappy hereafter. You say that you are right and we are lost. How do we know this to be true? We understand that your religion is written in a book. If it was intended for us as well as you, why has not the Great Spirit given to us, and not only to us, but why did he not give to our forefathers, the knowledge of that book, with the means of understanding it rightly? We only know what you tell us about it. How shall we know when to believe, being so often deceived by the white people?

"*Brother;* You say there is but one way to worship and serve the Great Spirit. If there is but one religion; why do you white people differ so much about it? Why not all agreed, as you can all read the book?

"*Brother;* We do not understand these things.

"We are told that your religion was given to your forefathers, and has been handed down from father to son. We also have a religion, which was given to our forefathers, and has been handed down to us their children. We worship in that way. It teaches us to be thankful for all the favors we receive; to love each other, and to be united. We never quarrel about religion.

"*Brother;* The Great Spirit has made us all, but he has made a great difference between his white and red children. He has given us different complexions and different customs. To you He has given the arts. To these He has not opened our eyes. We know these things to be true. Since He has made so great a difference between us in other things; why may we not conclude that He has given us a different religion according to our understanding? The Great Spirit does right. He knows what is best for his children; we are satisfied.

"*Brother;* We do not wish to destroy your religion, or take it from you. We only want to enjoy our own.

"*Brother;* We are told that you have been preaching to the white people in this place. These people are our neighbors. We are acquainted with them. We will wait a little while, and see what effect your preaching has upon them. If we find it does them good, makes them honest and less disposed to cheat Indians; we will then consider again of what you have said.

"*Brother;* You have now heard our answer to your talk, and this is all we have to say at present.

"As we are going to part, we will come and take you by the hand, and hope the Great Spirit will protect you on your journey, and return you safe to your friends."

As the Indians began to approach the missionary, he rose hastily from his seat and replied, that he could not take them by the hand; that there was no fellowship between the religion of God and the works of the devil.

This being interpreted to the Indians, they smiled, and retired in a peaceable manner.

It being afterwards suggested to the missionary that his reply to the Indians was rather indiscreet; he observed, that he supposed the ceremony of shaking hands would be received by them as a token that he assented to what they had said. Being otherwise informed, he said he was sorry for the expressions.

The Algonkian Prophet Tenskwatawa*

James Mooney, writing in 1892, summarized what was known from contemporary records concerning the doctrine of the Shawnee prophet Tenskwatawa (The Open Door), relative of Tecumseh.

It is impossible to know how far the prophet was responsible for the final shaping of the doctrine. Like all such movements, it undoubtedly grew and took more definite form under the hands of the apostles who went out from the presence of its originator to preach to the various tribes. A religion which found adherents alike in the everglades of Florida and on the plains of the Saskatchewan must necessarily have undergone local modifications. From a comparison of the various accounts we can arrive at a general statement of the belief.

The prophet was held to be an incarnation of Manabozho, the great "first doer" of the Algonquian system. His words were believed to be the direct utterances of a deity. Manabozho had taught his people certain modes of living best suited to their condition and capacity. A new race had come upon them, and the Indians had thrown aside their primitive purity of life and adopted the innovations of the whites, which had now brought them to degradation and misery and threatened them with swift and entire destruction. To punish them for their disobedience and bring them to a sense of their duty, Manabozho had called the game from the forests and shut it up under the earth, so that the tribes were now on the verge of starvation and obliged to eat the flesh of filthy hogs. They had also lost their old love for one another and become addicted to the secret practices of the poisoner and the wizard, together with the abominable ceremonies of the calumet dance. They must now put aside all these things, throw away the weapons and the dress of the white man, pluck out their hair as in ancient times, wear the eagle feather on their heads, and clothe themselves again with the breechcloth and the skins of animals slain with the bows and arrows which Manabozho had given them. They must have done with the white man's flint-and-steel, and cook their food over a fire made by rubbing together two sticks, and this fire must always be kept burning in their lodges, as it was a symbol of the eternal life, and their care for it was an evidence of their heed to the divine commands. The firewater must forever be put away, together with the medicine bags and poisons and the wicked juggleries which had corrupted the ancient purity of Midé rites. Instead of these the prophet gave them new songs

* James Mooney, *op. cit.*, pp. 675–76.

and new medicines. Their women must cease from any connection with white men. They were to love one another and make an end of their constant wars, to be kind to their children, to keep but one dog in a family, and to abstain from lying and stealing. If they would listen to his voice and follow his instructions, the incarnate Manabozho promised that at the end of four years (*i.e.*, in 1811) he would bring on two days of darkness, during which he would travel invisibly throughout the land, and cause the animals which he had created to come forth again out of the earth. They were also promised that their dead friends would be restored to them.

The ideas as to the catastrophe that was to usher in the new era seem to have varied according to the interpreter of the belief. Among the Ottawa, and perhaps among the lake tribes generally, there was to be a period of darkness, as already stated. Among the Cherokee, and probably also among the Creek, it was believed that there would be a terrible hailstorm, which would overwhelm with destruction both the whites and the unbelievers of the red race, while the elect would be warned in time to save themselves by fleeing to the high mountain tops. The idea of any hostile combination against the white race seems to have been no part of the doctrine. In the north, however, there is always a plain discrimination against the Americans. The Great Father, through his prophet, is represented as declaring himself to be the common parent alike of Indians, English, French, and Spaniards; while the Americans, on the contrary, "are not my children, but the children of the evil spirit. They grew from the scum of the great water, when it was troubled by an evil spirit and the froth was driven into the woods by a strong east wind. They are numerous, but I hate them. They are unjust; they have taken away your lands, which were not made for them."

A Speech by Tecumseh*

Tecumseh, the Shawnee war leader who attempted to unite the Indians of the southeast and of the Great Lakes region, is reported to have spoken as follows to Governor William Henry Harrison at a conference in 1811.

Brother: I wish you to listen to me well. As I think you do not clearly understand what I before said to you, I will explain it again. . . .

Brother, since the peace was made, you have killed some of the Shawnees, Winnebagoes, Delawares, and Miamis, and you have taken our land from us, and I do not see how we can remain at peace if you continue to do so. You try to force the red people to do some injury. It is you that are pushing them on to do mischief. You endeavor to make distinctions. You wish to prevent the Indians doing as we wish them—to unite, and let them consider their lands as the common property of the whole; you take tribes aside and advise them not to come into this measure; and until our design is accomplished we do not wish to accept of your invitation to go and see the President. The reason I tell you this, you want, by your distinctions of Indian tribes in allotting to each a particular tract of land, to make them to war with each other. You never see an Indian come and endeavor to make the white people do so. You are continually driving the red people; when, at last, you will drive them into the Great Lake, where they can't either stand or walk.

Brother, you ought to know what you are doing with the Indians. Perhaps it is by direction of the President to make those distinctions. It is a very bad thing, and we do not like it. Since my residence at Tippecanoe we have endeavored to level all distinctions—to destroy village chiefs, by whom all mischief is done. It is they who sell our lands to the Americans. Our object is to let our affairs be transacted by warriors.

Brother, this land that was sold and the goods that were given for it were only done by a few. The treaty was afterwards brought here, and the Weas were induced to give their consent because of their small numbers. The treaty at Fort Wayne was made through the threats of Winnemac; but in future we are prepared to punish those chiefs who may come forward to propose to sell the land. If

* Edward Eggleston and L. E. Seelye, *Tecumseh and the Shawnee Prophet*, Dodd, Mead and Co., N.Y., 1878, pp. 182–86.

you continue to purchase of them it will produce war among the different tribes, and at last, I do not know what will be the consequence to the white people.

Brother, I was glad to hear your speech. You said that if we could show that the land was sold by people that had no right to sell, you would restore it. Those that did sell did not own it. It was me. These tribes set up a claim, but the tribes with me will not agree with their claim. If the land is not restored to us you will see, when we return to our homes, how it will be settled. We shall have a great council, at which all the tribes will be present, when we shall show to those who sold that they had no right to the claim that they set up; and we will see what will be done to those chiefs that did sell the land to you. I am not alone in this determination; it is the determination of all the warriors and red people that listen to me. I now wish you to listen to me. If you do not, it will appear as if you wished me to kill all the chiefs that sold you the land. I tell you so because I am authorized by all the tribes to do so. I am the head of them all; I am a warrior, and all the warriors will meet together in two or three moons from this; then I will call for those chiefs that sold you the land and shall know what to do with them. If you do not restore the land, you will have a hand in killing them.

Brother, do not believe that I came here to get presents from you. If you offer us any, we will not take. By taking goods from you, you will hereafter say that with them you purchased another piece of land from us. . . . It has been the object of both myself and brother to prevent the lands being sold. Should you not return the land, it will occasion us to call a great council that will meet at the Huron village, where the council-fire has already been lighted, at which those who sold the lands shall be called, and shall suffer for their conduct.

Brother, I wish you would take pity on the red people and do what I have requested. If you will not give up the land and do cross the boundary of your present settlement, it will be very hard, and produce great troubles among us. How can we have confidence in the white people? When Jesus Christ came on earth, you killed him and nailed him on a cross. You thought he was dead, but you were mistaken. You have Shakers among you, and you laugh and make light of their worship. Everything I have said to you is the truth. The Great Spirit has inspired me, and I speak nothing but the truth to you. . . . Brother, I hope you will confess that you ought not to have listened to those bad birds who bring you bad news. I have declared myself freely to you, and if any explanation should be required from our town, send a man who can speak to us. If you think proper to give us any presents, and we can be convinced that they are given through friendship alone, we will accept them. As we intend to hold our council at the Huron village, that is near the British, we may probably make them a visit. Should they offer us any presents of goods, we will not take them; but should they offer us powder and the tomahawk, we will take the powder and refuse the tomahawk. I wish you, brother, to consider everything I have said as true, and that it is the sentiment of all the red people that listen to me.

Pushmataha's Reply to Tecumseh*

When Tecumseh sought to enlist the Choctaws and other south-eastern Indians in his cause, he was opposed by all except some Creeks. Pushmataha, leading man of the Choctaws, spoke as follows during Tecumseh's visit in 1811.

It was not my design in coming here to enter into a disputation with any one. But I appear before you, my warriors and my people not to throw in my plea against the accusations of Tecumseh; but to prevent your forming rash and dangerous resolutions upon things of highest importance, through the instigations of others. I have myself learned by experience, and I also see many of you, O Choctaws and Chickasaws, who have the same experience of years that I have, the injudicious steps of engaging in an enterprise because it is new. Nor do I stand up before you tonight to contradict the many facts alleged against the American people, or to raise my voice against them in useless accusations. The question before us now is not what wrongs they have inflicted upon our race, but what measures are best for us to adopt in regard to them; and though our race may have been unjustly treated and shamefully wronged by them, yet I shall not for that reason alone advise you to destroy them, unless it was just and expedient for you so to do; nor, would I advise you to forgive them, though worthy of your commiseration, unless I believe it would be to the interest of our common good. We should consult more in regard to our future welfare than our present. What people, my friends and countrymen, were so unwise and inconsiderate as to engage in a war of their own accord, when their own strength, and even with the aid of others, was judged unequal to the task? I well know causes often arise which force men to confront extremities, but, my countrymen, those causes do not now exist. Reflect, therefore, I earnestly beseech you, before you act hastily in this great matter, and consider with yourselves how greatly you will err if you injudiciously approve of and inconsiderately act upon Tecumseh's advice. Remember the American people are now friendly disposed toward us. Surely you are convinced that the greatest good will result to us by the adoption of and adhering to those measures I have before recommended to you; and, without giving too great a scope to mercy or forbearance, by which I could never permit myself to be seduced, I earnestly pray you to follow my advice in this weighty matter, and

* H. B. Cushman, *History of the Choctaw, Chickasaw and Natchez Indians.* Greenville, Texas, 1899, pp. 315–18.

in following it resolve to adopt those expedients for our future welfare. My friends and fellow countrymen! you now have no just cause to declare war against the American people, or wreak your vengeance upon them as enemies, since they have ever manifested feelings of friendship towards you. It is besides inconsistent with your national glory and with your honor, as a people, to violate your solemn treaty; and a disgrace to the memory of your forefathers, to wage war against the American people merely to gratify the malice of the English.

The war, which you are now contemplating against the Americans, is a flagrant breach of justice; yea, a fearful blemish on your honor and also that of your fathers, and which you will find if you will examine it carefully and judiciously, forbodes nothing but destruction to our entire race. It is a war against a people whose territories are now far greater than our own, and who are far better provided with all necessary implements of war, with men, guns, horses, wealth, far beyond that of all our race combined, and where is the necessity or wisdom to make war upon such a people? Where is our hope of success, if thus weak and unprepared we should declare it against them? Let us not be deluded with the foolish hope that this war, if begun, will soon be over, even if we destroy all the whites within our territories, and lay waste their homes and fields. Far from it. It will be but the beginning of the end that terminates in the total destruction of our race. And though we will not permit ourselves to be made slaves, or, like inexperienced warriors, shudder at the thought of war, yet I am not so insensible and inconsistent as to advise you to cowardly yield to the outrages of the whites, or willfully to connive at their unjust encroachments; but only not yet to have recourse to war, but to send ambassadors to our Great Father at Washington, and lay before him our grievances, without betraying too great eagerness for war, or manifesting any tokens of pusillanimity. Let us, therefore, my fellow countrymen, form our resolutions with great caution, and prudence upon a subject of such vast importance, and in which such fearful consequences may be involved.

Heed not, O, my countrymen, the opinions of others to that extent as to involve your country in a war that destroys its peace and endangers its future safety, prosperity and happiness. Reflect, ere it be too late, on the great uncertainty of war with the American people, and consider well, ere you engage in it, what the consequences will be if you should be disappointed in your calculations and expectations. Be not deceived with illusive hopes. Hear me, O my countrymen, if you begin this war it will end in calamities to us from which we are now free and at a distance; and upon whom of us they will fall, will only be determined by the uncertain and hazardous event. Be not, I pray you, guilty of rashness, which I never as yet have known you to be; therefore, I implore you, while healing measures are in the election of us all, not to break the treaty, nor violate your pledge or honor, but to submit our grievances, whatever they may be, to the Congress of the United States, according to the articles of the treaty existing between us and the American people. If not, I here invoke the Great Spirit, who takes cognizance of oaths, to bear me witness, that I shall endeavor to avenge myself upon the authors of this war, by whatever methods you shall set me an example. Remember we are a people who have never grown insolent with success, or become abject in adversity; but let those who invite us to hazardous attempts by uttering our praise, also know that the pleasure of hearing has never elevated our spirits above our judgment, nor an endeavor to exasperate us by a flow of invectives to be provoked the sooner to compliance. From tempers equally balanced let it be known that we are warm in the field of battle, and cool in the hours of debate; the former, because a sense of duty has the greater influence over a sedate disposition, and magnanimity the keenest sense of shame; and though good we are at debate, still our education is not polite enough to teach us a contempt of laws, yet by its severity gives us so much good sense as never to disregard them.

We are not a people so impertinently wise as to invalidate the preparations of our enemies by a plausible harangue, and then absolutely proceed to a contest; but we reckon the thoughts of the pale-faces to be of a similar cast with our own, and that hazardous contingencies are not to be determined by a speech. We always presume that the projects of our enemies are judiciously planned, and then we seriously prepare to defeat them. Nor do we found our success upon the hope that they will certainly blunder in their conduct, but upon the hope that we have omitted no proper steps for our own security. Such is the discipline which our fathers have handed down to us; and by adhering to it, we have reaped many advantages. Let us, my countrymen, not forget it now, nor in short space of time precipitately determine a question in which so much is involved. It is indeed the duty of the prudent, so long as they are not injured, to delight in peace. But it is the duty of the brave, when injured, to lay peace aside, and to have recourse to arms; and when successful in these, to then lay them down again in peaceful quiet; thus never to be elevated above measure by success in war, nor delighted with the sweets of peace to suffer insults. For he who, apprehensive of losing the delight, sits indolently at ease, will soon be deprived of the enjoyment of that delight which interesteth his fears; and he whose passions are inflamed by military success, elevated too high by a treacherous confidence, hears no longer the dictates of judgement.

Many are the schemes, though unadvisedly planned, through the more unreasonable conduct of an enemy, which turn out successful; but more numerous are those which, though seemingly founded on mature counsel, draw after them a disgraceful and opposite result. This proceeds from the great inequality of spirit with which an exploit is projected, and with which it is put into actual execution. For in council we resolve, surrounded with security: in execution we faint, through the prevalence of fear. Listen to voice of prudence, oh, my countrymen, ere you rashly act. But do as you may, know this truth, enough for you to know, I shall join our friends, the Americans, in this war.

The Doctrine of Smohalla,
Prophet of the Northwest*

Smohalla, of the "Columbia River Indians," began to preach about 1850. One account of his doctrine was recorded in the 1880s by an army officer.

I will tell you about it. Once the world was all water and God lived alone. He was lonesome, he had no place to put his foot, so he scratched the sand up from the bottom and made the land, and he made the rocks, and he made trees, and he made a man; and the man had wings and could go anywhere. The man was lonesome, and God made a woman. They ate fish from the water, and God made the deer and other animals, and he sent the man to hunt and told the woman to cook the meat and to dress the skins. Many more men and women grew up, and they lived on the banks of the great river whose waters were full of salmon. The mountains contained much game and there were buffalo on the plains. There were so many people that the stronger ones sometimes oppressed the weak and drove them from the best fisheries, which they claimed as their own. They fought and nearly all were killed, and their bones are to be seen in the hills yet. God was very angry at this and he took away their wings and commanded that the lands and fisheries should be common to all who lived upon them; that they were never to be marked off or divided, but that the people should enjoy the fruits that God planted in the land, and the animals that lived upon it, and the fishes in the water. God said he was the father and the earth was the mother of mankind; that nature was the law; that the animals, and fish, and plants obeyed nature, and that man only was sinful. This is the old law.

I know all kinds of men. First there were my people (the Indians); God made them first. Then he made a Frenchman [referring to the Canadian voyagers of the Hudson Bay company], and then he made a priest [priests accompanied these expeditions of the Hudson Bay company]. A long time after that came Boston men [Americans are thus called in the Chinook jargon, because the first of our nation came into the Columbia river in 1796 in a ship from Boston], and then King George men [the English]. Later came black men, and last God made a Chinaman with a tail. He is of no account and has to work all the time like a woman. All these are new people. Only the Indians are of the old stock. After awhile, when

* James Mooney, *op. cit.*, pp. 720–21.

God is ready, he will drive away all the people except those who have obeyed his laws.

Those who cut up the lands or sign papers for lands will be defrauded of their rights and will be punished by God's anger. Moses was bad. God did not love him. He sold his people's houses and the graves of their dead. It is a bad word that comes from Washington. It is not a good law that would take my people away from me to make them sin against the laws of God.

You ask me to plow the ground! Shall I take a knife and tear my mother's bosom? Then when I die she will not take me to her bosom to rest.

You ask me to dig for stone! Shall I dig under her skin for her bones? Then when I die I can not enter her body to be born again.

You ask me to cut grass and make hay and sell it, and be rich like white men! But how dare I cut off my mother's hair?

It is a bad law, and my people can not obey it. I want my people to stay with me here. All the dead men will come to life again. Their spirits will come to their bodies again. We must wait here in the homes of our fathers and be ready to meet them in the bosom of our mother.

DOCUMENT NO. 40

A Boarding School Experience*

Francis La Flesche, Omaha, attended a mission boarding school in the 1860s. The following is from the preface to a book which he wrote about his schoolboy years.

Among my earliest recollections are the instructions wherein we were taught respect and courtesy toward our elders; to say "thank you" when receiving a gift, or when returning a borrowed article; to use the proper and conventional term of relationship when speaking to another; and never to address any one by his personal name; we were also forbidden to pass in front of persons sitting in the tent without first asking permission; and we were strictly enjoined never to stare at visitors, particularly at strangers. To us there seemed to be no end to the things we were obliged to do, and to the things we were to refrain from doing.

From the earliest years the Omaha child was trained in the grammatical use of his native tongue. No slip was allowed to pass uncorrected, and as a result there was no child-talk such as obtains among English-speaking children,—the only difference between the speech of old and young was in the pronunciation of words which the infant often failed to utter correctly, but this difficulty was soon overcome, and a boy of ten or twelve was apt to speak as good Omaha as a man of mature years.

Like the grown folk, we youngsters were fond of companionship and of talking. In making our gamesticks and in our play, we chattered incessantly of the things that occupied our minds, and we thought it a hardship when we were obliged to speak in low tones while older people were engaged in conversation. When we entered the Mission School, we experienced a greater hardship, for there we encountered a rule that prohibited the use of our own language, which rule was rigidly enforced with a hickory rod, so that the new-comer, however socially inclined, was obliged to go about like a little dummy until he had learned to express himself in English.

All the boys in our school were given English names, because their Indian names were difficult for the teachers to pronounce. Besides, the aboriginal names were considered by the missionaries as heathenish, and therefore should be obliterated. No less heathenish in their origin were the English substitutes, but the loss of their original meaning and significance through long usage had rendered

* Francis La Flesche, *The Middle Five,* University of Wisconsin Press, Madison, 1963, pp. xvi–xx.

277

them fit to continue as appellations for civilized folk. And so, in the place of Tae-noo'-ga-wa-zhe, came Philip Sheridan; in that of Wa-pah'-dae, Uysses S. Grant; that of Koo'-we-he-ge-ra, Alexander, and so on. Our sponsors went even further back in history, and thus we had our David and Jonathan, Gideon and Isaac, and, with the flood of these new names, came Noah. It made little difference to us that we had to learn the significance of one more word as applied to ourselves, when the task before us was to make our way through an entire strange language. So we learned to call each other by our English names, and continued to do so even after we left school and had grown to manhood.

The names thus acquired by the boys are used in these sketches in preference to their own, for the reason that Indian words are not only difficult to pronounce, but are apt to sound all alike to one not familiar with the language, and the boys who figure in these pages might lose their identity and fail to stand out clearly in the mind of the reader were he obliged to continually struggle with their Omaha names.

In the talk of the boys I have striven to give a reproduction of the peculiar English spoken by them, which was composite, gathered from the imperfect comprehension of their books, the provincialisms of the teachers, and the slang and bad grammar picked up from uneducated white persons employed at the school or at the Government Agency. Oddities of speech, profanity, localisms, and slang were unknown in the Omaha language, so when such expressions fell upon the ears of these lads they innocently learned and used them without the slightest suspicion that there could be bad as well as good English.

The misconception of Indian life and character so common among the white people has been largely due to an ignorance of the Indian's language, of his mode of thought, his beliefs, his ideals, and his native institutions. Every aspect of the Indian and his manner of life has always been strange to the white man, and this strangeness has been magnified by the mists of prejudice and the conflict of interests between the two races. While these in time may disappear, no native American can ever cease to regret that the utterances of his father have been constantly belittled when put into English, that their thoughts have frequently been travestied and their native dignity obscured. The average interpreter has generally picked up his knowledge of English in a random fashion, for very few have ever had the advantage of a thorough education, and all have had to deal with the difficulties that attend the translator. The beauty and picturesqueness, and euphonious playfulness, or the gravity of diction which I have heard among my own people, and other tribes as well, are all but impossible to be given literally in English.

The talk of the older people, when they speak in this book, is, as well as I can translate it, that of every day use.

Most of the country now known as the State of Nebraska (the Omaha name of the river Platt, descriptive of its shallowness, width, and low banks) had for many generations been held and claimed by our people as their own, but when they ceded the greater part of this territory to the United States government, they reserved only a certain tract for their own use and home. It is upon the eastern part of this reservation that the scene of these sketches is laid, and at the time when the Omahas were living near the Missouri River in three villages, some four or five miles apart. The one farthest south was known as Ton'-won-ga-hae's village; the people were called "wood eaters," because they cut and sold wood to the settlers who lived near them. The middle one was Ish'-ka-da-be's village, and the people designated as "those who dwell in earth lodges," they having adhered to the aboriginal form of dwelling when they built their village. The one to the north and nearest the Mission was E-sta'-ma-za's village, and the people were known as the "make-believe white-men," because they built their houses after the fashion of the white settlers. Furniture, such as beds, chairs, tables, bureaus, etc., were not used in any of these villages, except in a few instances, while in all of them the Indian costume, language, and social customs remained as yet unmodified.

In those days the Missouri was the only highway of commerce. Toiling slowly against the swift current, laden with supplies for the trading posts and for our Mission, came the puffing little steamboats from the "town of the Red-hair," as St. Louis was called by the Indians, in memory of the auburn locks of Governor Clark, —of Lewis and Clark fame. We children used to watch these noisy boats as they forced their way through the turbid water and made a landing by running the bow into the soft bank.

The white people speak of the country at this period as "a wilderness," as though it was an empty tract without human interest or history. To us Indians it was as clearly defined then as it is to-day; we knew the boundaries of tribal lands, those of our friends and those of our foes; we were familiar with every stream, the contour of every hill, and each peculiar feature of the landscape had its tradition. It was our home, the scene of our history, and we loved it as our country.

FRANCIS LA FLESCHE

[1900]

The Ghost Dance—Wovoka*

Porcupine, a Cheyenne, visited Wovoka, the Paiute Messiah, with a delegation in the fall of 1889. The following excerpts are from Porcupine's account of what he saw and heard at Walker Lake in Nevada.

I went to the agency at Walker lake, and they told us Christ would be there in two days. At the end of two days, on the third morning, hundreds of people gathered at this place. They cleared off a place near the agency in the form of a circus ring and we all gathered there. This space was perfectly cleared of grass, etc. We waited there till late in the evening, anxious to see Christ. Just before sundown I saw a great many people, mostly Indians, coming dressed in white men's clothes. The Christ was with them. They all formed in this ring in a circle around him. They put up sheets all around the circle, as they had no tents. Just after dark some of the Indians told me that the Christ (father) was arrived. I looked around to find him, and finally saw him sitting on one side of the ring. They all started toward him to see him. They made a big fire to throw light on him. I never looked around, but went forward, and when I saw him I bent my head. . . . He sat there a long time and nobody went up to speak to him. He sat with his head bowed all the time. After awhile he rose and said he was very glad to see his children. "I have sent for you and am glad to see you. I am going to talk to you after awhile about your relatives who are dead and gone. My children, I want you to listen to all I have to say to you. I will teach you, too, how to dance a dance, and I want you to dance it. Get ready for your dance, and then when the dance is over I will talk to you." He was dressed in a white coat with stripes. The rest of his dress was a white man's, except that he had on a pair of moccasins. Then he commenced our dance, everybody joining in, the Christ singing while we danced. We danced till late in the night; then he told us we had danced enough.

The next morning after breakfast was over, we went into the circle and spread canvas over it on the ground, the Christ standing in the midst of us. He told us he was going away that day, but would be back the next morning and talk to us. . . . He had no beard or whiskers, but very heavy eyebrows. He was a good-looking man. We were crowded up very close. We had been told that nobody was to talk, and that even if we whispered the Christ would know it. . . . He would talk to us all day.

* James Mooney, *op. cit.*, pp. 803–04, 784–85.

That evening we all assembled again to see him depart. When we were assembled he began to sing, and he commenced to tremble all over violently for a while and then sat down. We danced all that night, the Christ lying down beside us apparently dead.

The next morning when we went to eat breakfast, the Christ was with us. After breakfast four heralds went around and called out that the Christ was back with us and wanted to talk with us. The circle was prepared again. The people assembled, and Christ came among us and sat down. . . .

*   *   *

"I found my children were bad, so I went back to heaven and left them. I told them that in so many hundred years I would come back to see my children. At the end of this time I was sent back to try to teach them. My father told me the earth was getting old and worn out and the people getting bad, and that I was to renew everything as it used to be and make it better."

He also told us that all our dead were to be resurrected; that they were all to come back to earth, and that, as the earth was too small for them and us, he would do away with heaven and make the earth itself large enough to contain us all; that we must tell all the people we met about these things. He spoke to us about fighting, and said that was bad and we must keep from it; that the earth was to be all good hereafter, and we must all be friends with one another. He said that in the fall of the year the youth of all good people would be renewed, so that nobody would be more than forty years old; and that if they behaved themselves well after this the youth of everyone would be renewed in the spring. He said if we were all good he would send people among us who could heal all our wounds and sickness by mere touch and that we would live forever. He told us not to quarrel or fight or strike each other, or shoot one another; that the whites and Indians were to be all one people. He said if any man disobeyed what he ordered his tribe would be wiped from the face of the earth; that we must believe everything he said, and we must not doubt him or say he lied; that if we did, he would know it; that he would know our thoughts and actions in no matter what part of the world we might be.

The Ghost Dance Among the Sioux*

Short Bull, a Sioux, returned from a visit to Wovoka to become a leader of the Ghost Dance ceremonies on the Pine Ridge Reservation. There he delivered the following sermon in October, 1890, which reveals the transformation which Wovoka's teaching underwent in the hands of the Sioux.

My friends and relations: I will soon start this thing in running order. I have told you that this would come to pass in two seasons, but since the whites are interfering so much, I will advance the time from what my father above told me to do, so the time will be shorter. Therefore you must not be afraid of anything. Some of my relations have no ears, so I will have them blown away.

Now, there will be a tree sprout up, and there all the members of our religion and the tribe must gather together. That will be the place where we will see our dead relations. But before this time we must dance the balance of this moon, at the end of which time the earth will shiver very hard. Whenever this thing occurs, I will start the wind to blow. We are the ones who will then see our fathers, mothers, and everybody. We the tribe of Indians, are the ones who are living a sacred life. God, our father himself, has told and commanded and shown me to do these things.

Our father in heaven has placed a mark at each point of the four winds. First, a clay pipe, which lies at the setting of the sun and represents the Sioux tribe. Second, there is a holy arrow lying at the north, which represents the Cheyenne tribe. Third, at the rising of the sun there lies hail, representing the Arapaho tribe. Fourth, there lies a pipe and nice feather at the south, which represents the Crow tribe. My father has shown me these things, therefore we must continue this dance. If the soldiers surround you four deep, three of you, on whom I have put holy shirts, will sing a song, which I have taught you, around them, when some of them will drop dead. Then the rest will start to run, but their horses will sink into the earth. The riders will jump from their horses, but they will sink into the earth also. Then you can do as you desire with them. Now, you must know this, that all the soldiers and that race will be dead. There will be only

* James Mooney, *ibid.*, pp. 788–89.

five thousand of them left living on the earth. My friends and relations, this is straight and true.

Now, we must gather at Pass Creek where the tree is sprouting. There we will go among our dead relations. You must not take any earthly things with you. Then the men must take off all their clothing and the women must do the same. No one shall be ashamed of exposing their persons. My father above has told us to do this, and we must do as he says. You must not be afraid of anything. The guns are the only things we are afraid of, but they belong to our father in heaven. He will see that they do not harm. Whatever white men may tell you, do not listen to them, my relations. This is all. I will now raise my hand up to my father and close what he has said to you through me.

A Creek Observer on the Effects of Allotment*

Pleasant Porter, a leading man of the Creek Nation, described to an investigating committee in 1897 what he saw as the effects of the work of the Dawes Commission on the Five Civilized Tribes.

It was a mistake to have changed these people's relations with the government. . . . The Indians . . . haven't had time to grow up to that individuality which is necessary to merge them with the American citizen. The change came too soon for them. . . . There will be a remnant that will survive, but the balance is bound to perish, do what you may for them. There is that sense of right and wrong which will bind men together and preserve the peace and maintain virtue and provide for offense without. That is the institution out of which a nation grows. Each of these groups [the Five Tribes] must have had that; but you rub that out, you transplant them into what they have no knowledge of; . . . there is no life in the people that have lost their institutions. Evolving a thing out of itself is natural, transplanting it is a matter of dissolution, not growth. There may be a few that will grow . . . but the growth will not be natural; and I don't see anything now that it has gone this far but to come to it heroically and pay no regard now to our prejudices or sentiment; do the matter up in a business-like way, for every delay changes conditions. . . .

If we had our own way we would be living with lands in common, and we would have these prairies all open, and our little bunches of cattle, and would have bands of deer that would jump up from the head of every hollow, and flocks of turkeys running up every hillside, and every stream would be full of sun perch. Those things are what we were used to in our early life. That is what we would have; and not so much corn and wheat growing, and things of that kind. But we came up against it; this civilization came up against us and we had no place to go.

Q. You told us a moment ago they were dying off pretty fast?

A. Yes, sir, the older people are.

Q. Is there any special cause for that?

A. Nothing; there is no new disease; I don't see anything other than the want of hope.

* Indian Territory Division Files, 4412/04, pp. 127–31. Quoted in Angie Debo, *And Still the Waters Run,* Princeton Univ. Press, Princeton, N.J., 1940, pp. 131–32.

A Cherokee Delegation Writes Home from Washington*

In 1895 a delegation of Cherokees opposing the work of the Dawes Commission in Washington wrote a letter to Principal Chief Mayes of the Cherokee Nation analyzing the situation of the Five Civilized Tribes.

Yet, in the struggle to shield our country from the calamities which the scheme contemplated by the friends of the Dawes report would certainly bring upon it, we had to labor under great disadvantages. It did seem as if the world was about to rise in arms against us. We saw that even the press had been largely subsidized in favor of the dissolution of our government and the invasion of our rights. Before the committee on territories of the House, in order to make the impression on members of Congress that the people of the several tribes were in favor of a territorial government, it was stated by lobbyists sent from Ardmore that there were fifty-five newspapers in Indian Territory, and that all of them excepting five were in favor of a territorial government. But care was taken not to let it be known that all these papers favoring a territorial government had been mounted[?] in the Indian Territory either by intruders or non-citizen white men for the express purpose of subverting the governments of the Indians and turning the country over into the hands of speculators and inferior politicians, who imagine that, in event of such change as they contemplate for the Indian country, they would be importuned to fill the territorial offices, and possibly to represent the dear people in the halls of Congress. Nevertheless, these papers have their influence. They are circulated at Washington as well as throughout the country at large. We met with some of them in the Department of Justice, where officers of the Government appeared to have formed their opinions in reference to our country from the stories told in their columns. . . . While we on our side of the great debate between the United States and the Cherokee Nation, have, for the most part, supinely rested in the belief that all was peace and safety, they with a zeal which knew no pause, have been sapping the very foundations of our government.

Furthermore, many of the great dailies that a few years ago

---

* Cherokee Papers, Report of S. W. Gray, Roach Young and J. F. Thompson to Hon. S. H. Mayes, 1895. Quoted in Angie Debo, *op. cit.*, pp. 27–30.

pleaded so persistently for the liberation of the slaves, are now insisting upon "opening" our country for the settlement and occupancy of the whites. Still further, as an evidence of the influence which the press has against us, even benevolent associations which were organized a few year[s] ago to urge Congress to keep the treaties which had been made with Indian tribes, are now advising the erection of a territorial government in our country and allotment of our lands in violation of our treaties and without our consent. It is worthy of remark, too, as indicating the course of public sentiment in relation to our country, that even the pulpit, which some time ago, was so exuberant of love for the slave has no good word to speak in behalf of the Indians of Indian Territory. No church assembly now passes resolutions against a violation of our treaties, the abrogation of our government and an invasion of our right of property. . . .

Under these circumstances, we cannot refrain from the indulgence of a reflection. The history of human affairs convinces us that it is always a misfortune to hold the position of a weaker party. East of the Mississippi we were a happy people. The United States wanted our country there; reluctantly we parted with it, and to this day have not received all that was promised us for it. The Government wanted the six million acres of our strip lands;[1] we agreed to part with those lands, but the terms of the agreement entered into at Tahlequah and ratified by act of the National Council, were changed by act of Congress without our consent, and yet, after changing those terms to its own liking, the Government has not complied with them. And now, they want us to enter into another agreement—an agreement with the Dawes Commission. But what assurance have we, even if we were disposed to come to an agreement with that Commission, that the terms of such agreement would not be swept aside and others, to which we could never assent, imposed upon us? We think it would be but fair on [the] part of the Government to comply with the agreements already made with our people, before asking us to enter into others of a nature more serious in their character than any hitherto proposed.

. . . [With regard to the failure of the United States to carry out a recent pledge to remove the intruders—] The newspapers, too, are interesting themselves in the matter. The question has been raised as to where the intruders can go, if they are to be removed from our country, as if their were no space on the continent outside of our lands, where even millions can find homes, if they only have a desire to do so. . . . We opine, however, that the same energy which they have displayed in their efforts to wrest from us a large portion of our property, will enable them to acquire homes even amongst the most astute of their fellow citizens. But there seems to be a sinister motive for keeping the intruders in our country. It was the

[1] Lands in Oklahoma Territory opened to white settlement in 1893.

contents of the wooden horse emptied inside the walls of Troy, that enabled the Greeks to take that ancient city.

It is seen by the keen eye of speculation, that, if our country were revolutionized as contemplated in the scheme of the Dawes Commission, it would become easy for capitalists and monied men of less degree to soon become the owners of millions. But what about the other side? What about our people, who are, now, the legal owners and sovereigns of these lands? Why the question is [e]asy of answer. Crushed to earth under the hoofs of business gread, they would soon become a homeless throng, more scoffed at and abused than a Coxey's army. No territorial or state legislation can protect the Indian in his rights. Business has no moral consciousness; when a statute comes in its way, it will invoke the aid of a 'higher law' and grasp the Indian's property anyhow.

. . . It is wonderful, too, to see with what unanimity the papers exclaim that *"Carthage must be destroye[d]."* . . . Even the heavy Quarterlies, such as the *North American Review,* are being operated in the interests of our enemies. . . .

. . . As far as the Indian people are concerned, the present are days to try men's souls; and he who is made of stuff so lofty of nature, as to rise superior to all selfish considerations, and, in face of the popular clamor of the times, boldly speak out in favor of the rights and freedom of the Indians, becomes an object worthy to be venerated by the good and great in all lands.

The Native American Church*

In 1944 after many years of conflict with missionaries and the Bureau of Indian Affairs the main body of the Native American Church was incorporated. Following are the preamble and the articles of incorporation.

Whereas, The "human rights" of all citizens of our country are guarranteed and protected by amendment 1 to the Constitution of our Country, and

Whereas, The Indians of the United States, we contend, are likewise protected by, and come within the meaning of and the protection of the Constitution, and

Whereas, These members of the Indian Tribes of the United States belonging to the Native American Church, do by these presents declare and publish to the world that they too, in the exercise of their native religion, call upon all liberty loving people of our country for tolerance, and that they likewise too, declare their inherent right to protection in the free exercise of their religious beliefs and in the unmolested practice of the rituals thereof, under amendment 1 to the Constitution of the United States and in the further pursuance thereof, do hereby propose the adoption of the following, to wit:

1. That the National name of our church shall be "The Native American Church of the United States."

2. That we as a people place explicit faith, hope and belief in Almighty God, and declare full, competent and everlasting faith in our church through which and by which we worship God.

3. That as a people, we pledge our faith and our allegiance and our lives if need be, as we are now doing, to the protection of our now common Country, its institutions and the Constitution and Government thereof.

4. That we further pledge ourselves to work in unity for, with and through the sacramental use of peyote and its religious use as such by "The Native American Church of the United States" to the interest of and the cause of religion and the cause of our fellowmen, wherever they may be, and in allegiance to the Church to be chartered and recognized by the United States of America as follows:

We, therefore, recommend that the original Articles of Incorporation of "The Native American Church" and the amendments thereto, now on file in the office of the Secretary of States of the State of Oklahoma, be amended to carry out the purposes set forth in this

* J. S. Slotkin, *The Peyote Religion: A Study in Indian-White Relations,* Free Press, Glencoe, Ill., 1956, pp. 137–39.

preamble and we, the undersigned, being all of the officers and trustees of the aforesaid corporation, do by these presents amend the aforesaid original Articles and amendments thereto in the following particulars, to wit:

AMENDED ARTICLES OF INCORPORATION

ARTICLE I

The name of this corporation shall be and remain "The Native American Church of the United States. (formerly "Native American Church.")

ARTICLE II

The purpose for which this corporation is formed is to foster and promote religious believers in Almighty God and the customs of the several Tribes of Indians throughout the United States in the worship of a Heavenly Father and to promote morality, sobriety, industry, charity, and the right living and cultivate a spirit of self-respect and brotherly love and union among the members of the several Tribes of Indians throughout the United States, with the right to own and hold property for the purpose of conducting its business or services.

ARTICLE III

That the place where the principal business of the corporation is to be transacted is at El Reno, Oklahoma.

ARTICLE IV

The number of trustees of the corporation shall be five, and until their successors are elected and qualified, shall consist of one member of said Church, for each Tribe throughout the United States belonging to or incorporated as a member of said Church.

ARTICLE V

The said corporation shall consist of as many subdivisions as are Tribes represented in its membership and which said separate Tribe shall each in turn seek recognition in their respective States by applying for Charters in accordance with the laws of their respective States but that the name of the parent organization shall be "The Native American Church of the United States."

The National Congress of American Indians*

In 1944 a national association of Indians was founded which was called the National Congress of American Indians. The membership was exclusively Indian. In 1954 the organization was incorporated. Following is the preamble to the constitution.

We, the members of Indian tribes of the United States of America invoking the Divine guidance of Almighty God in order to secure to ourselves—the Indians of the United States and the Natives of Alaska—and our descendants the rights and benefits to which we are entitled under the laws of the United States, the several states thereof, and the Territory of Alaska; to enlighten the public toward a better understanding of the Indian people; to preserve Indian cultural values; to seek an equitable adjustment of tribal affairs and tribal claims; to secure and to preserve rights under Indian treaties or agreements with, the United States; to promote the common welfare of the American Indian and to foster the continued loyalty and allegiance of American Indians to the flag of the United States do establish this organization and adopt the following Constitution and By-Laws.

* National Congress of American Indians Brochure, Washington, D.C., 1957.

A Hopi Religious Movement*

A part of the Hopi tribe, sometimes called "traditionalists," expressed their point of view to the President of the United States in 1949.

Hopi Indian Empire
Oraibi, Arizona
March 28, 1949

THE PRESIDENT
The White House
Washington, D.C.

TO THE PRESIDENT:

We, the hereditary Hopi Chieftains of the Hopi Pueblos of Hotevilla, Shungopovy, and Mushongopavy humbly request a word with you.

Thoroughly acquainted with the wisdom and knowledge of our traditional form of government and our religious principles, sacredly authorized and entrusted to speak, act, and to execute our duties and obligations for all the common people throughout this land of the Hopi Empire, in accordance with the fundamental principles of life which were laid down for us by our Great Spirit, Masau'u and by our forefathers, we hereby assembled in the Hopi Pueblo of Shungopovy on March 9, 13, 26, and 28 of this year 1949 for the purpose of making known to the government of the United States and others in this land that the Hopi Empire is still in existence, its traditional path unbroken and its religious order intact and practiced, and the Stone Tablets, upon which are written the boundaries of the Hopi Empire are still in the hands of the Chiefs of Oraibi and Hotevilla Pueblos.

Firmly believing that the time has now come for us the highest leaders of our respective pueblos to speak and to reexamine ourselves, our sacred duties, our past and present deeds, to look to the future and to study carefully all the important and pressing policies that are coming to us from Indian Bureau at the present time, we met here.

What we say is from our hearts. We speak truths that are based upon our own tradition and religion. We speak as the first people in this land you call America. And we speak to you, a white man, the

---

* Quoted in Arnold M. Rose (editor), *Race Prejudice and Discrimination: Readings in Intergroup Relations in the United States,* Alfred A. Knopf Publisher, New York, 1951, pp. 42–48.

last people who came to our shores seeking freedom of worship, speech, assembly and a right to life, liberty and the pursuit of happiness. And we are speaking to all the American Indian people.

Today we, Hopi and white man, come face to face at the cross-road of our respective life. At last our paths have crossed and it was foretold it would be at the most critical time in the history of mankind. Everywhere people are confused. What we decide now and do hereafter will be the fate of our respective people. Because we Hopi leaders are following our traditional instructions we must make our position clear to you and we expect you to do the same to us.

Allow us to mention some of the vital issues which have aroused us to action and which we recognize to be the last desperate move on the part of the leaders in Washington, D.C. They are as follows:

1. From the Land Claims Commission in Washington, D.C. a letter requesting us to file in our claim to land we believed we are entitled to before the five-year limit beginning August 13, 1946 is expired. We are told that after the five-year limit is expired we can not file any claim.

2. We are being told by the Superintendent at Keams Canyon Agency about leasing of our land to some Oil Companies to drill for oil. We are told to make decision on whether to lease out our land and control all that goes with it or we may be refused to do so. But, we were told if we refused then these Oil Companies might send their smart lawyers to Washington, D.C. for the purpose of inducing some Senators and Congressmen to change certain laws that will take away our rights and authority to our land and placing that authority in another department where they will be leasing out our land at will.

3. We've heard that a $90,000,000 is being appropriated for the purpose of carrying out the provisions of the Act No. S.2363 which reads: To promote the rehabilitation of the Navajo and Hopi Tribes of Indians and the better utilization of the resources of the Navajo and Hopi Indian Reservation, and for other purpose.

4. Recently we were told about the Hoover Commission's proposal to Congress the launching of a program to convert the country's 400,000 Indians into "full, tax-paying citizens" under state jurisdiction.

5. Now we heard about the North Atlantic security treaty which would bind the United States, Canada, and six European nations to an alliance in which an attack against one would be considered an attack against all.

Now these vital issues coming to us from Washington touch the very core of the Hopi life, a peaceful life. By this we know it is time for us to speak and act. It is now time for us as highest leaders of our respective people to come to a definite understanding of our positions before we go forward into the future and before you embark upon your new program. We want the people everywhere to know our stand, the Hopi people. It is of utmost importance that we do this now.

The Hopi form of government was established solely upon religious and traditional grounds. The divine plan of life in this land was laid down for us by our Great Spirit, Masau'u. This plan cannot be changed. The Hopi life is all set according to the fundamental principles of life of this divine plan. We can not do otherwise but to follow this plan. There is no other way for us. We also know that the white people and all other races everywhere are following certain traditional and religious principles. What have they done with them? Now we are all talking about the judgment day. We all are aware of that fact because we are all going to that same point no matter what religion we believed in. In the light of our Hopi prophecy it is going to take place here and will be completed in the Hopi Empire. So for this reason we urge you to give these thoughts your most careful consideration and to reexamine your past deeds and future plans. Again we say let us set our house in order now.

This land is a sacred home of the Hopi people and all the Indian Race in this land. It was given to the Hopi people the task to guard this land not by force of arms, not by killing, not by confiscating of properties of others, but by humble prayers, by obedience to our traditional and religious instructions and by being faithful to our Great Spirit Masau'u. We are still a sovereign nation. Our flag still flies throughout our land (our ancient ruins). We have never abandoned our sovereignty to any foreign power or nation. We've been self-governing people long before any white man came to our shores. What Great Spirit made and planned no power on earth can change.

The boundaries of our Empire were established permanently and were written upon Stone Tablets which are still with us. Another was given to his white brother who after emerging of the first people to this new land went east with the understanding that he will return with his Stone Tablet to the Hopis. These Stone Tablets when put together and if they agree will prove to the whole world that this land truly belongs to the Hopi people and that they are true brothers. Then the white brother will restore order and judge all the people here who have been unfaithful to their traditional and religious principles and who have mistreated his people.

Now, we ask you Mr. President, the American people and you, our own people, American Indians, to give these words of ours your most serious considerations. Let us all reexamine ourselves and see where we stand today. Great Spirit, Masau'u has granted us the Indians, the first right to this land. This is our sacred soil.

Today we are being asked to file our land claims in the Land Claims Commission in Washington, D.C. We, as hereditary Chieftains of the Hopi Tribe, can not and will not file any claims according to the Provisions set up by Land Claims Commission because we have never been consulted in regards to setting up these provisions. Besides we have already laid claim to this whole western hemisphere long before Columbus's great, great grandmother was born. We will not ask a white man, who came to us recently, for a piece of land that is already ours. We think that white people should be thinking about asking for a permit to build their homes upon our land.

Neither will we lease any part of our land for oil development at this time. This land is not for leasing or for sale. This is our sacred soil. Our true brother has not yet arrived. Any prospecting, drilling and leasing on our land that is being done now is without our knowledge and consent. We will not be held responsible for it.

We have been told that there is a $90,000,000 being appropriated by the Indian Bureau for the Hopi and Navajo Indians. We have heard of other large appropriations before but where all that money goes we have never been able to find out. We are still poor, even poorer because of the reduction of our land, stock, farms, and it seems as though the Indian Bureau or whoever is planning new lives for us now is ready to reduce us, the Hopi people, under this new plan. Why, we do not need all that money and we do not ask for it. We are self-supporting people. We are not starving. People starve only when they neglect their farms or when they become too lazy to work. Maybe the Indian Bureau is starving. Maybe a Navajo is starving. They are asking for it. True, there are the aged, the blind and the crippled need help. So we will not accept any new theories that the Indian Bureau is planning for our lives under this new appropriation. Neither will we abandon our homes.

Now we cannot understand why since its establishment the government of the United States has taken over everything we owned either by force, bribery, trickery, and sometimes by reckless killing, making himself very rich, and after all these years of neglect of the American Indians have the courage today in announcing to the world a plan which will "convert the country's 400,000 Indians into 'full, tax-paying citizens' under state jurisdiction." Are you ever going to be satisfied with all the wealth you have now because of us the Indians? There is something terribly wrong with your system of government because after all these years, we the Indians are still licking on the bones and crumbs that fall to us from your tables. Have you forgotten the meaning of Thanksgiving Day? Have the American people, white people, forgotten the treaties with the Indians, your duties and obligations as guardians?

Now we have heard about the Atlantic security treaty which we understood will bind the United States, Canada and six other European nations to an alliance in which an attack against one would be considered an attack against all.

We, the traditional leaders want you and the American people to know that we will stand firmly upon our traditional and religious grounds. And that *we will not bind* ourselves to any foreign nation at this time. Neither will we go with you on a wild and reckless adventure which we know will lead us only to a total ruin. Our Hopi form of government is all set and ready for such eventuality. We have met all other rich and powerful nations who have come to our shores, from the Early Spanish Conquistadors down to the present government of the United States all of whom have used force in trying to wipe out our existence here in our own home. We want to come to our own destiny in our own way. We have no enemy. We will neither show our bows and arrows to anyone at this time. This is our only way to everlasting life and happiness. Our tradition and religious training forbid us to harm, kill and molest anyone. We, therefore, objected to our boys being forced to be trained for war to become murderers and destroyers. It is you who should protect us. What nation who has taken up arms ever brought peace and happiness to his people?

All the laws under the Constitution of the United States were made without our consent, knowledge, and approval, yet we are being forced to do everything that we know are contrary to our religious principles and those principles of the Constitutions of the United States.

Now we ask you, American people, what has become of your religion and your tradition? Where do we stand today? The time has now come for all of us as leaders of our people to reexamine ourselves, our past deeds, and our future plans. The judgment day will soon be upon us. Let us make haste and set our house in order before it is too late.

We believe these to be truths and from our hearts and for these reasons we, Hopi Chieftains, urge you to give these thoughts your most earnest considerations. And after a thorough and careful consideration we want to hear from you at your earliest convenience. This is our sacred duty to our people. We are

Sincerely yours,

CHIEF TALAHAFTEWA, *Village Chief, Bear Clan, Shungopovy*
BASOWAYA, *Advisor, Katchin Clan, Shungopovy*
ANDREW HERMEQUAFTEWA, *Advisor, Blue Bird Clan, Shungopovy*
CHIEF SACKMASA, *Village Crier, Coyote Clan, Mushongopavy*
CHIEF JAMES PENGAYAWYMA, *Village Chief, Kokop Clan (fire), Hotevilla*
CHIEF DAN KATCHONGOVA, *Advisor, co-ruler, Sun Clan, Hotevilla*

A Tribal Council Chairman's Views*

Chairmen of Tribal Councils were frequently oriented in greater or lesser degree toward cultural assimilation. The following letter from Chairman Paul Jones of the Navajo Tribal Council was written in reply to Oliver La Farge, President of the Association on American Indian Affairs in 1955.

Dear Mr. LaFarge:

I regret that the pressure of duties has delayed my answering your first inquiry and the joint statements of June 26th by your association and three other associations interesting themselves in Indian affairs, which has apparently been followed by a subsequent release on the same subject dated "August–September 1955". I have given careful thought to your criticism of the present policy of the Commissioner of Indian Affairs, particularly his release of May 16th liberalizing the past policy in respect to patenting allotted lands to competent Indians, and have endeavored, in consideration with associates, to weigh your criticism against the apparent objectives of the Bureau of Indian Affairs.

My comments may be summarized as follows:

1. Few problems in Indian affairs can be answered in black or white, and certainly not this one. Here in Navajoland, as you well know, we have been engaged over many years in a quest for education and my acquaintanceship with Indians of other tribes has made me aware of similar efforts elsewhere. Innumerable individuals among the Indian tribes have progressed by means of education which they or their families have somehow earned or secured, toward complete self-sufficiency, independence, and freedom of American citizenship in all the fullest meaning of the word.

Perhaps the most conspicuous mark of the type of freedom and independence I refer to is home ownership. We have a great demand for home ownership on this reservation, particularly among the younger people and the veterans who have come back from the war. There has been deep frustration over the fact that they cannot even have the benefits of the G. I. Bill to the extent of getting Federal Housing Administration loans to finance the construction of homes for themselves and their families simply because there is no security which can be offered to a lending institution by way of a mortgage on individual property. There is no individual property. It is all tribal property.

* *The New York Times*, Letter to the Editor, October 30, 1955, p. 59.

Let me say at once that the vast reaches of our 16 million acre reservation are, for the most part, incapable of individual ownership, because the grazing capacity is so limited (about 22 acres needed for one sheep) that only by moving flocks over considerable areas of land can Navajo families get the maximum use of the tribal property.

A great exception is the allotted land areas west of the reservation and at other points around the reservation. Among the Navajos occupying these allotted areas are many who wish to have fee ownership of their interests for the sake of leasing them for uranium developments or oil leases, or just for general purposes of grazing or farming operations. I suppose the desire for individual ownership is very deep in most of us. Can anyone really say that this is evil or contrary to the best interests of the innumerable Indians who are moving toward complete self-realization and independence through economic self-sufficiency?

Do you own your own home? Do not the overwhelming majority of your directors and members of your association own their own homes? Many of us would like to do likewise and I have under consideration at this time, proposing legislation to the next Congress, a bill which would authorize the establishment of town sites at the growing communities in the Navajo Reservation now hold dewn in undeveloped condition where no Navajo and no outsider will make a substantial investment in buildings because they must stand on tribal property and cannot, at the present time, get adequate protection except by a 25-year lease. Our younger people would find satisfaction for their aspirations toward home-owning if they could buy land in such town sites, particularly those who are employed in the uranium mines, mills, lumber operations, or other commercial activities in these communities.

For these reasons, we may soon be asking the Commissioner of Indian Affairs to authorize patents in fee under such new laws.

2. There is undoubtedly, at many points, a conflict between tribal or communal operation of lands and requests for individual ownership of Indian lands. Those of us who are in official positions in tribal organizations are pulled both ways in this matter. I certainly desire to preserve our tribal traditions and practices, but this should not preclude—and certainly has not prevented the steady rise of the individual seeking a way of life more consistent with the American pattern in the communities surrounding them. I do not think that it is for any organization to decide, no matter how well meaning it may be, that the Indians must, of necessity, be preserved in a museum of collective or tribal ownership and practice if they do not wish it.

Undoubtedly, there will be casualties among the individuals who move off among the white men to live and do business in the ordinary way of other American citizens in the surrounding communities. However, we must confront the fact that there are casualties among the white men too. The price of freedom is the liability of taking a blow occasionally as well as the privilege of enjoying economic success and independence. It is perfectly clear historically that the paternalism of the Bureau of Indian Affairs has not developed independence or well being among the Indians, but has been inclined to develop a certain dependence or intellectual pauperism and a lack of initiative. Initiative is one of the main characteristics of American life and many thousands of our Indians are capable of it. Your remarks are always addressed to the tribal welfare but what have you done by way of trying to trace the fortunes of the many thousands of Indians who have moved into American life quite successfully?

When you speak of the alienation of land under the Allotment Act of 1887, stopped by Secretary Ickes after some 91 million acres of land had been alienated, is there any way of your determining how much of this alienation facilitated the establishment of Indian owners in independent economies? Land is capital and many of these patents in fee may have founded successful Indian families. In other words, the mere fact that the lands were alienated is not conclusively wrong.

No doubt during all those years, under the Allotment Act of 1887, there were conflicts between individual ownership and tribal interests in lands just as there will be in the acts which are referred to terminating or seeking to terminate Indian tribal ownership to make way for individual ownership. My point is that the individuals are pressing hard for their individual rights and most of them would like to acquire those same Indian lands for their homes in the Indian communities although they clearly would have the right, as American citizens, to traffic in those lands as others do. No man can be free and independent unless he owns his own property.

3. In objecting to facilitating patents in fee, I do not find reference in any of your statement to a very grave problem in respect to allotted lands. The heirs to allotted parcels are accumulating very rapidly. I believe I am right in saying there are several hundred thousand, and every time children are born in one of the families, the interests are further divided. I do not suppose the Commissioner's policy would solve this problem which is already rather overwhelming in its proportions, but at least it would stop its steady increase insofar as lands are concerned for which patents are issued. Have you ever given thought to finding a constructive solution for this problem of divided interest in allotted lands?

4. You say in criticizing the Commissioner's policy in your latest release: "If the land to be patented and sold out of Indian ownership contains the only water acceptable to the Tribe for irrigation, let the Tribe go dry. If it contains the only entry to tribal grazing lands, let the herds go up unpastured. If the tribal land base is destroyed, let the Indians stop being Indians."

It happens that we have known the Commissioner of Indian Affairs,

Glenn L. Emmons, intimately over a period of many years and I must state quite frankly that this is an unreasonable, if not hysterical, description of his policy. While my reading of his release of May 16th leads to the perfectly clear conclusion that in the quest for individual rights and independence which certainly marks the development of the Indian population of this country today, the Commissioner has sought to give an increased measure of fulfillment to those who seek the ownership of their own allotted lands, he certainly does not trample underfoot all other interests. The concluding line of the release says, "In critical cases which may seriously affect the protection and use of Indian lands remaining in trust status, and when in your judgment the application of a competent Indian for a patent in fee should be denied, you should submit the case to this office with your recommendation for an exception to this policy."

Quite clearly all other interests are not to be trampled underfoot.

It might be appropriate to refer to the old adage that one cannot make an omelet without breaking eggs. Certain breaks with past policy would seem to be inevitable. One break of the present Commissioner, Glenn L. Emmons, for which we Navajos will be forever grateful, is the inability of the Bureau over successive decades to give schools to the Navajos. In two years the present Commissioner, with the backing of Congress, has secured a seat in school for every child of school age. For the first time in history Navajos can go to school.

5. We have grave problems in respect to allotments on or about the Navajo reservation. One by one cases have been brought to my attention in which Navajo allottees were persuaded by the government to surrender their allotment interest by promises of other allotments in lieu thereof, only to find that they lost everything and gained nothing. There have been no lieu lands instead of what they lost. In many cases, these are invaluable mineral areas. These Navajos would not have lost their lands had they been patented, but as the matter stands, there is now no legal remedy for them.

Furthermore, the attempts to consolidate their lands in the area commonly called the checkerboard area east of the reservation may or may not have been to their best interests. You speak of the federal government and the Indian tribe having spent "millions of dollars in recent years to consolidate their grazing and timber lands". During the period of complete domination of the Bureau of Indian Affairs, namely in the 1930s under John Collier and your present assistant, Mr. Wm. K. Zimmerman Jr., Assistant Commissioner, who later served as Commissioner of Indian Affairs, in the last administration, many exchanges were made which were clearly to the advantage of the white man in those areas. We are examining this entire picture in order to advise our Navajos correctly in the future, and we are even now presented with cases in which Navajos have even in recent years been persuaded to surrender their allotted interests only to find that the Bureau of Land Management was incapable of getting other lands for them. Again some of the lands surrendered or in the process of being surrendered had valuable mineral rights.

Now that the Tribe is better organized and has an effective legal department and a thoroughly competent tribal mining engineer and a director of Land Use and Surveys, we are finding that all of these policies of the past were certainly not universally to the benefit of the Navajos.

Our experience strongly points to the conclusion that enlightened self-interest and self-help by the tribe in protecting its own affairs and the interest of its members, is far more effective than paternalism we have known in the past. Individuals have also suffered substantial disadvantages in not protecting their own interests—in not knowing how to do so, and of course they could not know without education. They had only paternalism to rely upon.

I make these observations because again it is certainly not clear that we can defend now the policy, Secretary Ickes and John Collier lauded in your release, and denounce the Allotment Act of 1887 as an unmitigated evil.

CONCLUSION

In a letter of August 5th enclosing your release of August–September 1955, you say that your association "pledged itself to the Indian tribal councils, on July 1, to tell their fellow-citizens of this surprise blow in the Bureau's remorseless campaign to end the Indian's right to be Indian."

This can only be described as hysterical. From the point of view of many years of observation of Indian Affairs, in addition to intimate personal experience with the Navajos, in the Bureau of Indian Affairs, as interpreter in court and as an American citizen generally, I am constrained to observe that the policy of this administration in opening the door for competent Indians to find their way into the stream of American economic life just like other citizens, is a decision of courage and wisdom. If there should be any diminution in the total holdings of Indian tribes and Indians by reason of the new policy permitting patents in fee of allotted lands, any honest view of the matter would have to credit statistically on the Indian side the lands held by the allottees or bought by Indians for homes and farms. Neither your organization, its affiliates, or the Bureau of Indian Affairs can begin to measure the ownership of individual Indians in the communities of this country, but thousands of such ownerships measure the success of "competent" Indians in moving into the stream of American life and enjoying and exercising the rights, benefits and responsibilities of citizenship just like other American citizens.

Actually, rehabilitation is an individual matter. Education, self-reliance, and economic independence, are incidents of individual development among Indians just as they are among other citizens. Policies in the past have demonstrated rather overwhelmingly that no matter how much money is spent, the government cannot buy rehabilitation of a whole Tribe; it can buy education·and facilitate self-effort and individual initiative so that individual Indians and their families take their places in the American community like other families. Home ownership becomes a natural objective. Incidentally, at this point you lose sight of these innumerable Indians who attain real independence and so does the Bureau of Indian Affairs.

The allotted land policy of permitting patents in fee may well be one of the transition steps for innumerable individual Indians. Enough has been said to indicate that the wrongness of the Commissioner's policy is by no means as easy to prove as your release would seem to suggest. The Commissioner's farsighted policies in respect to other matters, and his achievements in two years of what preceeding generations of Commissioners have never been able to accomplish in getting all Navajo children in school for the first time in history, is enough evidence for us of his ability and good intentions. We will certainly stop, look and listen before condemning any of his policies.

Kindest regards.

Sincerely yours,
PAUL JONES, Chairman
Navajo Tribal Council

A Seneca Spokesman*

The controversy over the construction of the Kinzua Dam brought up again the perennial legal issues in Indian Affairs. The following testimony was given in 1960 before the U.S. House of Representatives sub-committee on Indian affairs.

My name is George D. Heron. I live on the Allegany Reservation in New York, and I am president of the Seneca Nation of Indians. . . . my friends from Pennsylvania have said that the Treaty of November 11, 1794, was abrogated when all Indians became citizens in 1924. I would like to point out that the 1794 Treaty was signed by the *Seneca Nation,* not by individual Seneca Indians, and the Nation has not yet become a citizen. It remains today exactly what it was 165 years ago—in the words of the courts as reported to us by our attorney, Mr. [Arthur] Lazarus, a "quasi-sovereign dependent nation." More important, our tribal lawyer tells me that the Supreme court of the United States has held not once, but at least a dozen times, that the grant of citizenship does not affect any Indian treaty rights or in any other way change the special relationship of Indians and their property to the Federal government. I am not an educated man, but it seems very strange to me that these lawyers from Pennsylvania are willing to say that the Supreme Court ruled against the Senecas, when it did not even hear the case, while at the same time they are ignoring a whole series of actual Supreme Court decisions which go against their arguments.

I am proud to be an American citizen, and have four years in the United States Navy to prove it. I am just as proud to be a Seneca Indian. And I do not see any reason why I cannot be both. . . .

Lastly, I know it will sound simple and perhaps silly, but the truth of the matter is that my people really believe that George Washintgon read the 1794 Treaty before he signed it, and that he meant exactly what he wrote. For more than 165 years we Senecas have lived by that document. To us it is more than a contract, more than a symbol; to us, the 1794 Treaty is a way of life.

Times have not always been easy for the Seneca people. We have known and we still know poverty and discrimination. But through it all we have been sustained by a pledge of faith, unbroken by the Federal government. Take that pledge away, break our Treaty, and I fear that you will destroy the Senecas as an Indian community. . . .

On behalf of the Seneca Nation, may I thank you for granting us this hearing.

* Quoted in Jack D. Forbes, *The Indian in America's Past,* Prentice-Hall, Inc., Englewood Cliffs, N.J., 1964, p. 70.

A National Whiskey Advertisement*

In 1965 the executive director of the National Congress of American Indians spoke out, along with officials of several Sioux tribal organizations, against a whiskey advertisement. This action was prompted by the policy of the NCAI in promoting a better understanding of Indians among the American public. The letter resulted in the withdrawal of the advertisement. Both ad and letter are here reprinted from a national Indian journal.

IF THE SIOUX HAD HAD SOFT WHISKEY THEY WOULD NEVER HAVE CALLED IT FIRE WATER.

The Indians didn't call whiskey "fire water" for nothing. (Why do you think they were yelping all the time?)
And basically, distilling methods haven't changed much since those days. Except for Soft Whiskey, of course.
Soft Whiskey swallows easy. It's gentle going down. You could say we've gotten rid of the evil spirits.
But don't fool yourself. Soft Whiskey isn't for old squaws. It's 86 proof. And it can do anything any other 86 proof can do. It just does it softer.
How did we put out the fire?
For one thing, we distill in small batches instead of giant ones.
The rest of the process will have to remain our secret. You see, other distillers have been trying to develop a Soft Whiskey for years. It was many many moons before we even hit upon it. 12 years to be exact.
After all that work, we rather enjoy the idea of being the only Soft Whiskey.
Not to admit it would be speaking with forked tongue.

Dear Sir:

In reference to our conversation yesterday, I wish to draw some specific examples on why this advertisement is extremely detrimental to the Indian people as a whole and to the Sioux Nation and its constituent tribes in particular.

1) Why is Sioux picked out as opposed to other Indian tribes? Are the Sioux entirely different from other tribes? Are they more noted for drunkenness or for drinking? Do they yelp when they drink hard liquor? (Your initial answer yesterday was that there was no danger or malice involved as these people have been dead for 200 years.) The implication being: Indians are a funny little group from America's past and so it is safe to portray them as a funny little people and so let's just pick any tribe and talk stilted and be 'sophisticated.'

* *Indian Voices*, Tahlequah, Okla., May, 1965, pp. 18–19.

2) Do Indians yelp? I believe I have only heard 'yelp' referred to dogs? Is the inference that Indians are dogs? (Certainly not, you are in complete sympathy with Indians, in fact the company employs Indians, you even KNOW an Indian.) The inference that is actually behind 'yelp' is that in some manner or means Indians are not really people, they are an interesting 'SPECIES' found on the North American Continent. Any complaint they would have in reference to the 'fire' in the water would have to be a 'yelp,' 'bark,' 'growl,' 'whinny,' 'hiss,' 'bay,' 'chirp,' 'moo,' 'ugh,' 'snarl,' but certainly couldn't be in the form of an intelligent complaint. Again we have the image that if you don't speak English you don't speak intelligently. I should remind you that many Indians have mastery of two languages. I should be most interested in your ability to speak an Indian language.

3) 'We have gotten rid of the evil spirits.' Do Indians live in a religious universe where they are terrified by evil spirits? Is this not a "sophisticated" way of degrading a people in terms of your own understanding of them. My 5 years in Seminary have been sufficient to inform me of the absolute terror your ancestors dwelt in. I would only remind you of the mild insanity of the Salem witch hunts to feel that your inference to "evil spirits" is much more appropriate to your group than to mine.

You also have a reference to 'old squaws'. Pray tell me, what is an old squaw? Do Indians have 'squaws?' Do you still refer to Negro males as 'bucks'? Are the Minority races still 'species' for you?

The advertising format you use is apparently the 'new sophistication' that is described in *Time Magazine.* There Arthur C. Fatt, Chairman of Grey Advertising is quoted as follows: 'Up till recently we were concerned with whether or not people saw our advertisements. Now we are more concerned with what impression the advertisement makes.' Now I believe that we could cooperate with you to provide some real good Indian ads that would make an impression. Let's take the massacre scene of Wounded Knee where a band of Sioux were slaughtered by U.S. Cavalry and let's show a caption 'Before the Massacre we all had a shot of ———, it was smooth on us but rather hard on the Indians, but they didn't yelp for long.' Or let's show a picture of the beautiful Minnesota lake country with the notation '——— helped us steal this land, ——— and a smooth talker is too hard for the Sioux to handle.' You see, I believe that Indians would cooperate with your firm in good natured fun if we only had the chance. But you can also understand how the point of view makes a great deal of difference in what is fun and what is not.

You said over the phone that you generally don't check with representatives of the minority groups before portraying one of them in your ads. I would suggest that you begin a new policy in that respect in the very near future. All groups are trying to overcome an image that THEY DID NOT CREATE. There is no reason to type Mexican-Americans as 'dirty,' Italian-Americans as 'gangsters' or

American Indians as 'drunken,' although your people have found
in 300 years that a drunken Indian is much easier to make treaties
with.

There is still a great number of people in this country that do
not believe that your industry contributes a great deal to constructive social development in this country. I would be more concerned
if I were running ———— with making a new social image for liquor
than I would for profiteering on the incorrect images of minority
groups. I would like to see someone in your industry sponsor a boys'
camp on one of the reservations and work cooperatively with one
of the Indian tribes. Then next summer I would like to see them
run a good ad in magazines with a picture of that camp with the
notation 'The Spirit Industry fights Spiritual Poverty.' I believe that
that ad would show humane sophistication. Your present type of
sophistication shows a narrow provincial view of this country based
upon inadequate knowledge of the great social concern for all people
in this country.

I am enclosing some information for you on the Sioux Indians of
South Dakota but would have you know that there are also Sioux
tribes in Montana, Minnesota, North Dakota, Nebraska. I am also
sending the Sioux tribes a copy of this letter and would suggest that
your president send them all a letter of explanation of the intent of
the advertisement and apology for using the use of the Sioux name
without permission. I would hope that your firm would begin to lead
your industry into a more constructive use of its resources for the
good of all people in this country.

Sincerely yours,
Vine Deloria, Jr.
Executive Director
National Congress of American Indians

The Chicago Declaration*

The following are excerpts from a "Declaration of Indian Purpose" prepared at a Chicago conference of Indians from all over the United States in June, 1961.

LAW AND JURISDICTION

In view of the termination policy and particularly Public Law 280, many Indian people have been vitally concerned and fearful that their law and order systems will be supplanted, without their consent, by state law enforcement agencies which, perhaps, might be hostile toward them. In *U.S.* v. *Kagama* (1885) 118 U.S. 375, 383, the Court, speaking of Indians, said:

"They are communities dependent on the United States; . . . ; dependent for their political rights. They owe no allegiance to the States, and receive from them no protection. Because of the local ill feeling of the people, states where they are found are often their deadliest enemies. From their very weakness and helplessness, so largely due to the course of dealing of the Federal Government with them and treaties in which it has been promised, there arises a duty of protection, and with it the power."

That statement by the Supreme Court is considered to be as true today as when written.

The repeated breaking of solemn treaties by the United States has also been a concern which is disheartening to the tribes and it is felt that there is no apparent concern by the Government about breaking treaties.

RECOMMENDATIONS

1. Return of Indian Lands: We urge the Congress to direct by appropriate legislation the return in trust of that part of the Public Domain formerly owned by an Indian tribe or nation which the Secretary of Interior shall determine to be excess and non-essential to the purpose for which such land was originally taken or which was covered by a reversionary clause in the treaty or cession or other lands declared to be surplus to the government's needs. Restore all Indian lands that were consumed by termination policy.

2. Indian Claims Commission: We urge that Congress ascertain the reasons for the inordinate delay of the Indian Claims Commission in finishing its important assignment. The Congress should request the views of the attorneys for the tribes on this in order to

* *American Indian Chicago Conference,* The University of Chicago, June 13–20, 1961, pp. 13–16, 19–20.

balance the views already expressed to Congress by the attorneys for the United States.

The woeful lack of sufficient personnel to handle the case load in the Justice Department, we believe, is the *sole cause* for the delay, so damaging to the tribes, in expediting the Commission's work.

The law clearly directs that each tribe be represented by counsel and there would seem to exist no possible reason why the Justice Department should not be required to increase its personnel in the Indian Claims Section of the Lands Division to remove this just criticism. Simple justice suggests that this be speedily done or else irreparable damage to the tribes will result. We believe the Congress will want to correct this situation as promptly as possible.

3. Title to Reservations: The Secretary of the Interior, if he has the authority, or the Congress should act to determine the legal beneficiaries of reservations created under the Indian Reorganization Act or other authority for "Landless and Homeless Indians," also reservations established by executive order or prior act of Congress, where the naming of the beneficial users has been left indefinite or ambiguous. As Indians improve such lands, or as mineral wealth or other assets of value are discovered, ownership is in jeopardy unless clearly defined.

4. Submarginal Lands: Submarginal and other surplus lands adjoining or within the exterior boundaries of Indian reservations and purchased for the benefit of the Indians, should be transferred to the tribes under trust.

5. Land Purchase Funds: The land purchase funds authorized by the Indian Reorganization Act should again be appropriated on an annual basis, to permit tribes to add to their inadequate land base, to purchase heirship lands and allotments on which restrictions are removed, and otherwise improve their economy.

6. Voting on the Indian Reorganization Act: Amend the Indian Reorganization Act to permit tribes to vote on its acceptance at any time.

7. Protect Indian Water Rights: Adopt legislation to protect all Indian water rights of Indian reservations against appropriators who, because the government may be negligent in providing for Indian development, are able to establish a record of prior use.

9. Heirship Lands: Adopt a manageable and equitable heirship lands bill.

10. Amend P.L. 280: Amend P.L. 280 (83rd Congress) to require Indian consent to past and future transfers of jurisdiction over civil and criminal cases to the state in which a reservation is located, and to permit such transfers to take place, with Indian consent, on a progressive or item by item basis.

11. Reservation Boundaries: In order that Indian tribes may be properly protected in their reservation and may proceed with the orderly development of their resources, it is recommended that authority, if required, and funds be appropriated for the immediate survey and establishment of reservation boundaries.

TAXATION

Grave concern has arisen as a result of the recent rulings of the Bureau of Internal Revenue which in substance directly violate the solemn treaty obligations made with the American Indian.

In fact, within the past few years, there has been a steady trend by both the federal and state taxing departments to encroach upon the rights of the Indian in the taxing of Indian property.

Recently, the Bureau of Internal Revenue has boldly claimed that it has the right to levy upon and collect income taxes upon income received by Indians which is derived from the sale of livestock grazed upon restricted Indian lands. Already the Internal Revenue Service has levied upon, assessed and collected income taxes upon income received from restricted Indian production.

The taxing department of the federal government has arbitrarily made these rulings which are wholly contrary to the solemn provisions of the treaties made with the American Indian. These rulings have been made and are being enforced notwithstanding the fact that it was never intended that the Indian was to be taxed in any manner upon his restricted Indian lands, or upon the income derived from the same.

In fact the greater amount of Indian lands located in the western part of the nation are dry and arid lands and suitable for grazing purposes only. In other words, the Indian is by nature restricted as to the use of his lands since the same can only be used for grazing purposes.

Therefore, in order to further prevent the establishment of such arbitrary rules of the Bureau of Internal Revenue, and to correct the rules already existing, we deem it necessary that legislation be enacted which will clearly spell out the intent and purposes of the existing treaties and agreements made with Indian tribes. Specifically, a clear statement must be made by law that income received by an enrolled member of an Indian tribe, which is derived from tribal, allotted and restricted Indian lands, whether by original allotment, by inheritance, by exchange or purchase, or as a leasee thereof, while such lands are held in trust by the United States in trust, is exempt from Federal and State income taxes.

TREATY RIGHTS

It is a universal desire among all Indians that their treaties and trust-protected lands remain intact and beyond the reach of predatory men.

This is not special pleading, though Indians have been told often enough by members of Congress and the courts that the United States has the plenary power to wipe out our treaties at will. Governments, when powerful enough, can act in this arbitrary and immoral manner.

Still we insist that we are not pleading for special treatment at the hands of the American people. When we ask that our treaties be respected, we are mindful of the opinion of Chief Justice John

Marshall on the nature of the treaty obligations between the United States and the Indian tribes.

Marshall said that a treaty ". . . is a compact between two nations or communities, having the right of self-government. Is it essential that each party shall possess the same attributes of sovereignty to give force to the treaty? This will not be pretended, for on this ground, very few valid treaties could be formed. The only requisite is, that each of the contracting parties shall possess the right of self-government, and the power to perform the stipulations of the treaty."

And he said, "We have made treaties with (the Indians); and are those treaties to be disregarded on our part, because they were entered into with an uncivilized people? Does this lessen the obligation of such treaties? By entering into them have we not admitted the power of this people to bind themselves, and to impose obligations on us?"

The right of self-government, a right which the Indians possessed before the coming of the white man, has never been extinguished; indeed, it has been repeatedly sustained by the courts of the United States. Our leaders made binding agreements—ceding lands as requested by the United States; keeping the peace; harboring no enemies of the nation. And the people stood with the leaders in accepting these obligations.

A treaty, in the minds of our people, is an eternal word. Events often make it seem expedient to depart from the pledged word, but we are conscious that the first departure creates a logic for the second departure, until there is nothing left of the word.

We recognize that our view of these matters differs at times from the prevailing legal view regarding due process.

When our lands are taken for a declared public purpose, scattering our people and threatening our continued existence, it grieves us to be told that a money payment is the equivalent of all the things we surrender. Our forefathers could be generous when all the continent was theirs. They could cast away whole empires for a handle of trinkets for their children. But in our day, each remaining acre is a promise that we will still be here tomorrow. Were we paid a thousand times the market value of our lost holdings, still the payment would not suffice. Money never mothered the Indian people, as the land has mothered them, nor have any people become more closely attached to the land, religiously and traditionally.

We insist again that this is not special pleading. We ask only that the United States be true to its own traditions and set an example to the world in fair dealing. . . .

CONCLUDING STATEMENT

To complete our Declaration, we point out that in the beginning the people of the New World, called Indians by accident of geography, were possessed of a continent and a way of life. In the course of many lifetimes, our people had adjusted to every climate and condition from the Arctic to the torrid zones. In their livelihood and family relationships, their ceremonial observances, they reflected the diversity of the physical world they occupied.

The conditions in which Indians live today reflect a world in which every basic aspect of life has been transformed. Even the physical world is no longer the controlling factor in determining where and under what conditions men may live. In region after region, Indian groups found their means of existence either totally destroyed or materially modified. Newly introduced diseases swept away or reduced regional populations. These changes were followed by major shifts in the internal life of tribe and family.

The time came when the Indian people were no longer the masters of their situation. Their life ways survived subject to the will of a dominant sovereign power. This is said, not in a spirit of complaint; we understand that in the lives of all nations of people, there are times of plenty and times of famine. But we do speak out in a plea for understanding.

When we go before the American people, as we do in this Declaration, and ask for material assistance in developing our resources and developing our opportunities, we pose a moral problem which cannot be left unanswered. For the problem we raise affects the standing which our nation sustains before world opinion.

Our situation cannot be relieved by appropriated funds alone, though it is equally obvious that without capital investment and funded services, solutions will be delayed. Nor will the passage of time lessen the complexities which beset a people moving toward new meaning and purpose.

The answers we seek are not commodities to be purchased, neither are they evolved automatically through the passing of time.

The effort to place social adjustment on a money-time interval scale which has characterized Indian administration, has resulted in unwanted pressure and frustration.

When Indians speak of the continent they yielded, they are not referring only to the loss of some millions of acres in real estate. They have in mind that the land supported a universe of things they knew, valued, and loved.

With that continent gone, except for the few poor parcels they still retain, the basis of life is precariously held, but they mean to hold the scraps and parcels as earnestly as any small nation or ethnic group was ever determined to hold to identity and survival.

What we ask of America is not charity, not paternalism, even when benevolent. We ask only that the nature of our situation be recognized and made the basis of policy and action.

In short, the Indians ask for assistance, technical and financial, for the time needed, however long that may be, to regain in the America of the space age some measure of the adjustment they enjoyed as the original possessors of their native land.

The NCAI as Spokesman*

The following is part of an editorial from the national organ of the National Congress of American Indians.

. . . We think that the time is ripe for a realistic thoughtful study of the place of the American Indian in American society and in American history and that policy be hereafter based upon this study. It is necessary for a person to stop every now and then and review his life, ponder the facts of where he has been and where he is going, and set some new and more understanding goals for himself. Philosophers call this reflection and it is this quality, more than the making of olive oil, that the early Greeks have given to the world. We cannot, for example, understand how anyone can refuse to admit the failure of the colonial powers to set up stable governments in their former colonies when the United States has been so embroiled in the Congo, Viet Nam, Cuba, South America and other places since the last war. Failures in foreign policy are a large scale version of the failures in Indian policy made over the last century. While democracy is great, the all-important fact of a successful democracy is historical background. While the American economy is obviously quite efficient, again historical background is the key to reproducing it somewhere else.

There is not necessarily conflict for a group of people who are different in their wants and desires from the majority of the people in their country. And we do not feel that Indians necessarily want to be different or should be different. What annoys us, confuses people wanting to help Indians, and causes untold confusion in making Indian policy, is the assumption that INDIANS HAVE TO BE DIFFERENT. . . . or HAVE TO BE THE SAME. The Indian is always presented with the choice: keep your beads and braids and we won't let you have any refrigerators or other modern conveniences OR take all our material goods and surrender everything that is particularly Indian, beginning with your land.

Society today is moving very fast toward a new concept of itself. We shall soon be able and willing to provide a decent living for all of our citizens. Does this necessarily mean that we must all want the same things, all live in the cities and suburbs, all enjoy the same books, dances, movies, games, churches? Must we all share the same intangible values? And what will these values be?

The soul of a person is extremely complex. Even more so must

* *The Sentinel,* Vol. XI, No. 1, Winter 1966.

be the soul of a nation. Perhaps compassion is that quality that coordinates everything in a soul to provide that humaness that we look for in people and nations. We have the compassion at present, but we lack an essential ingredient that will allow compassion to work and that is variety. We must have a variety of real values and differences so that any person has many real options for living in our society. We believe that allowing total development of Indian communities on their own basis will be a major step in providing that variety in American life which is so necessary to a healthy society. We believe that the assumption that Indians necessarily have to be like everyone else should be stricken from the books and minds of people. Likewise the idea that Indians necessarily have to be different. Give Indian tribes the economic and educational means to be what they want to be and see what happens. The same with other groups.

We never again hope to see in America: bombed Sunday schools, State Troopers chasing little Amish children, landless Indians wandering from city to city.

Selected Bibliography

GENERAL

Collier, John. *Indians of the Americas, The Long Hope*. The New American Library, New York, 1947.

Fey, Harold E. and D'Arcy McNickle. *Indians and Other Americans, Two Ways of Life Meet*. Harper and Bros., New York, 1959.

Hagan, William T. *American Indians*. University of Chicago Press, Chicago, 1961.

McNickle, D'Arcy. *The Indian Tribes of the United States, Ethnic and Cultural Survival*. Oxford University Press, London and New York, 1962.

Spicer, Edward H. *Cycles of Conquest. The Impact of Spain, Mexico, and the United States on the Indians of the Southwest, 1533–1960*. University of Arizona Press, Tucson, 1962.

Underhill, Ruth. *Red Man's America: A History of the Indians of the United States*. The University of Chicago Press, Chicago, 1953.

Washburn, Wilcomb E. *The Indian and the White Man*. Doubleday & Company, Garden City, 1964.

Wissler, Clark. *Indians of the United States*. Doubleday & Company, New York, 1948.

CHAPTER 1

Corkran, David H. *The Creek Frontier, 1540–1783*. University of Oklahoma Press, Norman, 1967.

Hunt, George T. *The Wars of the Iroquois, A Study in Intertribal Trade Relations*. The University of Wisconsin Press, Madison, 1940.

Vaughan, Alden T. *New England Frontier, Puritans and Indians, 1620–1675*. Little, Brown and Co., Boston and Toronto, 1965.

Wallace, Anthony F. C. *King of the Delawares: Teedyuscung, 1700–1763*. University of Pennsylvania Press, Philadelphia, 1949.

CHAPTER 2

Deardorff, Merle H. *The Religion of Handsome Lake: Its Origin and Development*. Bureau of American Ethnology Bulletin 149, pp. 77–107, Washington, 1951.

Eggleston, Edward and Lillie Eggleston Seeyle. *Tecumseh and the Shawnee Prophet*. Dodd, Mead and Co., New York, 1878.

Mooney, James. *The Ghost Dance Religion and the Sioux Outbreak of 1890*. Bureau of American Ethnology 14th Annual Report, Part 2, Government Printing Office, Washington, 1896.

313

Starkey, Marion L. *The Cherokee Nation.* Alfred A. Knopf, New York, 1946.

CHAPTER 3

Debo, Angie. *The Road to Disappearance.* University of Oklahoma Press, Norman, 1941.
Emmitt, Robert. *The Last War Trail, The Utes and the Settlement of Colorado.* University of Oklahoma Press, Norman, 1954.
Gibson, A. M. *The Kickapoos: Lords of the Middle Border.* University of Oklahoma Press, Norman, 1963.
Jackson, Helen (H. H.). *A Century of Dishonor, A Sketch of the United States Government's Dealings with Some of the Indian Tribes.* Roberts Brothers, Boston, 1886.
Kroeber, Theodora. *Ishi in Two Worlds: A Biography of the Last Wild Indian in North America.* University of California Press, Berkeley and Los Angeles, 1962.
Priest, Loring Benson. *Uncle Sam's Stepchildren: The Reformation of United States Indian Policy, 1865–1887.* Rutgers University Press, New Brunswick, N.J., 1942.

CHAPTER 4

Debo, Angie. *And Still the Waters Run.* Princeton University Press, Princeton, N.J., 1940.
La Flesche, Francis. *The Middle Five: Indian Schoolboys of the Omaha Tribe.* The University of Wisconsin Press, Madison, 1963.
Meriam, Lewis and Associates. *The Problem of Indian Administration.* The Johns Hopkins Press, Baltimore, 1928.
Slotkin, J. S. *The Peyote Religion: A Study in Indian-White Relations.* The Free Press, Glencoe, Ill., 1956.

CHAPTER 5

Berry, Brewton. *Almost White.* The Macmillan Co., New York, 1963.
Thompson, Laura. *Culture in Crisis: A Study of the Hopi Indians* Harper and Bros., New York, 1950.
Wilson, Edmund. *Apologies to the Iroquois.* Farrar, Straus and Cudahy, New York, 1959.
MacGregor, Gordon. *Warriors without Weapons. A Study of the Society and Personality Development of the Pine Ridge Sioux.* University of Chicago Press, Chicago, Ill., 1946.

Index